I, Elizabeth Clare Prophet, Messenger for the Great White Brotherhood, do witness to the chelas and the world to the presence in my heart of my Lord and Saviour Jesus Christ. I witness to his Sacred Heart, one with my heart. I witness to his all-consuming love and mercy and grace upon my soul and the souls of all true Lightbearers, all true chelas of the will of God.

I witness to the sacred fire he has placed in my heart. It is a burning fire that kindles my soul, my chakras, all of my house. This fire I often feel as a physical fire. And whenever I give concentrated devotion, decrees and meditation to Jesus' Heart within my heart and my heart in his, the burning fire increases until it becomes such an all-consuming passion, and compassion, that I must leave off from this ecstasy lest I be transported from the realm of daily practicalities.

About the Photographs

Throughout this book you will find photos which are mementos of the past. Though some may not be in pristine condition, nonetheless they are priceless gems.

Our hope is that these pictures will help you make a greater connection with the magnanimous heart of Mark Prophet (the Ascended Master Lanello) and the courageous heart of Elizabeth Prophet.

On Fire for God

Adventures on the Mystical Path with Elizabeth Clare Prophet

Alex and Margaret Reichardt
with
Other Devotees of Elizabeth Prophet

Excelsior Publications, LLC
Virginia Beach, Virginia

This book is a work of non-fiction. The events and situations described are true accounts by those who worked and lived with Elizabeth Clare Prophet.

ON FIRE FOR GOD
Adventure on the Mystical Path with Elizabeth Clare Prophet
by Alex and Margaret Reichardt
with Other Devotees of Elizabeth Prophet

Excelsior Publications, LLC
Post Office Box 64625, Virginia Beach, VA 23467-4625
www.MarkandElizabethProphet.com

Select pictures are used by permission of: Terry Canady, Judy Sue Christenson, Louis Difo, Ruth Farnam, Rosemary Galgano, Donald Galvin, Marshall Haley, Susan Harrow, Janice Haugen, Guy Hudson, Ruth Jones, John and Carol Magazino, Tom Miller, Kenneth McNeel, Theresa McNicholas, Mary Paull, Erin Prophet, Adella Pugh, Andrea Selestow, Larry Stanley and other individuals.

The photographs in this book are intended for your personal enjoyment. For any other use, please contact us to obtain the appropriate written permission.

Bible quotes are taken from the King James Version.

ISBN 978-1-60530-955-2

Book cover, logo and interior design
by Living Arts Media, Bozeman MT

Printed in the United States of America

Gratitude

We can never sufficiently express our love and gratitude to God for sending his Messengers, Mark and Elizabeth Prophet to our assistance. They have led us from darkness and our own returning karma into the Light. Let us be mindful of all the Herculean effort of both these Messengers, the Masters and the Angels.

* * *

Without the priceless assistance we received while writing this book, it would never have been completed. Our gratitude goes first and foremost to Lanello, the Ever-Present Guru, who watches over his many disciples as a father watches over his newborn infant.

Also to all our friends who helped shape, perfect and ensure the accuracy of this book, a great big thanks. Your support, encouragement and prayers were invaluable.

—Alex and Margaret Reichardt
Virginia Beach, Virginia

> *Every effort has been made to ensure that all necessary permissions for material used in this book have been obtained. Any omission is unintentional and we will gladly correct any errors in future editions of this book.*

Note: We have used "He" and "Him" to refer to God. These terms are for readability only and are not intended to exclude women or the feminine aspect of God.

Elizabeth Clare Prophet,
Messenger for the Ascended Masters

I tell you frankly, as it is known by the Hierarchy today, beloved, were it not for this Messenger clothed upon with the mantle of Lord Gautama, you would not receive direct instruction and initiation. And it would be more arduous for you to make your way to the etheric retreats without the sponsorship of that mantle holding the balance for you. Recently El Morya so gave this instruction to the staff of the Messenger.

When the Messenger did come before the Lords of Karma to receive the assignment of this life, she was given the opportunity of two paths: the one, to become a Guru in the Himalayas with a small band of disciples, unknown to the world and therefore far from the reaches of the arrows and slings of outrageous fortune, far from the attack of the fallen ones, the attack of the press and the agencies of government and the people who are angry against the Light; and the other, to come forward and be in the public eye and therefore be vulnerable to every level of opposition from all planes.

She was shown how only a few disciples would benefit from her mission in the serenity of the Himalayan fastnesses. She was shown the many thousands of souls who would receive benefit, who would have the opportunity for the ascension and who could be sponsored through her mantle should she take the course that would place her, then, at the forefront of the battle and subject to all onslaughts coming out of Church and State.

You can see the path that she has chosen. Therefore El Morya did state that more than 95 percent of those who have found this path and who are ascending to God would not have had this teaching had she not made this decision.

–Buddha of the Ruby Ray, October 12, 1991

Contents

Past Embodiments of Elizabeth Clare Prophet

Nefertiti

Hypatia

Martha of Bethany

Clotilda

Guinevere

Yeshe Tsogyal

Biographical Sketch of the Messenger
Elizabeth Clare Prophet

Elizabeth Clare Prophet was born on April 8, 1939, in Long Branch, New Jersey, under the sign of Aries. She grew up in Red Bank, New Jersey, a small town not far from the Atlantic Ocean. During her entire life, the ocean is where she wanted most to be. Born of immigrant parents, Elizabeth was an only child with no relatives closer than Switzerland.

Elizabeth's love for Saint Germain began at the age of three. Her babysitters read the teachings of the Ascended Master Saint Germain in the I AM Discourses to her. At the tender age of four, when most little girls were content to play with their dolls, Elizabeth wanted to know more about God. She asked to be taken to Sunday School but it was not until age five that she was able to go. This turned out to be a big disappointment. All she did was color. Her mother or a neighbor took her to almost every Protestant church in town. Here she attended the adult services but was still dissatisfied. They did not have the answers she was seeking. Finally at age nine she found what she had been looking for in the Christian Science Church.

By the time she was in high school her yearning to find God and learn about her mission was so strong that she found herself alone much of the time. After she went to Antioch College and majored in political science, she interned at the United Nations. All the while she was looking for Saint Germain.

Then at age 22 she met Mark Prophet. Finally she discovered her mission and at the same time she found Saint Germain. Once that happened, she locked in and never looked back. Ever since she has remained faithful to her calling: going after the lightbearers who have lost their way, and even the rebel angels.

Elizabeth spoke about her mission in her lecture given October 10, 1992.

Nine Cats, Nine Lives
by Elizabeth Clare Prophet

I remember leaving the Great Central Sun. I remember going before Alpha and Omega in the Great Throne Room, bowing before them and asking their leave to go and descend into the lower octaves where the rebel angels, those who had rebelled against God and his Christ, were moving against the children of Light. I specifically asked permission to go and find them and woo them back to God. I received the blessing of beloved Alpha and Omega to do this.

This is the teaching that they gave me before I departed: I would go forth and for many long centuries I would be mother and teacher to the rebel angels. They said the mission did not have great chance of success but they would support me in my efforts. They said that these reprobate ones would woo me and flatter me and support me, so long as I was to them mother and teacher. But when the time of their judgment would come, Alpha and Omega would send me the message. It is then that they would rise up and make war against me.

And so I remember clearly the record of descending down what I could only describe as a chute of light like a large tunnel. And I simply went down and down and down until I came to the octaves of Earth to which I was sent. Apart from saying that this was in a timeless epoch, I cannot give you a date for it. I also did journey to Earth with Sanat Kumara as part of those who would come and help to establish the rekindling of the Threefold Flame in those in whom it had gone out.

Mark and Elizabeth Prophet are the Two Witnesses for the Aquarian Age. Part of their mission is passing the Word from God to man. They were not chosen as Messengers of the Ascended Masters because they had mastery in all areas. They were chosen because they were strong enough to withstand the opposition to the messages the Masters spoke through them.

> *And I will give power unto my two witnesses,*
> *and they shall prophesy a thousand two hundred*
> *and threescore days, clothed in sackcloth.*
>
> (Rev. 11:3)

Sackcloth denotes that the Witnesses come forth bearing their personal karma and by the practical demonstration of cosmic law prove that every man and woman can overcome karma by invoking the fires of the Holy Spirit. The advantage of having the Witnesses "clothed in sackcloth" is to give all of us hope. No matter how heavy our burden of past karma or the weight of sin that so easily besets us, it can be made light by devotion to the I AM Presence and by service to God and man.

Saint Germain clarified the position of the Messenger in his Pearl of Wisdom of August 3, 1975:

> *In every age the Lord has sent his emissaries to initiate spirals of renewed Self-awareness. Our Messenger is the taper which we hold in our hand to kindle anew the crystallization of the God flame within you. Through the release of the spoken Word at conferences, through the blessing of your chakras with special jeweled focuses which we have secured especially for this purpose, our Messenger is appointed to be the instrument of a greater concentration of the light of hierarchy in the body of God upon Earth.*

Elizabeth told us over the years that she and Mark have a covenant with God. Should they compromise God's laws, even in small matters, by cosmic law the Masters could no longer use them and they would no longer be able to bring forth the Word of God. She also reminded us that she is merely the vessel. Of her own self she can do nothing. It is the Father that doeth the work through her. To think otherwise is idolatry.

During Elizabeth's 12 years with Mark they had four children. Their organization, The Summit Lighthouse, moved from Virginia to Colorado Springs. After Mark's transition into the ascended state, Elizabeth under the Masters direction moved the activity to Pasadena, California, then to Camelot in Calabassas, California, and finally to the Inner Retreat in Montana.

Elizabeth's past embodiments were only stepping-stones to her victorious fulfillment in this age of a journey begun long ago. Sometimes she was embodied as a saint and sometimes as European royalty. Each lifetime brought her closer to this one and her role as Messenger for the Ascended Masters and one of the Two Witnesses.

Elizabeth Clare Prophet's Previous Embodiments
As revealed by the Messengers

Nefertiti 1390 BCE Egypt
When Nefertiti was fifteen years old, she married Amenhotep IV who was one year older and became king upon his father's death. As Nefertiti, one of the most famous women in antiquity, she and her husband, Pharaoh Ikhnaton (Mark Prophet this time around), established the worship of the one God, Aton, in preference to the worship of many gods of the black priests. They therefore ushered in a new era of monotheism. Some have hypothesized that she was the power behind the throne and thus responsible for the innovations during Ikhnaton's rule. They had six daughters.

Ikhnaton built a dazzling new capital, Tel El Amarna, and moved in the royal family and 50,000 followers. This new city became a focal point for their new religion with temples and Palaces of light. In retaliation, the black priests brutally murdered Nefertiti and Ikhnaton and many of their followers and destroyed their new city. They sought to obliterate all reference to them from Egyptian history. Yet archeologists and historians have been able to uncover various artifacts and piece together their lasting legacy.

Martha of Bethany 1st century AD

Martha, devotee and follower of Jesus, is portrayed in the Bible as the one who prepared the meal for her visitors. She was intent on how she might feed the Lord, while her sister, Mary, was intent on how she might be fed by the Lord. They lived in Bethany with their brother, Lazarus, and were apparently good friends of Jesus. They provided hospitality for him and his disciples when they traveled from Jerusalem.

When Lazarus died, it was Martha who eagerly ran out to meet Jesus on the road, proclaiming her unshakable faith in him, saying that her brother would not have died had Jesus come earlier. "But I know, that even now, whatsoever thou wilt ask of God, God will give it thee." Jesus then made his great statement to her, "I am the resurrection, and the life: he that believeth in me, though he were dead, yet shall he live; and whosoever liveth and believeth in me shall never die. Believest thou this?" Martha said "Yea, Lord: I believe that thou art the Christ, the Son of God, which should come into the world." (John 11:20-27)

Elizabeth talked about this life in her lecture on October 10, 1992 entitled "Nine Cats, Nine Lives" and in her book: *In My Own Words*:

"Harriet Beecher Stowe (Nineteenth century author) stated that Martha was a natural born leader. Interestingly, my childhood playmate was the re-embodiment of Harriet

Beecher Stowe. We were inseparable from age two to nine this life.

"Mary (Martha's sister) re-embodied as Mary Baker Eddy, spiritual head and founder of Christian Science. I chose to be a Christian Scientist when I was a child until the age of twenty-two when I met Mark Prophet."

Hypatia of Alexandra 370 – 415 AD Egypt

Hypatia was known for her intellectual brilliance and possessed great moral authority. History records her as the first notable woman in mathematics. She also taught philosophy and astronomy. In 400 AD, she became the head of the Platonist school at Alexandria teaching the works of Plato and Aristotle. Her reputation as a gifted orator spread throughout the ancient world, and Christians and foreigners alike traveled great distances to be counted as her loyal students.

Hypatia died a martyr. She was killed by a Coptic Christian mob who blamed her for religious turmoil. Some historians suggested that her murder by a mob at age forty-five heralded the virtual cessation of scientific advancement for the next thousand years, and marked the end of the Hellenistic Age.

Guinevere, Queen of Camelot Fifth Century

Guinevere was the beautiful wife of Arthur, "King of the Britons" during fifth century Britain, residing in his many-towered castle, Camelot. Arthur also had a mighty champion named Lancelot and a magical helper named Merlin. Merlin was a prophet, poet and wizard and an advisor to the king. Various authors chose to write about fabled King Arthur including Geoffrey Chaucer, whose fourteenth-century tales included lands filled with knights and ladies of the court. This magical age was the "brief, shining moment" of Camelot.

St. Clotilda, c. 474 – 545 AD

Clotilda was a Burgundian princess, widely known for her beauty, who became the queen of Clovis I, the Frankish king. She was a devoted Catholic and instrumental in the conversion of her husband to Christianity. This resulted in the establishment of the Frankish kingdom as a Catholic nation. Together they built the Church of the Apostles Peter and Paul in Paris, later renamed Sainte-Geneviève. After her husband's death she spent her life caring for the poor.

Yeshe Tsogyal 757 – 817

Yeshe Tsogyal helped establish Buddhism in Tibet. Yeshe is said to have been a princess who was married to a king at the age of twelve. She ran away to study meditation for three years with a Buddhist master and traveled to Nepal. She realized the need to escape from samsara, was compassionate and made offerings to the needy. She is known to have had the gift of instant recall and was able to write down verbatim, word for word, the teachings of Padma Sambhava. It is because of her efforts that we have the priceless teachings of Padma Sambhava vouchsafed to us to this day.

St. Clare of Assisi 1194 – 1253

Clare was a devotee of St. Francis. She was born of noble descent in Assisi, Italy. Before Clare was born, her mother received a message from God: "Thou shalt bring forth a light which shall enlighten the whole world clearly." Therefore she was given the name of Clare.

At 18 Clare joined St. Francis' order after hearing his sermons in the public square. Her relatives tried to persuade her to return home—to no avail. Her mission was to support Francis as he extended his ministry to the people.

Those in the order of St. Francis adhered to an austere lifestyle. They slept on the ground, owned no property, and received sustenance from alms. Clare was sick for the last 27 years of her life as the result of her extreme asceticism. She was very close to God.

Catherine of Siena 1347 – 1380

From her earliest childhood Catherine began to see visions and to practice extreme austerities. At the age of seven she consecrated her virginity to Christ. In her sixteenth years she took the habit of the Dominican Tertiaries. After three years of celestial visitations and conversation with Christ, she rejoined her family and began to tend to the sick. She served the poor and tirelessly labored for the conversion of sinners.

Though always suffering terrible physical pain, she lived for long intervals on practically no food except the Blessed Sacrament. She was radiantly happy and full of practical wisdom and could impart the highest spiritual insight. She began to gather disciples around her, both men and women, who formed a spiritual fellowship.

Though unschooled, Jesus taught her to write so she began to dispatch letters to those in leadership positions. Later on, she dictated the book of her meditations and revelations, "The Dialogue of Saint Catherine of Siena."

She beseeched her Divine Bridegroom to let her bear the punishment for all the sins of the world, and to receive the sacrifice of her body for the unity and renovation of the Church. She received the stigmata. At the age of 33, she died. She had laid down her life for the Church that it might survive.

Sir Thomas More's daughter Margaret 1505 – 1544

Margaret More was the oldest child of Sir Thomas More, Chancellor in the reign of King Henry VIII. She was his favorite child and confidante and he called her Meg. As his daughter, Margaret was to learn firsthand her father's stand for truth and justice: he would not compromise.

In 1514 Thomas quarreled with the king and was imprisoned in the Tower of London. While in prison, More demonstrated remarkable composure and legendary good humor. During these trying days, his chief comfort was in visits and letters from his daughter Margaret.

More's imprisonment was a hardship to his family. Margaret visited her father in the Tower and begged him to reconsider his decision. But he would not. She was to find out to her great anguish that he would be preferring death to wrongdoing. This would be a great lesson for her.

In 1535 he was tried in Westminster Hall as he had fully expected, sentenced to death and was being taken along the river back to the Tower. Margaret was waiting for her last look. She broke through the guard of soldiers, threw her arms round his neck, and kissed him, sobbing "Oh, my father! Oh, my father!" He blessed her, and consoled her that whatsoever she might suffer, it was the Will of God. Having parted with him, she again ran back to him, and clinging round his neck, kissed him over and over again. At this sight, the guards themselves wept.

On July 6, he was executed. His head was on the post of the London Bridge. Margaret bribed the executioner to give it to her.

Years later on a stump to Great Britain, Elizabeth knelt in solemn prayer at the foot of his statue, reliving the entire scene. She realized that in this present life she still had unresolved issues surrounding the execution of her father. She said that Thomas More was the best and greatest father she ever had. He had taught her courage.

Marie Antoinette 1755 – 1793

"Courage! I have shown it for years; think you I shall lose it at the moment when my sufferings are to end?"
– Marie Antoinette

Marie Antoinette was born in Vienna, Austria. She was the youngest and most beautiful daughter of Francis Stephen I and Maria Theresa, Emperor and Empress of the Holy Roman Empire. Marie Antoinette was brought up believing her destiny was to become queen of France. She married the crown prince of France in 1770. Four years later she became queen when her husband was crowned King Louis XVI.

The stories of Antoinette's excesses are vastly overstated. In fact, rather than ignoring France's growing financial crisis, she reduced the royal household staff, eliminating many unnecessary positions that were based solely on privilege. In the process she offended the nobles, who added their condemnation to the scandalous stories spread by royal hopefuls. It was the nobility that balked at the financial reforms the government ministers tried to make, not the King and Queen, who were in favor of change. In truth, Antoinette and Louis were placed in harm's way not alone by elements of their personalities but by the changing face of political and social ideology in the 18th century.

France was beginning to come upon hard times in the late 1780s. The harvest was poor and the people started going hungry. Marie Antoinette, being kind-hearted, came to the aid of the people. However, her small acts of kindness to help impoverished families were eclipsed by the political turmoil of the time. By 1795 the French Revolution had run its horrible course. The King and Queen and many others had been executed. After Marie Antoinette was executed, Saint Germain took her to the octaves of light to the retreat of the Great Divine Director.

Elisabeth of Bavaria, Empress of Austria & Queen of Hungary 1837 – 1898

Elisabeth was the daughter of the Bavarian duke Maximilian Joseph. She was regarded as the most beautiful princess in Europe. At the age of 16 she married her cousin, Franz Joseph, then Emperor of Austria. She later wrote that she regretted accepting his proposal for the rest of her life. Due to his many infidelities, the marriage was an unhappy one.

She bore the Emperor four children but was denied any major influence on her older children's upbringing. To ease her pain and illnesses, Elisabeth embarked on a life of travel.

Generally popular with her subjects, she offended Viennese high society by her impatience with the rigid etiquette of the court. She loved Hungary and in return, they built a monument in her honor. Several sites are also named after her. Her enthusiasm for Hungary, however, affronted German sentiment within Austria. She partly assuaged Austrian feelings by her care for the wounded in the Seven Weeks' War of 1866

The suicide of her only son, the crown prince Rudolf, in 1889, was a shock from which Elizabeth never fully recovered. Later that year, during a visit to Switzerland she was mortally stabbed by an Italian anarchist, Luigi Luccheni.

The Messenger revealed that as Elisabeth, she had some knowledge of the teachings of the Brotherhood, but not enough to counteract the total momentum of witchcraft and Satanism of Europe which was pitted against her lifestream and her mission. As a result the cult of the Mother was not fully realized in Austria.

As Messenger for the Great White Brotherhood and Mother of the Flame, she once again has the mission to bring forth the culture of the Divine Mother in this life.

Embodiments of Elizabeth Clare Prophet

Catherine of Siena

Clare of Assisi

Marie Antoinette

Elisabeth of Austria

Elizabeth Clare Prophet

Part One

Beautiful Dreamer
Elizabeth Clare Prophet

by Alex and Margaret Reichardt

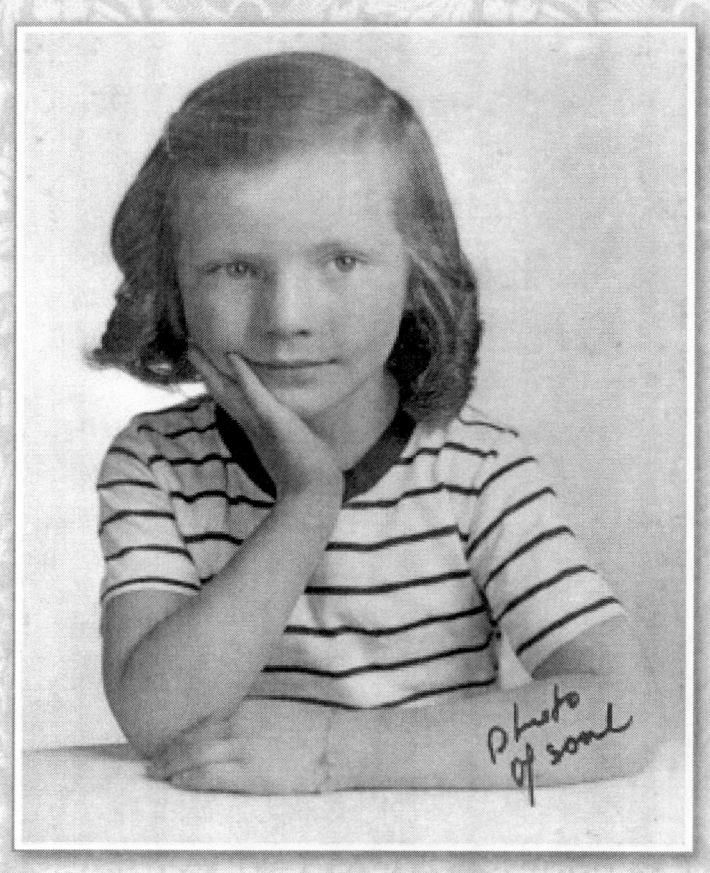

Elizabeth age 4

TRIP DOWN MEMORY LANE
Pray Your Flight Be Not in Winter
by Alex Reichardt

Will you remember? Will you remember, hearts and souls of light, that we can give forth the light, we can allow you to feel that light as in the mountaintop experience of your communion in the Holy of Holies, but the law requires that you come down from the mountain and sustain the flame of the law without anyone to continually nourish your lamps with oil?

Precious ones, do you understand that we all know that you can sustain the flame in our presence? It is out of our presence, neath the vine and the fig tree of your own God awareness, that you must prove the law, that you must stand and face and conquer every flaw of the human consciousness. Will you understand that these are the rules of the game?

–Godfre, *Pearls of Wisdom*, Vol. 19, No. 17

In a driving snow with near-zero visibility, we desperately needed to find a place to stay the night. Working feverishly around the clock, we had finally loaded our 17-foot U-haul with car in tow for our 2,300-mile journey. Exhausted from our white-knuckle trek, we were moving across hostile terrain in the dead of winter and now were ensnared in a blizzard. Wild animals, frigid conditions and black ice contributed to our fatigue.

For the last thirty-plus years, Margaret and I had been living a life that is almost impossible to describe– though bliss, happiness, ecstasy might be a start. Now we were going far away, in distance and essence. Leaving before dawn from Livingston, Montana, we continued through Billings over to Sheridan, Wyoming, and on south. In the

3

diminishing light, with few taillights to guide us, we were deep in thought. Only the sounds of the engine and the ice-caked windshield wipers punctuated the silence. Behind us were the best years of our lives, which had become our entire world. We had given our all for this dream come true. Would anybody believe we had found Shangri-La?

Through the icy headlights I glimpsed a forlorn motel in a clump of white firs. I jumped out to check for vacancies, leaving my wife in the cab and the engine running. Just in time! After being told "No vacancies," next came the warning: The highway was being shut down because of the treacherous conditions. I jumped back into the truck and hightailed it back onto the Interstate. The choice was clear: Make a run for it or be stranded. Half-buried vehicles in ditches along the road were a constant reminder of what our fate could be.

Crosswinds swept through canyons, causing our rig to sway back and forth. Navigating along a steep pass, I caught a quick glimpse in the rearview mirror of the wooden barrier closing the road behind us. A lone patrol car with emergency lights flashing stood guard to prevent anyone from entering. With still 200 miles before the next big city where we hoped to find a place to stay, the gas tank was half empty. Would we make it?

Four hours later–on empty–we finally came upon the silhouette of an isolated motel just outside Cheyenne and edged up to the front door. As we lay down for a much-needed rest, our thoughts once again wandered to the friends we had left behind and our amazing adventures with Elizabeth Clare Prophet.

* * *

I was Mark's personal assistant until his ascension in 1973, and I worked with Mother for 33 years. I helped her with various assignments, including design projects for the Church. Mother loved bringing forth the culture of the Divine Mother and beautifying the environment. She remembered many magnificent designs from the retreats of the Brotherhood. Although I had studied architectural design in college, Mother took this discipline to a higher level of perfection and taught me a great deal. I will always be grateful for that. And working closely with her gave me the opportunity to receive chelaship and initiations from the Masters through her–always given with profound love.

In 1997 my wife, Margaret, and I left Mother's staff and have continued studying and living the Teachings. Yes, this is the water of eternal life, free for the taking. We were there for the good times, the challenging times, and saw personally what Mark and Mother were made of. They are the Messengers[1] of the Great White Brotherhood[2], the Ones Sent–and they are true blue.

So we are publishing our stories, along with stories from others who also knew the Messengers personally, as an armchair adventure for all those following. Our first book, on our experiences with Mark Prophet, is titled *All for the Love of God: Life with Mark Prophet, a Modern-Day Mystic*. This second book is the story of Elizabeth Clare Prophet. We want you to see for yourself what it was like being around these Messengers, to experience once again their great love and encouragement.

---

[1] **Messenger.** Evangelist. One who goes before the angels bearing to the people of Earth the good news of the gospel of Jesus Christ and, at the appointed time, the Everlasting Gospel. The Messengers of the Great White Brotherhood are anointed by the hierarchy as their apostles ("one sent on a mission"). They deliver through the dictations (messages) of the Ascended Masters the testimony and lost teachings of Jesus Christ in the power of the Holy Spirit to the seed of Christ, the lost sheep of the house of Israel, and to every nation. A Messenger is one who is trained by an Ascended Master to receive by various methods the words, concepts, teachings, and messages of the Great White Brotherhood; one who delivers the law, the prophecies, and the dispensations of God for a people and an age.

[2] **Great White Brotherhood.** The group of ascended and unascended masters so called because their light is great enough to give them a white aura, although they may have any color of skin.

When I think of Elizabeth, first and foremost I think of her incredible attunement. With a keen sense of listening grace, she had one eye on God and the other on the needs of those He placed before her. She would do whatever the Master required of her without hesitation, whatever the personal cost. Early in life, she had learned the lesson "Obey immediately."

She wasted no time getting things done for the Masters. As one with a fiery mission, Elizabeth was determined to do it, come hell or high water. In the beginning she took very little time off, so concerned was she to reach the lightbearers. Even on vacations or trips, she would work on the Pearls that Mark dictated and edit the Teachings to prepare them for print.

Elizabeth never said she was perfect and warned against idolatry. She would remind us that like us, she too was striving to balance her karma and had her faults. She cautioned that idolatry is a trap on the Path and must be avoided, lest seeing a flaw in the teacher we become disillusioned with the teacher, the Teaching and therefore the Path.

When students came to Elizabeth for advice, she wouldn't tell them what to do. She would simply share a teaching with them relating to their problem and let them make their own decisions. This way they gained their individual self-mastery and the overcoming was theirs.

When students accepted the counsel of the Messengers as a higher vision or direction, all went well. When the student rejected their counsel and preferred to do it their way, they had to learn from their decisions. The Messengers would never interfere with anyone's free will. They would encourage us, saying, if you make a mistake, just get up, shake the dust off, and keep striving. Tomorrow is a brand new day, a white page, with no mistakes. Become one of the overcomers and don't let anything or anyone deter you. Tempus fugit! (time flies).

1

LONG LOST LOVE
Early Impressions
by Alex Reichardt

Beloved ones, I must tell you that when we looked for the Messenger who could carry this message and Truth through what would befall that Messenger in this century, we looked down this lifestream and found that strength and faith which would not be moved by the gossip or the calumny or the framing or whatever else might occur. For if the message is not borne by one who has the strength to meet the foes of the message with their anti-message, then how can our activity or our knowledge endure?
—Master Kuthumi, March 3, 1985

In 1958 my high school art teacher gave me two books from Saint Germain Press: *Unveiled Mysteries* and *The Magic Presence* by Godfre Ray King. She also told me about Mark Prophet, who was starting a new activity called The Summit Lighthouse. She explained that Mark had earned all nine gifts of the Holy Spirit while still a young man. Determined to find the purpose of existence, I signed up for the *Pearls of Wisdom*[1] and Keepers of the Flame

---

[1]*Pearls of Wisdom:* Messages from the Ascended Masters in the form of weekly letters to their students delivered through their Messengers Mark and Elizabeth Prophet, beginning in 1958. Many of these weekly Pearls have been collected and bound in annual volumes.

lessons.[2] These are the very teachings I had been looking for all my life. My soul was starved for the inner mysteries of God.

Now, these are no ordinary teachings. They are timeless teachings given for the next 2,000 years to help us meet the challenges of the Aquarian Age. Until now they were only given in the inner retreats of the Brotherhood.[3] At one time these retreats were physical. Due to mankind's disobedience to the Laws of God, preferring their own will to God's Will, these retreats were withdrawn to higher octaves. Mankind could only access them in their finer bodies while they slept. By cosmic dispensation this instruction is once again being made available to those seeking the higher way of life.

In late summer 1964 Mark sent out a personal invitation to the upcoming conference in Washington, D.C. In glowing terms he spoke of the great benefits for those who would make the effort. We would receive instruction on how to put on our Christ consciousness. We could walk in the footsteps of Jesus and other luminaries who had ascended from this plane of existence and achieved reunion with God—beings like Enoch, seventh from Adam, who "was not, for God took him," and Elijah, who was taken up in a "chariot of fire." Catching the flame, I took a leap of faith.

That's where I first met Elizabeth. There was something special about her that I immediately recognized and my soul responded. Both she and Mark seemed so familiar, like I must have known them before. When she looked at me it felt like she was looking through me, taking a reading at many deep levels, to the very core of my being.

You couldn't be in the Messengers' presence without experiencing a spiritual quickening and gaining some insight

---

[2]**Keepers of the Flame Fraternity:** A nondenominational spiritual order founded by Saint Germain. Its members are men and women who pledge to keep the flame for the incoming golden age of freedom, peace and enlightenment.

[3]**Brotherhood:** short for the Great White Brotherhood.

into your life. One day Mark told me that Elizabeth was just as capable as he was of reading the record of any lifestream. I soon learned how accurate this statement was. It amazed me how well Mark and Elizabeth knew me– inside out, from cover to cover, including earlier editions from past ages. They knew both my strengths and my shortcomings, but they didn't criticize or condemn me for any wrongdoing. Instead they preferred to hold the immaculate concept and present a higher way to help me overcome past momentums. It astounded me when they would answer my unspoken thoughts and questions.

During my first conference Mark did the lecturing and gave all the dictations from the Masters except one. He explained that receiving these dictations was a gift of the Holy Spirit.

These "dictations" are messages from the saints in heaven, known as Ascended Masters.[4] These Masters walked the path of Christhood, balanced their karma, and reunited with God in the ritual of the ascension. Some were the guiding lights of previous golden age civilizations of great beauty and culture–Lemuria, Atlantis, and South America. I realized this path was not only for Jesus, but for all those who would follow in his footsteps. He was the wayshower, asking us to take up our cross and follow him. Each one of us has the opportunity to make restitution for past mistakes and wipe the ledger clean.

Elizabeth and Mark had married the year before and had an infant. Mark was the first person to call her "Elizabeth." Before Mark she was called "Betty Clare." He explained that addressing someone by their full name, rather than their nickname, ties them into their original blueprint given at birth.

[4] **Ascended Masters:** Beings like you and me who were quickened by the Holy Spirit, followed the Path to union with the Higher Self, completed their mission on Earth, balanced at least 51 percent of their karma, and returned to the heart of God in the ritual called the ascension.

In those early days, Elizabeth was quietly listening, absorbing and internalizing the dictations, leaning on every word. She was one-pointed and very serious. Perhaps she was contemplating what Mark had told her: that he wouldn't be with her for very long. She was trained as a Messenger so she could take his place. And she knew that she would eventually have the responsibility of moving the organization forward–no small task.

Elizabeth made it plain for all to see that Mark was in charge. He was the Guru and the leader. When she spoke, though, it was with authority. Reporters called her "the woman with the silver voice." One moment her voice was as soft and sweet as an angel's. Another moment she was able to draw down the thunder of heaven!

Having recently graduated from college, I could relate to Elizabeth, who was one year older. Unassuming and reserved, she possessed great depth and a tender heart. It was apparent that Elizabeth and Mark were deeply in love with each other. The room felt aglow with so much light and love from the hosts of the Lord. I knew this was real, they were real. The Teachings were food for my soul. This is what I had been longing for. It filled me with great joy and I was raised up. I was coming home.

Most people attending this conference were older, a cut above the ordinary, conservative, well-dressed, warm, open and friendly. They possessed an inner light as though they had found something special. The women were in pastels and the men in suits and ties. I began to think of them as my mentors and made some lasting friendships. I wanted to learn as much as I could from the "old-timers"–some had studied the Ascended Masters' Teachings for decades. Many had come from the "I AM" Activity and were now being drawn into this one. There were also some younger people like myself taking the first steps on the Path.

Throughout the years many others joined our ranks, especially during that special time that Mother referred to as "being in the bosom of Abraham." This was the time we received a great deal of personal and inner instruction, much like Jesus gave his disciples in the Upper Room.

When Elizabeth was not on the platform, she was every bit the perfect hostess. She would go out of her way to make people feel comfortable and make sure their needs were met. She made a point of inquiring about their families and how they got into the Teachings. She was very supportive. If someone had a problem she promised to pray for them. At times the powers of darkness attacked Mark and he got hit with condemnation projected against him. Elizabeth had to remind him of who he was and support him with her prayers and calls.[5]

When Elizabeth first started giving lectures and dictations, some who were used to seeing Mark up front were skeptical. They wondered what qualifications this young woman had, having come more recently into the Teachings. They soon had a change of heart when they witnessed her delivery of the Word. She quickly turned their jaded view into one of respect and great love for her. This was enhanced by her invaluable assistance to them on their personal path.

I still remember one of her first lectures. She reminded us that we should start planning for eternity. What will we be doing after we ascend? We should look at our God-given talents and think about how we can use them after our ascension. We should nurture them and get an education. We would then have something of worth to give back to God for all He has given us.

One day Mark asked, "Aren't you interested in saving your soul?" His question caught me off guard. I had never really thought about that. And Elizabeth exhorted me, "When are you going to become a Son of God?" I began to realize there couldn't be any compromise

---

[5]**Calls:** Powerful prayers, fervent commands given by the authority of the God within. It's a known fact that in life-and-death matters, people spontaneously cry out to God with an intense fire of the heart.

on this path. Time was short and I had to accelerate, regardless of pain or price. This meant cutting my ties to the past, to worldly friends and the success cult.

As the years rolled on Elizabeth began balancing her assignments from the Brotherhood with more time out for her family and chelas.[6] This was special time that many cherish to this day.

God Is the Doer

Over the years, Elizabeth gave thousands of lectures and dictations, sometimes for hours on end. Once when she had been standing on the platform for six hours without a break, a student came up to her and asked, "Elizabeth, how can you do it?"

Her response was, "I didn't do anything. I am merely the vessel for the Master to speak through me."

At times when she was rebuking a soul, the fire that came down could hit the chela to the quick. One afternoon Elizabeth walked into the kitchen at La Tourelle. Suddenly she stopped, she turned to a disciple, the fire descended and he received a severe rebuke. She had no idea why this had taken place, and she wondered what this person had done to warrant such a severe discipline from the Master. Bystanders were shaken and perhaps thought she was too heavy-handed. Later that person came to Elizabeth and sheepishly confessed that he had deserved this chastisement, validating the Master's response through her.

After a few years, Elizabeth was given the title of Mother of the Flame and many began calling her "Mother." Then she received the mantle of "Guru Ma," meaning Teacher as Mother. Some began calling her "Guru Ma," or "Ma" for short.

---

[6]**Chela:** A Hindi term used to designate the disciple of a teacher or Guru; also, an exceptionally self-disciplined and devoted student of the Ascended Masters' teachings. In its highest manifestation, a chela is a devotee accepted by a specific Ascended Master for initiation. Derived from the Sanskrit word for "servant" or "slave."

2
ONE IN A MILLION
Mother, Messenger, Guru, Friend
by Margaret Reichardt

This is a path of Love expanded in your hearts in song and winged prayer with the Mother, whose heart's call has reached us in Darjeeling with many plans for this year of expansion and cutting free those ten thousand times ten thousand of Maitreya's bands.
–El Morya, *Pearls of Wisdom*, Vol. 29, No. 17

It took six months to get me to La Tourelle, though I lived only 20 minutes away. Instinctively I knew once I set foot on that property my life would change dramatically. Not that I was all that satisfied with my life, but familiarity breeds comfortability. After six months of cajoling by a very persistent friend, I was too embarrassed to say No one more time so I stepped off the cliff. But instead of falling I was lifted up. My first visit to The Summit Lighthouse at La Tourelle was for a Wednesday night Jesus' Watch service.[1] From the moment I entered the estate I was in bliss, my feet barely touching the ground.

---

[1]**"Watch with Me" Jesus' Vigil of the Hours** Everyone who watches with the Master one hour each week commemorates the vigil Jesus kept alone for the world in the Garden of Gethsemane" (*Jesus' Watch*, page 6). Available from The Summit Lighthouse, 800-845-8445 or www.tsl.org.

Mary Spelzhaus (Walt Whitman reembodied as a female) took me around to the violet dining room and explained the Chart of Your Divine Self.² I couldn't tell you what she said since I was floating around in euphoria. When she was finished we went to the chapel where the service was in progress. I sat in the back row so as not to disturb the others. Immediately I detected a strong odor of burning flesh. Looking around, I saw no other source for this unpleasant smell but me! There was a lot of human effluvia being burned up. Inasmuch as the Masters have told us that to get into the Teachings requires a sponsoring Master, I look back at this incident as an indication that my sponsoring Master must have been working overtime! I do not express my gratitude for him nearly enough.

From that time on, nothing of the world meant anything to me—not my career, not my friends, not my money, not my future, not my past. I lived for the next opportunity to go back to La Tourelle. On one such occasion, as I was walking through the wrought iron front gate and along the gravel driveway, I observed a queen standing by the entrance to the building. She didn't have a crown but she was a queen, all right. She had a self-assurance I had never before witnessed. She knew who she was and what she was about. The sound of her voice as she greeted me was an irresistible joy. Elizabeth. Music to my heart. I have known her before, I have known her forever.

Her voice comes from a deep harmony with God. So soothing. Once when I took a trip to New York City I decided to go to the Statue of Liberty. On the ferry ride to Liberty Island a little boy about five sat next to me with

²**Chart of Your Divine Self:** A full-color representation of three figures. The highest is the I AM Presence surrounded by color bands representing the good manifested by the soul, the middle figure is the Holy Christ Self (Mediator) and the lower figure, representing the disciple on the Path, is surrounded by the violet flame and encased in a tube of light showered down from the I AM Presence. Available from The Summit Lighthouse.

his mother. He was very fussy and fidgety. I was listening to a lecture given by Elizabeth Prophet through my cassette player headphones and decided to put them on the little boy. There was an immediate transformation. He calmed down and sat motionless during the entire time he heard Elizabeth speaking. This is exactly the same effect her voice has always had on me—except on a few occasions when she was giving me a stern rebuke.

I don't mean to say that Elizabeth (Mother) gave me a rebuke on only a few occasions. Once I joined staff, I received my share of reprimands. Most of the time, though, I could feel her great love shining through the penetrating censure. Somehow the pain of the scathing words accompanied by the searing fire soon gave way to my delight of living with the Messengers. To be in the same home with them, every day, was more than I had ever hoped for. The place was filled with light. There were angels everywhere. This is as close to heaven as anyone can get on this Earth. On more than one occasion Elizabeth questioned why I wasn't more grieved over her admonishment. I had no answer. It just seemed she had so much love for everyone, including me. And I knew she, too, received chastisements from the Ascended Masters and even from her own husband, Mark.

Elizabeth Becomes a Messenger

Elizabeth's three years of training was through Mark under the direction of many Masters, particularly El Morya and Saint Germain. It was intense. There was no leniency, since not much time was left before Mark was to leave this plane for the heaven world. Elizabeth shared just a little of the tests and initiations she went through.

For three years she wasn't allowed to listen to the news or read the newspapers. All contact with her former friends was prohibited. This was a most severe test for her. So grueling was her training that Mark at times privately wept. But Elizabeth knew she had to have such determination that she would do whatever was asked, no matter what it would cost her.

Morya directed that Elizabeth's training be tough so that she would learn to be tough. He wanted to ensure she did not end up making the same mistakes as his previous Messenger, Geraldine Innocente. Geraldine was the Messenger for the Bridge to Freedom from 1951 until she committed suicide on June 21, 1961. Right after her unfortunate death Morya appeared to Elizabeth in Boston and told her, "I have need of a feminine Messenger. You are to go to Washington to be trained under Mark Prophet." In this meeting Morya was abrupt when he talked to her because he had to go and serve on the planet Excelsior as a discipline for the failure of Geraldine Innocente, whom he had sponsored.

Elizabeth explained that this failure happened because the opposition to Geraldine was so virulent. There were actually a number of contributing factors, but most important was the lack of sufficient decrees given for her protection from the astral energies of death and hell attacking her. For this reason, Elizabeth was adamant about maintaining the decree tags for herself. She told us "If you want a Messenger in embodiment, you must decree for me."

Halfway through her ministry, Geraldine no longer believed in the authenticity of the Masters and began to make up the dictations. After her passing she was surprised to find that El Morya was indeed real.

One of Elizabeth's first assignments was to read three years of *Pearls* published by Mark, beginning in 1958. She was also to learn to decipher which of the dictations from the Bridge to Freedom were accurate and which were not. She came to the conclusion that the first years were fine. The later releases did not carry the Masters' radiation.

Elizabeth gave her first public dictation at the "Fruit of Freedom Independence Convocation" on July 5, 1964. The Ascended Master Rex spoke through her. Three months before Morya had dictated through her to a small group at Holy Tree House. Evelyn Dykman was present at the public dictation and Dorothy Lee Fulton was in attendance at the previous private dictation. Both shared their experience in their memoirs.

Elizabeth's Intense Training and First Dictation
by Evelyn Dykman

At various times Mark had told us about his training to become a Messenger—a training that went on over many, many lifetimes. He also told us that when Elizabeth came to be with him, she had to go through a severe period of training in order to become a Messenger and give dictations. Mark told us how serious it was and that sometimes during her training he felt that he would have to tell her not to go on, to just give up, because it was so hard for her. But she never gave up. She kept on until she finished what she came to do and was told by our beloved El Morya that she was ready to be a Messenger.

Mark gave the dictations at the first few conferences I attended. I remember that at my second or third conference there was something new in the air, a sense of excitement or exuberance, as we prepared for the dictation. When Elizabeth came out and took her place on the podium, the whole room felt different than usual. Then Mark came out and took his place. We could see by his face, as he sat there looking at us and then at Elizabeth, that something unusual was about to happen.

This was the day that Elizabeth gave her first dictation at a conference. What a blessing to be there! When she had finished, Mark stood up and said, "Did she not do a wonderful job?" And we said, "She certainly did!" We gave her all the applause of our hearts to show her that we appreciated being there to hear her. We were so happy for her and for all of us too, being able to experience this together.

Excerpted from *Sweet Mystery of Life* by Evelyn Dykman, available through The Summit Lighthouse

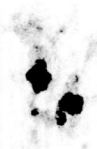
Surprise
by Dorothy Lee Fulton

It was an early morning service. We had gathered to hear the Master's dictation. Mark came to the podium and stood in his usual place. Introductory music was played. Mark waited for the Master to begin the dictation.

He nodded for the choir to sing again and stood and waited. Nothing happened. He turned and looked at Elizabeth Clare. She pointed to herself and said, "It's me, Mark."

Bewildered, he sat down. She took his place at the podium and immediately the dictation began. This was the first time Elizabeth had received and delivered a dictation. All of heaven and earth was blessed! And I was there to hear it.

Excerpted from *Here I AM* by Dorothy Lee Fulton
Messenger of Music

Mark and Mother
at Holy Tree House
Fairfax, Virginia

Mother gave her
first dictation at
Holy Tree House

3

LABOR OF LOVE
Love Is Stronger Than Death
by Margaret Reichardt

"It was with the passing of Mark that the full weight came upon the Messenger of that planetary karma as well as the initiation of the descent into Death and Hell and specifically the assignment to deal with those individuals who had plagued the house of Rakoczy and the entire Great White Brotherhood for centuries–personal enemies of mine and of yourselves who must be dealt with."
–Saint Germain, *Pearls of Wisdom*, Vol. 30, No. 2

Elizabeth ("Mother") knew Mark was going to leave. He had told her they wouldn't be together long. But is it ever possible to be fully prepared for the loss of the beloved?

She could have taken the easy way out–her ascension –since she had 51 percent of her karma balanced. But what about their four children? What of the activity? What of the Ascended Masters who needed to have their chelas contacted? How could she turn her back on those she loved so much?

I was with her daily after Mark made his ascension. I didn't do much except sit by her side during those quiet periods when she was processing her grief and coming to grips with her new life. At day's end, when everyone's needs had been met, when all duties had been dispatched, when her children were in bed and all was quiet, she was faced with the painful realization of her new life, her new identity, her new aloneness. So different now without her teacher, leader, comforter, protector, companion, twin flame. So different without someone stronger to lean upon. Now she had to be the strongest, now she had to be leaned on, now she had to take the weight of the world upon her shoulders. There were no words to describe her loss. Indeed, she did not allow her heartbreak to show when interacting with others or while at the altar, calling down God's light.

Everyone was astonished to witness how she rallied, how she led the memorial service, how she turned her attention to those around her who were suffering loss too. She nursed our wounds and shored up our spirit.

When it was time to tend to the needs of a child or a student, when there were matters that needed her attention, she set aside her pain, put on her bravest smile and carried on as if she had no needs of her own.

She told me that in these still, silent moments she was internalizing the essence of Mark. She was putting on his consciousness and strengthening the pathways of communication between them. She had the realization that her sense of loss, the agony she felt, was the result of looking outward. She realized she needed to strengthen her inner tie to Mark. The sense of separation is an illusion, though at times an overpowering one.

Most of the time she would go within, deep within. Most of the time she was silent. But at times she wanted to talk about Mark and she wanted to hear about Mark. So I told her my story. I told her how he never really got upset with me, even when I deserved it.

Mark's Great Love

One of my duties was to operate the radio. This was our way of communicating with Mark when he was off the property. (Remember the days before cell phones?) When using the radio you had to get your message across to Mark without broadcasting it all over Colorado Springs. It was talking in code and innuendoes. To me this was an impossible task and I dreaded having to do it. I wasn't good at it. Once I messed up big-time and gave certain information that caused a great inconvenience for him.

So I was waiting in the kitchen when Mark came back, fully expecting to get the dickens from him. Instead he said, "I understand that you're fearful of the radio and so I think I should train you." Then he sat with me and we practiced until I got the hang of it. I have never forgotten how the Messenger took his precious time to give me one-on-one instruction.

Mother and I talked about the time Mark bought me a waterbed. How could he have known I had been thinking about how nice it would be to have one? Then one day on no particular occasion Mark came to me and said, "I bought you a waterbed and we're going to set it up in your room this afternoon." Mark had it delivered and then he supervised the installation to ensure it was done correctly. This thoughtful gesture of Mark both astonished me and made me realize how much he cared about each one of us.

Mother Was Very Much in Tune with Her Children

When the fourth Prophet child was born in early 1972, I was assigned to her care while Mother worked on the Messengers' first book *Climb the Highest Mountain*. In this capacity I interacted with Mother every day throughout the day. I was amazed at how she always knew when her baby wanted to nurse. It didn't matter what she was doing writing, editing, counseling, cooking, whatever–when the baby wanted to nurse Mother appeared. How she knew where we were, I never figured out but she was there just as the crying would start. She was there before I finished dialing her. Regardless of the preoccupation, her consciousness extended to the whereabouts of her children. This was the sensitivity, the caring that made her a Messenger. This is the love that transformed her from Mark Prophet's 33-year-old widow to the head of a major new-age movement.

I will always be grateful for the lessons I learned at Mother's side. She did not seek solace but rather gave solace. She stood tall and mustered superhuman strength from deep within to be the pillar everyone learned to expect. No one could have done what she has done without a most extraordinary, ceaseless love such as our dear Mother has for God and His creation.

Mother draws down the Causal Body of Lanello and blesses the devotees at Mark's ascension service, 1973 La Tourelle

4

A MOVING EXPERIENCE
Land of Lanello
by Alex Reichardt

The One Sent is the Messenger who stands at the nexus of Life where the sphere of heaven and the sphere of Earth meet for the cosmic interchange of God and man.
–Sanat Kumara, *Pearls of Wisdom*, Vol. 22, No. 13

One of the last major decisions Mother and Mark made together in 1973, before he ascended, was to find the "place prepared"—as the first step toward a self-sufficient community. This was to be for those sons and daughters of God who would come together and worship the Lord God, free from the burdens of the world. Mark knew his time was short and was concerned about our future. He wanted to be sure a safe haven would be secured for the gathering of the elect. La Tourelle could no longer accommodate the many students who were coming to the quarterly conferences. The Messengers and the Masters wanted many more attending conferences and needed a bigger place. This is the "law of the vacuum." Prepare the chalice and it will be filled.

Just one month before Mark's transition, in the dead of winter, the Messengers went driving in a jeep through rough terrain east of Colorado Springs, near Peyton, Colorado.

Searching the unspoiled land in deep snowdrifts and snow-covered pines, they came upon it.

Mother described the setting as a natural amphitheater. They thought this location would be suitable. In their minds' eye they were already seeing a Golden Age civilization held in the heart of Saint Germain as a fait accompli. To Mother this move for the spiritual freedom of mankind was like Lincoln freeing the slaves over a century ago. They decided to go ahead with the purchase. That summer the "Land of Lanello" became the bustling site for the July conference.

Mother sent out the call and students around the world rallied, lending their support. In just three short weeks miracles were wrought! Through hard work and sheer determination, wilderness was tamed, giving birth to a veritable tent city—just as Mother and Mark had envisioned it.

Catastrophe Averted

Many challenges were overcome. In place of sagebrush and deer, we now had a large tent for worship with a campground, hot showers and even a Laundromat, thanks to the newly erected water tower.

The main tent had seating for 1,000. On the altar was a life-size statue of Mother Mary in gold leaf, flanked by portraits of the Ascended Hosts. Other tents included a bookstore, general store, kitchen and cafeteria. A makeshift gas stove was fired up to feed the 1,000 for 10 days.

Everything had to be planned down to the smallest detail. There was no running down to the corner store. This was real country, miles away from anywhere. Just as we were wondering whether we would get everything completed on time, the generator failed, threatening the refrigeration for our food. After fervent calls and a marathon of decrees, the light of God prevailed. All was in working order again and the class went ahead on schedule.

The first night arrived and every seat was filled. Many souls were quickened by the power of the Holy Spirit. This became a very moving experience none of us would ever forget!

Mother was touched looking out at the audience and seeing so many faces filled with gratitude and joy for all they were experiencing. She remarked that they appeared to her like many different daisies in the field. She would reflect on this experience at future conferences. Later she had a photographer take her picture as she sat dressed in blue, in a meditative pose in the middle of a sea of daisies. She did this both as a reminder of this event and also as a love tryst of the guru-chela relationship.

This open-air tent setting rekindled an ancient memory for many of us. It felt as though we had been together before, and we likened our experience to the children of Israel, in the tents in the wilderness worshiping the one God.

In a Field of Daisies
by Burt Kahn

It was an evening about four years ago following an Easter conference. Mother graciously invited my wife and me for dinner at her home on the Ranch. We were discussing the various focuses of the Ascended Masters, and I remarked to Mother that on our altar at home in our sanctuary, we had the photograph of her in a field of daisies. She asked me if I knew the significance of the photo, especially the daisies. I replied that I did not.

Mother told us when she was younger, she was looking out at a field of daisies and realized that the daisies represented us, and all the lightbearers of the world. It was her mission to gather all of us, her daisies, and give us the Teachings of the Ascended Masters. Ever since that night, when I look at one daisy or a field of them, I can see the faces of all of Mother's daisy children. We are all connected, one to the other, and ultimately to her, by a gossamer thread of light.

Lanello's Fiery Message

Lanello dictated and expressed his gratitude for the valiant effort that went into putting on this conference. But he goaded us to do better, saying he knew of 10,000 souls who would respond on the instant to this Teaching if they just had the contact. He admonished us that, had more postering been done, there would have been many more than 1,000 present. As a result we determined to put more effort into advertising future conferences.

Lanello, stressing the importance of unity, spoke of the poem "Hiawatha," which he wrote in his life as Henry Wadsworth Longfellow. Quoting Gitche Manito, the mighty, he said:

> All your strength is in your union;
> All your danger is in discord.

Lanello, in his address with K-17, spoke on preparation for cataclysm. He said, "Be the best prepared company of servers upon Earth, and then we will provide the way of escape." This dictation was a prelude to the three-day seminar on survival immediately following the Freedom Class.

Mother Was Tireless

Mother had a very rigorous schedule during this conference. Many students waited hours to be baptized by her, and this ceremony was not over until 1:00 am. Nonetheless, early the next morning Mother was back on the platform ready to impart the Sacred Fire once again to those the Lord had brought for liberation.

Mother affirmed that each person who received this baptism has the assurance of the support of the Two Messengers. She explained that as twin flames, she and Lanello hold the focus of the ascension for the body of God on Earth. Because of their office as the Two Witnesses, they are able to intercede before the Lords of Karma for all who make themselves worthy through righteousness and obedience to God's laws.

She explained that she was using an amethyst egg carved out of amethyst crystal to bless each one. Serapis Bey had anchored the ascension flame inside the amethyst egg at the previous Easter class. The egg hung on a chain that was a gift from Clara Louise Kieninger, Regent Mother of the Flame.[1]

Mother announced that Denny Cree, longtime Keeper of the Flame, had earned his ascension on May 13, two months earlier, having balanced 68 percent of his karma. This thrilled his wife, Iva, who was in the audience and heard the thunderous applause. Several years later, Mother confirmed that Iva went on to make her ascension, having balanced 53 percent of her karma.

They were both very devoted to the Masters and attended many conferences. We used to kid Denny about his name and would call him "De-Cree" as a pun on the word "decree,"[2] which was the capstone of his victory.

What It Will Take to Transform the Earth

The Goddess of Liberty said she needed only 1,000 dedicated individuals to transform the Earth—the very number of students who had rallied for this conference.

Archangel Michael relieved us of our fear and doubt. He said, "My momentum is great enough to charge you with a living faith that shall carry you home to the victory of your ascension."

Each night at the end of the last session we gathered around a large campfire and formed "the Circle of Oneness."

---

[1] **Clara Louise Kieninger**. See *All for the Love of God: Life with Mark Prophet, A Modern-Day Mystic*, page 44.

[2] **Decree:** More powerful than other forms of prayer, a specifically worded petition to the Godhead for constructive personal and planetary change, given aloud by a son or daughter of God in His name and in accordance with His will. "Thou shalt also decree a thing, and it shall be established unto thee: and the light shall shine upon thy ways." (Job 22:28)

This ritual was based on one of the first dictations from Lanello to staff after his ascension. Visualizing the Christ standing in the center and his apostles in a golden ring around us, we surrendered the day's burdens, all manifestations and happenings, deeds and thoughts less than the Christ Presence. Calling upon the law of forgiveness, we asked that our Christ Presence replace our untransmuted human substance. Interestingly enough, we were told that this had also been the custom of the American Indians.

A Transcendent Experience

Many agreed that this conference had been one of the most memorable experiences ever. Twenty-one dictations were delivered. Each dictation had a specific dispensation, many of which could be received only by those who had made the effort to be present.

The Elohim Astrea gave us much comfort with her words on how to pass our tests: "Forget not that at any hour of the day or night when the trial comes, when the fires of crucifixion are upon you, you can know that you can win if instantaneously you address the Almighty, if you address Jesus the Christ, the Holy Spirit and the Divine Mother, and then call to the mighty Elohim, call to Astrea to release the circle and sword of blue flame around the cause and core of all that opposes your God-identity. If you will do that, I will promise you that you will not fail one single test along the pathway of life."

The Ascended Lady Master Portia announced a decision made a year earlier by Saint Germain, Jesus and the Darjeeling Council. The Great White Brotherhood had anointed the Mother of the Flame, Elizabeth Clare Prophet, as the Vicar of Christ and head of the true Church. Portia explained, "Although it is not the preference of this Messenger to have this announcement made, I have explained and insisted that unless the announcement be released by Hierarchy into the ethers and anchored in the body of the

Keepers of the Flame, Hierarchy would not be able to precipitate all that we desire to bring forth."

After the Survival Seminar, Mother and 100 pilgrims hiked up to the 14,110-foot summit of Pike's Peak to anchor the light released during these 10 days. Through lightning and thunder, rain and hail they continued their climb up 12 miles of steep, rough terrain. Though wind-blown and soaked, they felt energized and victorious when they reached the top.

Mark's ascension brought an explosion in the membership. With Lanello as one of the Two Witnesses in heaven and Mother on Earth holding the balance and doing the clearance work, they were an unbeatable team to cut free the lightbearers.

Many joined staff, though Mother was concerned about taking on more mouths to feed. Nevertheless, she told me that Lanello wanted these people to be part of our "spiritual family." Setting her concerns aside, she allowed whoever Lanello wanted to join in our growing band.

Ma gives the sure sign of Victory on top of Pikes Peak
after a pilgrimage with conferees in 1973

5

CITY OF THE SUN
New Golden Age Civilization
by Alex Reichardt

There is required a body of God on Earth who are living just midpoint between the octaves. And that midpoint is your own Christ Self—your own Christ-realization—and that midpoint is the contact of the Word and the Messenger in your midst.

—Lanello

Just three months after Mark's ascension in 1973, planning was already under way for a self-sufficient community. In response to Lanello's request, Mother established the first Community of the Holy Spirit, overlooking the majestic 30-mile-long Lake Coeur d'Alene in Idaho. This was the land of sky-blue waters and pine-forested mountains near Harrison. This impressive project was to be built on a large 340-acre parcel, donated in part by two members of the activity.

Mother drew down the matrix for this community, proclaiming it God's dream for a Golden Age civilization come again, a place prepared for the Woman and her Seed. Included were Mother's retreat and a chapel, along with a very large farm and a food-processing plant. On the drawing board were schools for M.I. (Montessori International), preschool through high school, for children of community members and Keepers. These children would be taught Ascended Master Law along with a typical American education.

A large parcel of land was set aside for the future construction of a temple. This edifice was to be a replica of the temple in the golden City of the Sun residing in the etheric. Mother and the Board met with a prominent architect chosen to work on this remarkable venture. It was to be built by Keepers and staff. Plans drawn up for this self-reliant community received a favorable response from the local county planning commission.

Heart of the Lion
by Michael Kincheloe

We could walk down to the lake and it had the coldest water I have ever been in. Elizabeth talked to me about "the place prepared." She said since Mark had been Saint Mark and was called "The Lion of God," Coeur d'Alene was an appropriate setting because it means "Heart of the Lion."

The Ascended Master Cuzco Dedicated the Land

Prior to his ascension, Cuzco ruled a very advanced ancient civilization of the Incas in Peru. To this day there is a city in that country bearing his name as a memorial to his leadership and legacy.

Dictating through Mother with 24 disciples present, the Ascended Master Cuzco anchored the ascension flame in the property dedicating it to the ascension of all mankind. He stipulated that only those possessing undying loyalty and unflinching devotion to the Mother Flame would remain in this community. The responsibility for the ascension of a planet and its people rested upon the shoulders of those who made this place their home. This was a time of great expectation. There was nothing to stop us from total victory.

Afterward Mother and staff read together from the Book of Acts on the founding of the early church, recounting the miracles by John and Peter and the healings that took place. Mother explained that they received many signs and wonders of the Holy Ghost descending in their midst because of their total surrender and dedication to the flame of God.

> And the multitude of them that believed were of one heart and of one soul: neither said any of them that ought of the things which he possessed was his own; but they had all things common. (Acts 4:31–32)

The meaning of this was clear. If we were to ask God for His all, we would be required to give our all. This would necessitate the total commitment of each occupant to pass the tests of the ruby cross of selflessness, service, sacrifice and surrender (of the lesser self). Those accepted as residents were expected to give all they had in excess of their day-to-day needs. This was not to be of poverty, but of the abundant Life and a willingness to trust God to provide.

Vision of a Modern-Day Essene Community

Therefore, like the Essene community, this new "City of the Sun" would be dedicated as a haven of light. It was destined to lay the foundation for the next 2,000-year cycle of the Aquarian Age.

Later the plans changed and this dream took a new direction, foretelling of a divine destiny yet to come. After the infrastructure was well under way and the three once-dilapidated buildings were completely renovated, the couple who had offered their land backed out. The setting of the etheric blueprint became the matrix for another venture, mightier still. And the dream lived on as the future Royal Teton Ranch in Montana.

Mark and Elizabeth

Empowered by the Holy Spirit, Mark and Elizabeth
Prophet are Messengers of God for today. They deliver
the Word of Elohim as did the prophets of old. These
Messengers were anointed by Saint Germain, hierarch
of the Aquarian Age. Saint Germain is the "seventh
angel" spoken of in the Book of Revelation, and his
coming marks the hour when "the mystery of God
should be finished, as he hath declared to his servants
the prophets." (Rev. 10:7)

6

NO PAIN, NO GAIN
Six Months without Contact
by Margaret Reichardt

Pain is a weaning process. We have allowed our Messenger and chelas to know pain and the very depths of pain and loss and persecution, and so on, but only because our Messenger and certain chelas have welcomed whatever discipline or initiation. For as you know, only the chela can create the Guru and in so doing will have the full ministration of the Guru.
— Kuthumi, *Pearls of Wisdom*, Vol. 34, No. 33

Sometime in the summer after Mark made his ascension, life on staff took a turn and we started getting regular Sunday afternoons off. We often went on group trips to the mountains for a picnic lunch after the morning service. On one such jaunt Alex and I found ourselves sitting alone together on top of a big boulder. We discussed a message we had just received from Lanello. He said we should strive for balancing 100 percent of our karma while here. It is easier to balance karma on Earth than in the etheric.

Though we had daily contact for four years, it was not until this moment that I realized I had feelings for Alex. And from all appearances the feeling was mutual. Each time I looked at him, my heart did a little flip. This took me by surprise. I had vowed some years before that I would not get involved with anyone, having a sense of satisfaction with all I had been given as grace. I had the Messengers and the Masters. That was really all I needed.

Around this same time Alex wrote a letter to Mother requesting permission to date. Mother called me and asked what I thought. Yes! I would like to date Alex. I was thrilled.

The culture of staff life at that time made it advisable to keep budding relationships under wraps, thus avoiding the possibility that any coworker become unsettled about their monastic status. Now this secrecy posed quite a problem for me because I had to sit by silently and watch the pretty young girls expressing their interest in Alex as if there were no code of conduct. So we met at the Broadmoor Hotel, a few short blocks away. This was as far as we could go without a vehicle.

I no longer had my car because the year before Mark had decided to clear out the parking lot. A number of staff did not comply with his request. I could not bring myself to dispute or analyze any of the requests of the Messengers. To me there was no question that giving up the car was an initiation I had to pass. I found myself relieved without this previously prized possession. But I had surely made an emotional decision rather than a practical one. As soon as the school year started, my girls had no way to get there and it was too far to walk. So Mark assigned a car to me for this purpose.

But I didn't have the use of this vehicle for my secret dates with Alex so they were mostly walks around the Broadmoor lake. The code of conduct prevented us from even holding hands. No touching unless about to be married. Even so, we found ourselves getting serious. Hmmm. Was this going to work? He was a confirmed bachelor and I was a single mother of two teenage daughters and a son. The deck was stacked. Still . . .

About that time the Masters stepped in and Mother told us we could have no contact for six months. No dates, no talking, no looking. Shortly after, she sent Alex to Santa Barbara and then to Spokane to design an eatery at the World's Fair. I tried unsuccessfully to get him out of my mind. Then I went with Mother and some staff to Spokane for the Freedom '74 class. Here I was in the same city as Alex. Like a thirsty man in the desert, just missing the oasis.

Six months later, at the end of the summer, Alex was due to return to La Tourelle. I was uncontrollably elated and expectant—until Mother told me I had to leave staff. What? I had joined for life. Nevertheless, she said she wanted Alex back at La Tourelle and the two of us couldn't both be there. I wasn't used to questioning the decisions of the Messenger, but this was so shocking. What had we done?

"Dorothy Smith told me you two have broken the code of conduct and that cannot be permitted. You are out!" (Dorothy Smith was Alex's high school teacher who introduced him to the Teachings.)

I was dumbfounded. "Where did Dorothy get an idea like that? We have never once broken the code of conduct."

Silence was like a roaring in my ear. Mother stared at me quietly for a long time. I felt her gaze burning through to my soul, reading my deepest secrets. My world hung by a thread. Have I not sufficiently surrendered this relationship? Then I will do better. I will give up even my thoughts of Alex. I cherished being on staff. I needed to be on staff. There was no other life for me.

Finally, "OK, I believe you. Dorothy was only trying to make trouble because she wants to take your place. You may stay and you may date Alex."

Whew.

The Tower of La Tourelle

Mother's Office

In the Tower

7

FOLLOW YOUR HUNCHES
Don't Let That Person In
by Alex Reichardt

If you are not in attunement with God at all times, how can He act for you in time of danger or crisis or opposition? It means that in the presence of danger you must first make your attunement before you can receive assistance. In the life of a disciple there is not time for this, beloved ones. Attunement must be ready as an armor, as a sword of Truth. When you are in a battle, you cannot run back to the lines and put on your armor and your sword after the enemy has launched their attack; there you must be ready.

Attunement, therefore, is somewhat of a subconscious quality. It is begun with the outer mind; it is begun by its supplication, by the prayer to the Holy Christ Self to take command and continue the prayers and decrees of your heart throughout the twenty-four hours. This is an important request, and it should be made by you each morning before you even rise from your beds.

—Mother Mary, *Pearls of Wisdom*, Vol. 24, No. 58

"Voyages of Discovery," the 1974 Harvest Class, was held in the Crystal Ballroom at the Biltmore Hotel in Los Angeles. The class was quickly filling to capacity with over 500 people. Many conferees had already made their way to their seats when Mother, moving quickly down the main aisle, said to me, "Don't let that person in!" pointing to the crowd.

Her security was my responsibility. Therefore I had to figure out who she was concerned about. Looking out over the burgeoning crowd, I realized this must be my test. I knew she was counting on my attunement to make the right decision. After some inquiries, I finally zeroed in on one lady in the back. I learned she was suicidal and unbalanced. I asked her to leave. From past experience, I knew that just one person focalizing this type of negative energy could compromise the delivery of the Word from the Masters.

The next day we had a surprise visitor. A representative of the false hierarchy arrived at the door seeking admittance. Hostile and filled with dark energy, he seemed determined to disrupt the event. So I grabbed Edwin, another staff member, and we confronted him.

Gentle by nature, Edwin at 6'4" raised himself to his full stature, and with arms crossed said, "Sir, you may not enter the service." Taken aback, the man took one look at him, spun around and left. We never saw him again.

"I Want to Follow Her!"

After the break Mother was walking down the main stairway into the lobby when a stranger, catching a glimpse of her, said, "Whoever that woman is, I want to follow her!" Like many others, she had recognized something special about Mother, and her soul responded. Mother had an electrifying aura because of the Presence of God upon her.

Due to the mantles bestowed upon her as Messenger for the Great White Brotherhood, God was able to work through her. After a while I began to notice how people's lives were being transformed. Sometimes healing took place. Other times thorny issues were resolved. Even the vibration of a whole group of people could be raised when she entered a room. I had noticed the same thing happen when Mark was still in embodiment. She was following in his footsteps.

She realized that this was a result of her continual prayers and devotion to the heart of Jesus. She knew it was not she but the Lord who was blessing the people. Ever humble, she would always give the glory to God and not allow anyone to idolize her.

Another devotee who recognized Mother's light and attainment was Herbert.

A True Messenger
by Herbert Beigel
(Herbert dictated this story when he was 90, shortly before he passed on.)

Growing up I always prayed to Jesus to put me in the right religion. As a result he brought me to the book *Unveiled Mysteries*, by the Messenger of the "I AM" Activity, Guy Ballard. So I came into the "I AM" Activity three months after Guy Ballard ascended (he is now the Ascended Master Godfre). The "I AM" Activity is the same Teaching as The Summit Lighthouse, except that they are much stricter.

When Edna Ballard (Guy Ballard's wife, also a Messenger of the "I AM" Activity) ascended, I figured there must be a Messenger someplace so I started looking. There were lots of groups getting messages. They said very good things but they weren't Messengers and there was no mantle.

I heard about The Summit Lighthouse and waited until there was a conference close by. Finally one was advertised in Minneapolis. So my wife and I attended. It was immediately obvious that Elizabeth Clare Prophet was a true Messenger. She spoke with authority. There was radiation and she said the right things. After the service, Ma looked us up. She told us, "When you came into the class, you had so much light around you! I wanted to know who you were." Of course, I told her about my many years decreeing and our "I AM" Activity background.

If anyone has the dictations of the Ascended Masters, they have priceless gems. Study the dictations and you will learn something new each time you read or hear them. Studying them takes you deeper into the light and gives you more insight.

My motto is this: Keep praying the light! For one day we'll all be on the other side!

Mount Shasta

At the conference on Mount Shasta in the summer of 1975 Mother spoke about the mountain. She said that it had high spiritual energy, and then recounted how Saint Germain had contacted his disciple, Guy Ballard, while he was hiking on the mountain. This story can be found in Unveiled Mysteries, published by Saint Germain Press.

Later Mother talked about a Catholic priest who came up to her after the conference. He expressed his gratitude and thanked her for having the courage and strength of conviction to be who she was. He said her example helped him considerably to be who he was.

Mother greets students at the Motherhouse

Alex and Margaret at the Prom

Morya Mark

Merlita Mother

October 10, 1973

The special inscription autographed by Mother
in the new book *Light from Heavenly Lanterns*

8

True Blue
Life in the Temple
by Alex Reichardt

When you speak the Word of life, when you recite the beautiful sayings of the avatars who have gone before, when you read our dictations aloud, when you give dynamic decrees, when you recite the Hail Mary, you are the anchoring of the Word of the Logos itself. —Kuan Yin, *Pearls of Wisdom,* Vol. 26, No. 54

Seated in the chapel of the Motherhouse that memorable day in September, no one had any idea what was transpiring right outside. It was 1969 and Saint Germain was dictating. He announced to the incredulous group that El Morya was walking the grounds. Morya was establishing a powerful concentration of the Will of God in Santa Barbara, extending out to California, across America and to Europe. Of course nobody ventured out to see this cosmic event for fear of disturbing the dictation and breaking Mark's attunement.

Four years later El Morya came again. Now a miniature sanctuary stood where he had walked. In just three weeks, Morya's ardent chelas had transformed a neglected shed into a Will of God focus fit for a king. It already had the right silhouette with its tile roof, white stucco exterior and columns entwined with violet sun-kissed vines.

Mother was ecstatic and announced that it was like standing in Morya's temple at Darjeeling.

Mother had supervised the décor, to be sure it was right: blue-flame carpet, blue and gold paper of Moorish design. Three-flame sconces for Morya's three dots and a Spanish candelabrum as a focal point for the Great Central Sun. Actual photos of Morya and Kuthumi, as they appeared to Madame Blavatsky 100 years earlier, were hung above the altar. The central carved altar with an exquisite crystal chalice completed the matrix. The five chairs focused Mighty Cosmos' secret rays, which included Morya's Jacobean blue velvet chair and four chairs for his disciples.

The Ascended Hosts began to take note of this Shrine to the Will of God and started calling it the "Blue Room" as the disciples continued giving their devotions. To help maintain this forcefield, calls to the will of God were given daily.

In honor of this accomplishment, Mother autographed the new book *Light from Heavenly Lanterns* by El Morya.

Gems from the Heart of Morya

After the Mother of the Flame consecrated this little chapel on October 10, 1973, El Morya dictated an important message and a promise. He proclaimed his ray was anchored in the chalice and in our hearts. But to keep the flame alive, we needed to prime the pump. He said without the heart and the will fueled by faith and determination, outer rituals would fall into a state of neglect and decay. He then made a promise, "For every decree offered in the honor, the sacred tryst, of the holy Will, I shall multiply it still by the power of the ten and by the action of Truth."

Moving across the sands of time, he told of olden times when he was on the stage of life as King Arthur of Camelot with Saint Germain as Merlin. Once again he made his entrance as Thomas Becket, then as Sir Thomas

More, Lord Chancellor of England and servant of King Henry VIII.

The lesson that El Morya wanted us to take from his story is this: when we leave this plane of existence, the only thing we leave behind of worth is our principles as an example for others to follow.

Happy Memories of the Motherhouse
by Margaret Reichardt

The Motherhouse was a jewel in the heart of Santa Barbara. The Spanish-style building was centrally located on a large property on State Street above the city. French doors opened onto a patio in the back where many happy events took place.

The first time I saw this beautiful place was some days before the first conference held there, Easter 1970. I had arrived early to help with registration and was busy setting up. Anita Buchanan was nearby sewing blue chiffon curtains for the windows. Since I was a seamstress, I knew how challenging it was for her to make all these curtains. Chiffon is slippery and difficult to control. Although Anita was an excellent seamstress, she had measured wrong and one of the panels came out eighteen inches short! But there was no more fabric left, not at the Motherhouse and not at the store. Faced with this dilemma she prayed fervently to Saint Germain and told him he would have to produce a miracle. And he did!

Now Anita was no stranger to Saint Germain. In his embodiment as Christopher Columbus, Anita (Queen Isabella at the time) had sponsored his mission to the New World. To her amazement the panel was stretched and the curtains looked great. I did not witness this miracle but I did witness the hubbub after. Another account of this story can be found in Annice Booth's book *Memories of Mark: My Life with Mark Prophet.*

Ding Dong the Bells Are Gonna Chime!

The next time I went to the Motherhouse was to get married! It was the day after the Harvest Class 1974 "Voyages of Discovery," held at the Biltmore Hotel in Los Angeles. Alex and I had been dating for some months. And that's all it was—just dating. So one day I spoke with Mother and told her that, although I enjoyed going out to dinner and taking walks around the lake, I didn't see any purpose of continuing the relationship. Well, she had a different take. She told me Alex and I had been married many times before but that he also had been a monk in many embodiments. So it wasn't an easy step for him to think of marriage. She recommended I make arrangements to meet Alex at 2 pm the next day and tell him to fish or cut bait. Well, we met at 2 o'clock (the line of doubt and fear on the Cosmic Clock)[1] and it worked!

So now the Messenger, Elizabeth Clare Prophet, was marrying us. And what a beautiful cupid she was! Mother told Alex after we tied the knot, "Lanello is very happy you are getting married." This put the wind in our sails! We had three days for a honeymoon in gorgeous Santa Barbara.

The day after we got married, Dorothy Lee Fulton married her childhood sweetheart. In her memoirs *Here I AM* she tells the story of how Lanello had made sure Dorothy and Milton finally got together after many years of separation.

The Ascended Master Lanello surely does look after us!

---

[1]**Cosmic Clock:** A science of understanding personal psychology and karma by plotting the qualities of God and their perversions by man on the 12 lines of the clock, and using this chart to anticipate the tests to come in the cycles of time. This science was a gift of Mother Mary to mankind through Mark and Elizabeth Prophet. See *Predict Your Future: Understand the Cycles of the Cosmic Clock*, published by The Summit Lighthouse.

Wedding Bells ring for Margaret and Alex. Mother married us at the Santa Barbara Motherhouse. Afterwards we had a reception on the patio.

Conferees relaxing at the Motherhouse in Santa Barbara, California

Washington, D.C.

Anchoring
the Light

9

YANKEE DOODLE DANDY
Anchoring the Light in Our Nation's Capital
by Alex Reichardt

Precious ones, I address every Keeper of the Flame across the face of the Earth. I need you, each and every one, in my service in this hour. —Saint Germain, *Pearls of Wisdom*, Vol. 21, No. 6

Buoyed up by our rousing 1976 July class in Washington, D.C., Mother and 700 students went on a pilgrimage throughout the city to anchor the light from the Freedom conference in our national shrines and landmarks. Decree leaders using megaphones helped keep all our voices in sync as we marched to the beat of the drum, the flute, a guitar and accordion, hands clapping, along the streets. Mother announced that angelic hosts had joined us and were carrying banners of the World Mother and Maitreya. We could feel their presence as we sang patriotic songs and offered devotions to God. Our hearts felt reignited by the original fervor of the American patriots and their great dedication to freedom. We remembered the Master's statement that "the very atoms and cells of the land of America were recording this event."

Lincoln: Righting Ancient Wrongs

Walking past the reflecting pool, we approached the Lincoln Memorial. Once inside the rotunda, Mother shared her thoughts about this great president, saying he had paid the ultimate price for the Republic. She revealed it was his flame that had preserved the Union as one nation under God, uniting both North and South. She then gave us some remarkable teaching about the soul of Lincoln.

He was embodied in Egypt as Ramses II, the Pharaoh who would not let the children of Israel go. Because of this unpaid debt, he needed another opportunity to right this record. As president this time around, he was able to end slavery in America, thereby accruing good to his lifestream and balancing that karma. She explained that this showed how exact Cosmic Law really is, and that life gives each one of us the opportunity to balance misdeeds of the past.

George Washington Come Again

Seeing the majestic Washington Monument rising above the city brought back the great love and power of Godfre's dictation two days earlier. During his message, a powerful thunderstorm had caused the monument to be shut down for an hour. Mother reminded us that Godfre, in his previous life as George Washington, was a man of great honor and integrity. He was also embodied as Guy Ballard, Messenger of the "I AM" Activity in the 1930s, and made his ascension in 1939. His presence was tangible in the capital, especially at the Washington Monument.

Facing skyward at the top of this magnificent 555-foot granite and marble obelisk, is the inscription *Laus Deo*, or "Praise be to God!" From this vantage point is a beautiful panoramic view of the "Alabaster City" designed by Pierre Charles L'Enfant. It is a perfect cross: the White House is to the north, the Capitol to the east, the Jefferson Memorial to the south and the Lincoln Memorial to the west.

Except the LORD build the house, they labour in vain that build it: except the LORD keep the city, the watchman waketh but in vain. (Psalm 127: 1)

Washington's Prayer for America, Dated April 30, 1789

Almighty God, We make our earnest prayer
- that Thou wilt keep the United States in Thy holy protection,
- that Thou wilt incline the hearts of the citizens to cultivate a spirit of subordination and obedience to government;
- and entertain a brotherly affection and love for one another and for their fellow citizens of the United States of America at large.
And finally that Thou wilt most graciously be pleased to dispose us all
- to do justice,
- to love mercy and
- to demean ourselves with that charity, humility and pacific temper of mind which were the characteristics of The Divine Author of our blessed religion, and without whose example in these things we can never hope to be a happy nation.
Grant our supplication, we beseech Thee, through Jesus Christ our Lord.
Amen.

Continuing our prayer vigil, we went on to the White House. We were thrilled to see this magnificent building up close. Mother told us that this is an outer focus of the Great White Brotherhood, hence its name. She said the first family is supposed to set the example of the Holy Family for the people of this nation.

Several years earlier Mark had given us the inner meaning of the word government as "God-over-men." Mother said since the time of Noah, government was established for the protection of all people—including the unborn. Any nation that supports abortion will not endure and will go down in cataclysm, whether economic or physical. In a dictation Mother Mary said that we had just so much time to stop abortion before the judgment of Almighty God descends.

We then anchored the light of freedom in the National Archives. This is where our sacred documents are enshrined, including our Constitution and Declaration of Independence. Our eight-hour vigil came to an end as we continued anchoring the light at the Capitol and the Supreme Court.

We were inspired by the Statue of Freedom above the Capitol dome, framed by the golden rays of the setting sun. Most Americans have no idea of the significance of this work of art. This statue is of a classical female figure. Her right hand rests upon the hilt of a sheathed sword. Her left hand holds a laurel wreath of victory and the shield of the United States with thirteen stripes. Her helmet is encircled by stars and features a crest composed of an eagle's head, feathers and talons.

A brooch inscribed "U.S." secures her flowing robes as she stands on a cast-iron globe encircled with the national motto, E pluribus unum ("Out of many, one"). This design was inspired upon the sculptor Thomas Crawford, by a being of light. Known as the Goddess of Freedom,[1] she dictated through Mother and referenced this statue.

Even though it was now past 6 pm, we were surprised that after eight hours of decrees and songs, our voices had held out so well. We then boarded the buses and returned to George Washington University for a much-needed rest.

The Man Who Would Not Die

1977 was a banner year for Mother and Saint Germain! The magical moment came when she was asked to speak about Saint Germain's embodiment as the "Wonderman of

[1]**The Goddess of Freedom**: Refers to the Ascended Lady Master who holds the God consciousness of Freedom for the Earth.

Europe." Alan Landsburg decided to do a TV documentary on le Comte de Saint Germain—*The Man Who Would Not Die*—and she used this opportunity to expound on his previous embodiments.

Televising of this event took place in the perfect setting: Saint Germain's office at the Ashram of the World Mother in Los Angeles. As Mother was seated before the cameras, the portrait of Saint Germain, along with his flame and vibration, could be seen behind her by the millions who would be viewing this special.

This was an historic moment when Saint Germain's Messenger could bear witness to this Master of Freedom and Alchemy to the American people, known to them as their own Uncle Sam. Having done his research for the show, Leonard Nimoy commenting on this embodiment as the Wonderman of Europe said, "He was considered a genius in art, music, politics and alchemy—and although he looked to be forty, many believed he was at least 150 years old!"

During this interview for national television, Saint Germain used the opportunity to give a dictation titled "A Message to America and the People of Earth." Commenting afterward, Mother said this was a long-awaited and long-deserved tribute to the Master, who sponsored America and the freedom flame enshrined in its people. After the filming she remarked that she felt his presence closer to the physical than ever before, and that it would leave a lasting impression on the souls of those in the audience when it was viewed.

"You Are the Chosen Ones!"

In 1977 Saint Germain spoke to M.I. high school students at their graduation ceremony at the Ashram. He had come with an important assignment and a dispensation granted by the Lords of Karma. After informing them they are the chosen ones, Saint Germain told the students they are the leaders of the teenagers of America.

They Almost Seemed Alive
by Alex Reichardt

Mother really loved two blue and white ceramic
Fu Dogs that I had gotten for her. She said that Fu Dogs
are the guardians of the temple and protect against evil
spirits. When they first arrived, she noticed they needed
cleaning. Rolling up her sleeves, she carefully washed
each one herself, treating them as though they were alive.
She seemed to get great joy from doing this. I snapped
these pictures of her scrubbing them.

Mother enjoyed having pictures of the Masters
and statues around her. She said they focused their presence through them. Some of these treasures came from
monasteries in Tibet and China and were one of a kind
rare finds. She particularly cherished an old weathered
wooden statue of Kuan Yin and had it photographed
against the setting sun over the Pacific. By the serene
expression on Kuan Yin's face, it looked as though many
pilgrims had fingered this beautiful representative of
the Mother of Mercy.

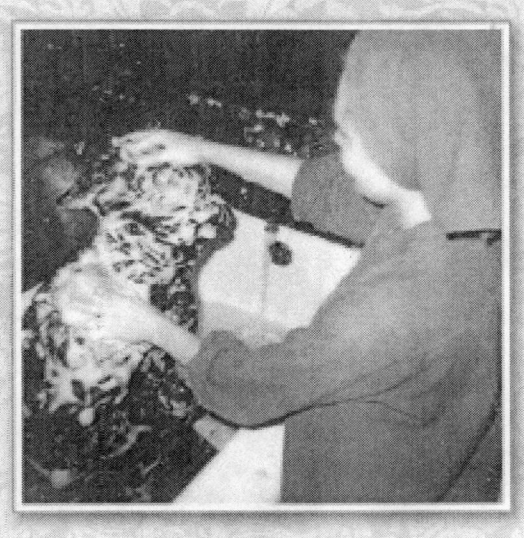

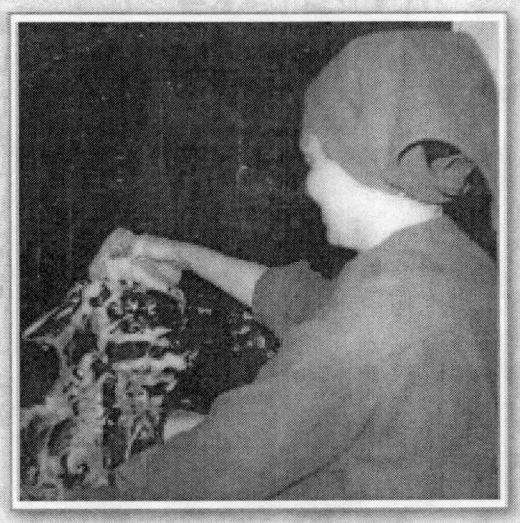

Mark and Mother
greet the conferees

La Tourelle

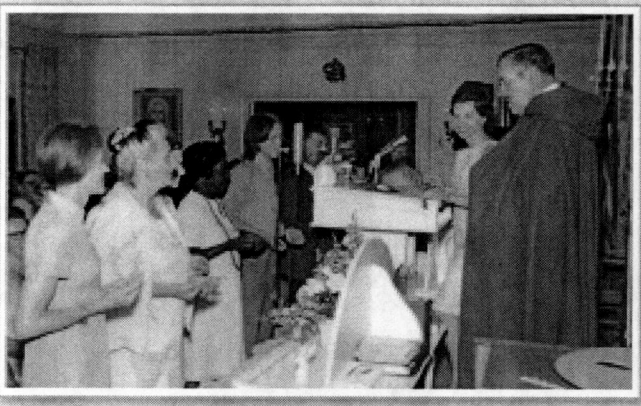

Knighting Ceremony

10

WILL WONDERS NEVER CEASE
The Messenger's Unshakable Faith
by Alex Reichardt

The Messenger then and now is the One Sent and the believers are those who sustain the light of the Spirit in the souls of humanity through the blessed Mediator personified in the anointed Messenger.
— Archangel Gabriel, *Pearls of Wisdom*, Vol. 22, No. 8

In 1976 Jesus came with a profound message. His pivotal dictation gave new impetus and direction to the mission of the Two Witnesses: going after the 144,000.[1] He was calling his Messenger and his Church to the New Jerusalem in the City of the Angels–Los Angeles, California.

We had found the perfect place–a college campus in the middle of Pasadena, just outside Los Angeles. Finally

---

[1]**144,000:** Eons ago Earth was such a dark planet it was to be dissolved. Sanat Kumara, the Ancient of Days, volunteered to come here from Venus to keep the flame of God burning. Sanat Kumara would endure this voluntary exile until his opportunity had come to an end or until some would catch that flame and turn around and serve God, establishing once again the Light on Earth. Accompanying Sanat Kumara on his long exile were 144,000 volunteers who vowed to stay with him until this mission was accomplished. Among this group were Gautama Buddha, Lord Maitreya and the Messengers Mark and Elizabeth Prophet. A city of light (Shamballa) was built for Sanat Kumara on an island in the Gobi Sea. This city was later withdrawn to the etheric octave because of the ungodly consciousness of some of the inhabitants. The Gobi Sea then became the Gobi Desert.

we would have the facilities and lebensraum we needed all in one place. This would give us barely enough time to move and open Summit University (S.U.) in September.

Midst the euphoria, the unthinkable happened. Pasadena College suddenly changed their mind and we were no longer welcome. All preparations and planning came to a grinding halt. Since there was no alternative, the consequences of this decision were serious. Mother was adamant. This was totally unacceptable. To accept this would put back the Darjeeling Council's plans by at least one year. There was no turning back.

How Mother Dealt with Crisis

With her unshakable faith in God, Mother went to the altar and gave invocations, placing the entire matter in Jesus' hands for a God-solution. She told us that this opposition to the onward march of light was also the rejection of the One Sent and needed immediate spiritual work.

Mother rallied staff and the membership to give their fervent calls and not let up until the Victory was secure. From that moment on, the round-the-clock tag began in earnest for the protection of Jesus' mission. Having turned the entire matter over to God, Mother began teaching S.U.

Without the Calls Nothing Would Have Happened

Mother's fiery calls and the rising momentum of decrees lit a fire so intense that the opposition literally melted away. Pasadena College again reversed their decision and the lease was signed. Once again the call had compelled the answer! Without this prayer vigil nothing would have happened and we would still be sitting in Colorado Springs.

Everything we owned was boxed, labeled, and numbered. Finally the caravan was on its way. We began to feel like the children of Israel in search of the Promised Land. A sense of expectancy was in the air as we set out for the Golden State enfired with a new sense of mission and purpose.

Situated at the base of the San Gabriel Mountains, the college campus with its 17 buildings seemed spacious and included residence halls with inner courtyards. There was even a small theater and library for students and staff to study the many releases from the Masters. We had gone from a 20-room mansion to a 12-acre campus. Yet within weeks all facilities were occupied. Our activity was expanding as rapidly as a new nova on the horizon. This was in fulfillment of El Morya's promise to astound us by the unfolding of future events.

Meanwhile, Mother and her editorial staff stayed behind at La Tourelle preparing the Teachings for publication. She wanted to ensure that the students continued receiving the Masters' words without interruption. Mother had made the commitment to El Morya that the Pearls would go out weekly, and she intended to keep her word. Finally they wrapped up their work and made their way to California.

No Room in the Inn

However when Mother arrived in Pasadena, she was in for a surprise. There was no space set aside for her office. Her needs had been forgotten. As head of the organization she could have easily taken over someone's office. But seeing everyone had already settled in, instead she went about trying to find a place to work. The only place left was a small cleaning closet on the third floor of Nease Hall. Here she could be near Graphics (located in the basement). So she exchanged the mops and brooms for her desk and files, and said nothing about it. I was amazed! Many never knew anything about this incident. This was so characteristic of our Messenger's selflessness and humility, placing the needs and comfort of others before her own.

This reminded me of the way Mother described herself: she is the Messenger, a gift of God to the chelas. As such the chelas can do anything they want with this gift.

They can love or hate, they can follow or oppose, they can support or deny. She was truly living by her word.

Like a Living Room on Venus

Our new home had a dark cavernous auditorium with fixed seating for 3,000 and no windows. Mother decided to create a proper forcefield for the Masters by having an altar built. She asked me to design a bell-shaped platform with a home for a statue of Gautama at the base and planters along the sides. When I asked if she would like to have a nice chapel some day, she replied, "Yes, but the priority and focus of the mission is contacting the light-bearers and any additional funds should go to that purpose."

Mother chose rose for the color scheme, as a focus of divine love. Rose-colored cascades and swags framed the new proscenium, and violet wool carpet on closeout completed the matrix. Non-stop construction for two weeks and the transformation was complete, just before the conference was to begin.

Then the defining moment! Sanat Kumara, Ancient of Days, dictated. He surprised us by thanking everyone who worked on the altar, saying it reminded him of a "living room on Venus." So often the Masters would express their gratitude for everyone's efforts, great and small, cheering us on. They loved encouraging us to keep the vision of God's kingdom on Earth through hard work and calling upon the Lord!

Finding a Home for Shiva

Some time later Mother called me into her office and showed me a large colored print of Shiva[2] the Art Department had just produced. She told me to go out and find a suitable frame for that poster—not just any frame but the "right one."

[2]The Hindu Trinity of Brahma, Vishnu and Shiva is parallel to the Western Trinity of Father, Son, and Holy Spirit. The three form the triad for the creation, preservation, and destruction of the universe. Shiva, the Destroyer (also known as the Restorer), is the fearsome one who drives away sin, disease and demons of delusion.

She said, "The right one exists somewhere and you will know it when you see it." Then the clincher. I couldn't spend more than $29.

Rummaging through shops in Pasadena, I finally wandered into an antique store. I was just about to leave when something caught my eye. Tucked away in a back corner was an old gilded frame, covered with soot. When I pulled it out I found it was in flawless condition. Checking the match, it was an exact fit. But a frame of this quality must be expensive. Looking at the faded tag, I was stoked — $29! This must be the one that Mother had seen with her inner sight. So I paid the clerk and left.

Mother was exuberant and said, "That's the right one!" She wasn't happy just because I had found the right home for a print, but because I was following my instincts and developing intuition along the way. To her this was far more important. She valued discernment as the most important quality on the Path and reminded us to develop it. One day the Messengers would not be here to give spiritual direction, and we would need to find our own way. So the print was framed and Mother began showing everyone the treasure.

Archangel Michael, the Great Liberator

September came and Summit University classes began on schedule. Beginning with Archangel Michael, Prince of the Archangels, the next seven quarters were sponsored by the seven Archangels. Mother reminded us that Archangel Michael, referenced in all the scriptures of the world, is the great liberator in the battle of Armageddon. Archangel Michael has at his command legions of angels serving under all the other Archangels. Since Mark revealed that one legion is composed of 144,000 angels, what a great boon this can be to all of us when we remember to call for this Archangel's assistance!

I AM in the glory of the resurrection flame and the Spirit of the Resurrection in the Great Central Sun. And the seraphim who march with me are numberless, beyond counting, through the Earth. They come and they possess the attribute of being able to absorb great quantities of human effluvia and the misqualifications of the human consciousness. Thus, the cleansing of layers of the Earth by the seraphim this day will bear many positive results in the Earth. And you should see those results, beloved ones, as the opening of the pathways for diligent souls to enter spiritual realms.

- Beloved Holy Justinius, Captain of Seraphic Bands,
Easter Sunday, April 3, 1994

More Homes for the Ascended Masters' Work

Next came the Ashram, dedicated to the World Mother. Located on Country Club Drive in West Los Angeles, California, it was a gift from local Keepers. The sizable property had two mansions, and provided a haven in the middle of the city where devotees could gather and give their devotions to Mother Mary and the Ascended Hosts of Light. Mother said that with the coming of Archangel Michael, leader in battle and defender of the Mother, he was anchoring his flame there for protection.

Within two years came the purchase of Camelot on Mulholland Highway in Calabasas, California, with its 218-acre campus. Located in the Santa Monica Mountains, it was designed in the 1920s by the architect Wallace Neff in a Spanish Colonial Revival style.

Change your Appearance!
by Margaret Reichardt

When Mother went stumping to Africa, she designed new garments for us. We called them "Guru Ma's" because they had "Love, Guru Ma" embroidered on the front. Made out of cotton, they consisted of loose-fitting pants and a tunic-length top. Colors coordinated with the color of the day: yellow on Sunday, pink on Monday, blue on Tuesday, green on Wednesday, purple on Thursday, white on Friday and violet on Saturday. A string of rudraksha beads completed the look. We certainly looked different, though they were designed to be worn on campus and not in town.

Some of us wore them. Others chose not to. It took me a long time and some coaxing by Mother to come around to wearing the "pj's." Once I started sporting these easy-care clothes, I found them very comfortable and was one of the last people to go back to normal street wear.

Mother also wore "Guru Ma" outfits and had an Afro hairdo. One day she was walking through the lower floor of the admin building on the Pasadena campus when Lanello told her she needed to change her appearance. He said to get dressed up, go to the beauty parlor, have her hair done and conduct the conference. Lanello told Mother that to make things happen in this world, she would have to be like the people she was trying to attract into the activity. That way people could better identify with her and feel more comfortable in her presence.

In a Field of Daisies

Queen Guinevere (Mother) at the Camelot Ball

 "You may take me
to the ball if you do
all the things you
promised…"

John & Carol

Lady Elaine and Sir Bedivere

Guinevere knights a disciple for valor

11

PUT YOUR BEST FOOT FORWARD
A Ball To Redeem Our Honor
by Alex Reichardt

When we examine then the equation of Camelot, our community of lightbearers, and we consider all of the souls upon Earth who will be drawn to this matrix of intense love, we look at the equation of power, and we are concerned that children of God understand that there is a price to be paid for power. If you then, above all desiring, desire to free your brothers and sisters on the Path, you will come to the place where you are willing to pay the price for the gift of power to implement the plan. That price is your sweet surrender to your holy vow.

—El Morya, *Pearls of Wisdom*, Vol. 24, No. 43

In the fall of 1976 Mother announced we were going to have a masked ball! El Morya had decided it was time to help balance the karma for the destruction of the original Camelot in fifth-century England and to redeem our honor. This event was to take place at the upcoming New Year's Class in Pasadena and include a pageant, a banquet, a grand promenade and waltz. The reenactment of this drama would take place in the large area behind the altar.

The Messenger revealed that many of us had been together long ago—at the original King Arthur's court and succeeding eras of Camelots. She explained that God was

69

once again drawing us together to balance the karma for the destruction of the original Camelot.

We were told many of the 12 kings who opposed Arthur back in old England had been or were in positions of authority on Mother's staff. Even Vivien, the woman who had seduced Merlin, had been on staff. There was a long list of them. Mother said they were all returning to choose to once again oppose Camelot or support it.

Mother, under the Masters' direction, personally chose the roles each one of us was to play—good, bad and indifferent—for this pageant. Margaret was Lady Elaine, a lady of the court, and I was Sir Bedivere, the knight and cupbearer who stayed with Arthur to the end.

Mother approved the sketches I proposed for the set design, which included a castle. A construction team worked non-stop until the day of the ball.

The Gala Event

Being in close proximity to Hollywood, for props we tapped into their vast resources for our full-scale production. There was also a white-canopied tent fit for a king and queen to preside over the celebrations. Mother was Guinevere and Tom Miller was King Arthur. To put this all in historical perspective, Mother revealed she had been embodied as Guinevere, El Morya was King Arthur and her own twin flame, Mark, was Lancelot.

For weeks we wondered how El Morya's direction for "a ball to redeem our honor" would outplay. Would there be a penance? Would we be ready? As the days flew by, many requests were made to ladies handy with a needle. These ladies burned the midnight oil putting on the finishing touches on our medieval garb.

Excitement mounted and the grand day finally arrived: December 31, 1976. The banquet began as we took our places at the tables. The cast for this command performance included Mother, the Board members and select staff. Dressed in lavish costumes, we came as knights and ladies, pages and squires. Seeing everyone take their part in this drama was quite an experience and made it all the more real for everyone involved.

The pageant began with vignettes of key episodes from the original Camelot mystery school. Throughout, Mother gave profound teaching on the mystical origin of Camelot and the search for the Holy Grail as the body and blood of the Christic Light.

She explained that the Great Karmic Board[1] had requested that we put on a specific character and garb of the day. This assignment was for those who had been the players with Guinevere and King Arthur and the original Camelot as the Once and Future Mystery School.

During the scene of the sword being pulled out of the stone, Mother said that the right to rule with the sword is only by spiritual attainment and the Sacred Fire of the heart, providing that one passes the initiation of the crucifixion. Therefore the caliber of each person's sword Excalibur is based on their development of the Threefold Flame. That determines the power and scepter of authority for each one's divine plan.

Camelot as a Mystery School

Mother announced that Camelot is a great opportunity for the chelas to pass the initiations of the Christ consciousness by putting on the garment of the LORD, the Mighty I AM Presence. Having passed his initiations individually and holding the balance for world karma, Arthur

---

[1]**Great Karmic Board:** A board of eight members (known as the Lords of Karma) that administers divine justice and determines the destiny of souls, countries and planets. In effect, they are the Supreme Court of this solar system. Before each incarnation, the Karmic Board gives us our assignment for this lifetime and tells us what karma we will be required to balance. After the transition called death, we go before the Karmic Board again to receive a life review. Some people remember receiving their assignment before birth, and some people who have had near-death experiences remember the life review.

earned the right to wield the sword Excalibur for this mission in fulfillment of his divine plan. Guinevere was at Camelot to help hold the balance as the divine feminine. She came with the wisdom of the Mother and the holy will of the Father as the counterpart of Arthur. Because Guinevere had the mantle of the purity of Camelot, she was assailed by witchcraft. The assailants knew if they were successful, the community would be destroyed.

The Three Dots of Morya •°•

Mother said the three dots represented Arthur (Morya) as Father, Guinevere (Mother) as the Christ and Lancelot (Mark) as the Holy Spirit. Mother revealed that Arthur, Lancelot and she were part of the entourage, along with the knights and ladies, that came to Earth to support Sanat Kumara.

The great love of these three sustained Camelot. Mother described their eternal bond as being almost inconceivable. It anchored the light necessary for the foundation of England and the New Jerusalem in America. In all their embodiments these three needed each other to fulfill their destiny, and could not have succeeded without the other two. Thus the dream of Camelot is fulfilled as the dream of the Holy Grail.

At the appointed time, the knights and ladies arrived in their finery. The hall began to take on the appearance of a page from history. Mother seemed transformed in this alchemy from the heart of Merlin, as she surveyed the scene of the 60-foot medieval cathedral rising above the castle turrets. With its luminescent stained-glass windows, it looked like it could have been used in another production of Camelot and the Knights of the Round Table. The revolving mirror ball and streamers cast a magical glow of ever-changing colors over the scene.

After the masquerade ball we sat glued to our seats as El Morya began speaking. With the deepest love and compassion of his heart, El Morya offered his forgiveness for any part anyone had played in the original destruction of Camelot. He then presented us a great opportunity to make amends. He expressed his gratitude for anyone who would make it their mission to build anew where we had left off as a grand opportunity, once again making the mystery school of Camelot a reality.

We could feel the great love and compassion of Morya's forgiving heart as we processed his message and internalized his request to make amends for past shortcomings. With hope in our hearts, we pledged to go forward once again with the message of the true Teachings of the Christ as the essence of the Holy Grail mystery teachings vouchsafed for the knights and ladies for eons.

One thousand devotees pledged to keep the flame and to carry the torch of Camelot as a beacon of light on behalf of Earth's evolutions.

Mother cautioned us to consider seriously the vow we were taking. It was not merely a promise but a pledge of our very life and being to this mission and holy cause.

> *A vow is more than a promise. It is more than a human word or a human contract. A vow is the pledging of one's life and being and soul to a mission or to a cause.*
>
> —Saint Germain, *Pearls of Wisdom*, Vol. 30, No. 2

A Night to Remember

After the dictation, the grand promenade began as the strains of The Procession of the Nobles by Nikolai Rimsky-Korsakov filled the hall. This sacred experience began to take on another dimension. Lest we reflect back that this was only a dream, photographs taken during this event provided a lasting record of what had transpired. Into the early morning hours we waltzed to lilting Strauss music.

Mother spoke to us about the three-quarter beat of the waltz music. This glorious Viennese music was inspired upon Johann Strauss Sr.[2] and son from the heart of Saint Germain. She described this action as an aspect of the violet flame, in sync with the rhythm of the heartbeat.

A professional dance team had taught us how to waltz without stepping on each other's toes. Jubilant conferees—and some children with limitless energy—waltzed and polkaed 'til almost dawn. This would be a life-transforming event we would carry with us as one of the highlights of our life.

12

THE STUFF THAT DREAMS ARE MADE OF
Without Mother There Would Be No Church
by Alex Reichardt

Nothing is more important than the maintenance of your attunement with God. And thus I urge you, and I urge the Mother of the Flame to urge you, to stop whatever you are doing at any time, any given moment, and to make a return to God before you wear away the delicate matrix, the delicate filigree of light that is a repository that we have placed around the brains, around the hearts of the chosen ones, of our disciples around the world. For, you see, even long before our disciples begin to call upon our name, we have a certain authority because of our office in Hierarchy to lend protection to souls of light. Otherwise, precious hearts, there would be no possibility of your finding the light.
—Sanat Kumara, *Pearls of Wisdom*, Vol. 17, No. 18

From the beginning the Messengers had an open-door policy for those coming into this activity. They were given the opportunity to balance their karma through good deeds and invoking the light, thereby expanding their Threefold Flame. Mother used to tell her staff that sometimes those closest to her were the ones who had the most karma to balance.

Mother's discernment and listening ear saved the day on many occasions. Often El Morya or another Master would tell her of an approaching problem she would have to deal with. She might even see a compromise of the honor flame in the aura of someone when directed to do so. One time I was walking with her toward the Pasadena Auditorium when she pointed out two staff members. She was concerned about them and noted there was something not right about their relationship. It soon came out that they were having an affair. The man was already married, and consequently they were dismissed from the community for not upholding the code of conduct.

Sometime later I happened to mention to Mother that I had seen this man in town and had a conversation with him. She asked me if I shook his hand. I had. She told me I shouldn't have done that and gave me the teaching on forcefields. She explained by shaking his hand, I would be exchanging my light for his darkness, and that since light, like water, seeks its own level, it benefits the person with the least amount of light, who has not earned it.

Lanello Removes a Portion of My Snakeskin

On the Pasadena campus one day, Mother told me she had a message for me from Lanello. He had removed a portion of my snakeskin (untransmuted human consciousness). She said he was able to do this because of my personal striving, thereby balancing karma that allowed the mercy of the Law to act. I was very grateful to her and Lanello for this grace. Her message confirmed for me the new sense of buoyancy that I had been feeling.

The Judgment on Hollywood

In a dictation through Mother at a conference, the Elohim Astrea pronounced the judgment upon Hollywood for the immorality and decadence coming out of the movie industry. Astrea then exhorted us to continue ratifying it with our calls and decree work. Afterward a large white sword appeared in the azure blue sky near the horizon, pointing directly at Hollywood. Mother said this was created by the sylphs of the air in response to the Elohim's judgment. The image was visible for some time and hundreds saw it, including myself. Quick on the draw, Kenneth McNeel photographed it for posterity. The photo captured the perfectly shaped sword against a cloudless sky and was a reminder of the Elohim's request for our continued calls.

Mighty Astrea's sword in the sky pointing at Hollywood.

Florence (Lady Kristine), Margaret, Larry and other Graphic Arts Department staff sing favorites from *The Sound of Music* in front of our homemade Swiss Chalet

Alex emcee, Anita and Tom singing "Edelweiss" to Mother from *The Sound of Music* at Mother's birthday party

Mother, faculty and S.U. students dancing near Nease Hall, Pasadena, California

13

A SIGHT FOR SORE EYES
The Cosmic Egg
by Alex Reichardt

Morya speaks. We advocate the amplification of the will of God, for "the will of God is good."

The affirmation of this childlike statement over and over again is the means whereby the mind can be stilled and the mounting crescendo of human emotions diminished.

The will of God is the thunder of universal love. It is the strength of the right arm of the Almighty. It is the fire of his devotion and the best gift to his children.

There is safety in it and the strength that fashions security for the ages and beyond.

—Morya, *Pearls of Wisdom*, Vol. 12, No. 9

Mother said if you want something in life, write a letter to the Karmic Board and burn it, and they will answer immediately. She used the example of the children, Jane and Michael Banks, in the 1964 movie Mary Poppins with Julie Andrews. The youngsters wrote their letter for the perfect nanny and burned it in the fireplace. Next day she mysteriously appeared at their front door with the very letter they had written, still intact.

In 1977 The Summit Lighthouse activity was experiencing great growth with Pasadena, the Ashram, new teaching centers and then Camelot. Since my training was in architectural design and seeing the pressing need, I decided to write a letter to the Karmic Board requesting to do design work for the Church. I then burned it and told no one.

To my amazement, the very next day Mother called me into her office at the Ashram and told me that I would be doing interior design and space planning for the Church, and that was the way I would get my chelaship.

Mother loved interior design and said that if she were not a Messenger she would have loved being a decorator. I soon realized that part of her mission was bringing forth the beauty and culture of the Divine Mother. Since she remembered her inner experiences in the retreats of the Brotherhood, she was able to recreate them. She was very exacting and would only accept designs that reflected the perfection that she had seen in the etheric. One such design was for the Will of God focus at the Ashram of the World Mother.

Gift to Mother for Her Home

The Ashram was located on a magnificent estate, albeit run down, in the heart of Los Angeles. It was given to Mother so that she would have a home and a place to hold services in the City of the Angels. This property had been purchased for a song, because the buildings, though structurally sound, were severely neglected and would require major surgery. One was a large Italianate Renaissance mansion, similar in design to the headquarters for the Tournament of Roses in Pasadena. A three-story Colonial Revival structure, connected to the main house by a pergola, became the Teaching Center.

Mother took a large vacant garden shed in an abandoned formal garden and created a room in the shape of an egg. This was to become El Morya's Will of God focus.

Spiritually this represented the Cosmic Egg. She was very specific how this should be designed and drew a sketch for the construction crew and me. When no one knew exactly how this should be executed, she gave a practical solution. She suggested taking an egg and boiling it and then measuring it to get the right proportions for the room.

After the walls were built, they were painted blue— a pure pigment with no muting. It looked like the blue sky on a clear day and we called it "Archangel Michael blue."Mother said this color would focus the vibration of the Masters and be a fitting chalice for their presence, especially El Morya and Archangel Michael.

In the center of the room was a life-size statue of Jesus of classical design on a pedestal with planting at the base. It was designed to make a complete 360-degree revolution hourly. We could feel the tangible presence of the Master assisting us as we sought to put on our Christ consciousness.

Before entering we were to give a minimum of 15 minutes of violet flame decrees for transmutation. This was accomplished in the two adjacent smaller circular Violet Flame Rooms painted amethyst, with crystal chandeliers and sconces. Outside was a meditation garden designed by Michael H., a Keeper who was a professional landscape designer. Meandering paths led to small grotto-like spaces with seating as a quiet space for chelas to reconnect with their Higher Self through prayer and meditation. This experience helped remind us that each of our paths is a personal one. When it was completed, Mother was very pleased with the results.

Students of the Masters loved giving their devotions in this beautiful focus of the Brotherhood. Some traveled long distances just to be there in the early morning hours giving their violet flame decrees and experiencing the presence of Jesus and El Morya in the Will of God focus. To them, it was life transforming!

One lady, who had been in the Teachings for several years, exclaimed how breathtaking it was after she had completed her vigil walking outside just in time to see the rising sun. To her it looked like the cover of the album *Harpstrings of Lemuria*, with its golden-pink glow rays reflected off the surrounding landscape and buildings.

A Startling Pronouncement

This same year, on October 26, 1977, Mother Mary inaugurated a spiral of healing and resurrection for Los Angeles and the sons and daughters of God on the Path of soul liberation through the Messenger Elizabeth Clare Prophet. In her first dictation at the Ashram, she told us to keep the flame and our ascension in this life "will immediately open the door for 1,000 souls to follow" each one of us.

She then announced the ascension of Marguerite Baker, a Keeper of the Flame of long standing. As a teacher of first-grade children, Marguerite had told the story of how the angels appeared in her classroom, as witnessed by all the children in response to their devotions. This resulted in a booklet about their inspiring experiences.

On Wednesday November 23, during the service Mother Mary charged us to be diligent in giving the Jesus Watch for Los Angeles on Wednesday evenings. She said she was taking this action even as the darkness increased because the fallen ones continually sought to tear down the Holy City. She pleaded for the children of God in the city, saying, "I have looked into the eyes of each and every soul within this city. I know the anguish of those who are seized by the entities of alcohol and drugs, of heroin, and the entities of sugar and of every impure substance that binds the brain, the blood vessels, and the nervous system to darkness."

She said, "I pray you then invoke the Archangels for the protection of this land, for your dwelling place, for your body temple. For never in all the history of the race has there been such a race for the destruction of souls and for their absolute salvation in Almighty God!" At the close of this and many other healing services, Mother made calls for the healing of those in attendance and for all of God's children not able to come to the altar.

Continually under Attack

Mother was living at the Ashram and found that she was not able to sleep. Initially we had nightly "tags" to help roll back the energy and protect the forcefield. After a while it became apparent she would have to move away from this metropolitan area with its millions of people and their consciousness.

Having been Mark's assistant, I understood this equation of light and darkness only too well. He was continually on the move trying to get out from under the scope of the fallen ones. That's probably why El Morya said that no one since Jesus Christ had experienced more attacks from the black magicians than Mark Prophet. Upon his ascension, Mother not only received his mantles but his "burden of light" as opposition as well. Therefore the necessity for the continual tags and decree support that sustained her. She even said, "If you want a Messenger in embodiment, you have to decree for me!"

Memories of a Bygone Era

Come with us on an armchair adventure back in time. Experience firsthand what it felt like attending a service at the Ashram of the World Mother with our Messenger, the presence of Mother Mary, and the chelas of the will of God! Each Wednesday evening Mother conducted the Jesus' Watch with Me One-Hour Service dedicated to Jesus and Mother Mary, followed by a darshan for staff and students. A wonderful opportunity awaits you! Watch your step . . . and don't be late!

Getting off the interstate, you drive down past a large corner property on Country Club Drive and park your car. You walk through the ornate gate in the wrought iron fence and boxwood defining the property from the street. You mount the steps just as the sun sets behind the tall palms in the distance. The scent of jasmine and honeysuckle fills the air. In front of you is a massive oak door. As it opens and you are bid welcome, the sound of soft classical music greets you. You notice the ivory and white walls. There seems to be a step up in vibration. To your immediate right is a bust of George Washington on a marble base. You are just in time for the buffet being served on the sideboard in the Great Divine Director dining room, with its oak-paneled walls, glistening crystal chandelier and country French dining set.

The home-cooked meal includes fresh organic vegetarian fare and some gourmet treats. After you fill your plate, you find a congenial spot in one of the comfortable chairs or sofas in El Morya's room on the other side of the foyer. You notice the wealth of books lining the bookcases along the wall. A portrait of El Morya hangs over the ornate fireplace. You walk across the royal blue Oriental rug on the polished oak floor and you take a seat. You join in the conversation, making some new acquaintances and renewing old ones.

Soon it is time for the service. Bhajans begin playing and chelas take their seats in the foyer. Shortly Mother arrives in a green sari and sits down in her "guru chair" on the main landing of the grand stairway in the foyer. A life-size gold-leafed statue of Mother Mary stands beside her. Behind is a full-length window overlooking the fountain and formal garden below. You learn that the Deodar trees, just beyond, were blessed by one of the Masters in a dictation.

Soon the Jesus Watch begins with joyful songs and devotions to the heart of Mother Mary and Jesus. Later Mother gives personal calls for everyone's healing and clears the world's weight from those present. She then gives personal teaching, which seems somehow to be an answer to your prayer and lifts your burden.

To seal the service, we sing to the blessed Mother of Jesus. The service is over and it's time to leave. You linger a bit longer with everyone else, giving thanks for such a blessing and determine to return next week for another feast of light!

Ashram of the World Mother
by Raoul Quintero

I remember when the staff moved from Colorado to California and then to Los Angeles. I came from New York City and I was a window cleaner. Mother knew that and told me that there would be an opportunity for me to clean the windows at the Ashram. I loved working there to make it clean and bright and afterward being at the services. And oh, what beautiful services we had!

She was very happy with the work we all did and after the work was done, she came and gave us lessons from the Masters. One time I remember that we were sitting around Mother on the floor and she was sitting in a chair giving us a teaching. I don't remember what she was saying. All I know was that I was very devoted, and the way I took it was that she was giving me thanks for cleaning the windows and I got a little bit of the Teachings.

I remember how beautiful that mansion was! Those big beautiful white stairs going up to the landing with the life-size statue of Mother Mary, and the Jesus Watch services Mother used to lead. I loved to go because a lot of times, she would end the service by singing "Sancta Maria." I used to love to sing to Mother Mary.

The Jesus "Watch with Me" is a wonderful service! Give this service from the Jesus' Vigil of the Hours pamphlet and see if you agree. I never saw anything so beautiful. It's about 38 pages. You give that very carefully with devotion—week after week—and it starts to open your mind.

I started doing this service 2½ years ago, and I began to take in the words a little bit at a time. Jesus gives you to eat but you have to meditate, you have to open up your heart and say, "I want to help!"

We need one who is ascended, like our beloved Jesus. He represents the Christ in every one of us. He received a lot of power and that is fantastic! Attune with him and he will be there helping you.

I believe that and that's what I'm doing. And as you give your decrees and the violet flame, you get cleaner and clearer. Then you give an opportunity to your Christ Self to come closer and closer to you. It's a question of pacing.

That's why I like Mother Mary's Rosary—the scriptural rosary to Mother Mary. She wants us to give it at 5 am. Then she can go to the world and help people. She can help with war or with the unborn souls, the youth and the children. You have to have faith. Without faith you cannot believe in God.

Thank you for giving me life, my dear God, for giving me sight and understanding. I want to pay for that. I want to prepare myself. Jesus said that if you are in attunement and you are sincere, if you are honest and you are in love with the Truth, the resources and whatever you need to spread the Teachings would be there. You have to do your part. And I said, "Well, I will do that!" It's like jumping into the sea.

Grand Staircase

Saint Germain's
Office

The Ashram

Ma said Job
thought he was
a "people."

Mother started out with Job, the guard dog,
but decided Archangel Michael was most
capable of doing the job of guarding her.

14

FAITHFUL AND TRUE
Archangel Michael Promises to Become Physical
by Alex Reichardt

I seal you out of my own heart flame, and I guarantee your protection if you will not fail to call to me, giving my decrees at least twenty minutes each day. And when you give all the decrees and songs on either Archangel Michael cassette, inserting your fiats for the nations and all souls of Light, you will find such extraordinary intercession in your lives through the legions in my command as to make you wonder why you had never locked in to that decree momentum before.
—Archangel Michael, *Pearls of Wisdom*, Vol. 37, No. 41

When we moved to Pasadena, California, security for our Messenger became paramount. So Mother established an honor guard for the protection of herself and her family, and made me responsible. Although Mark had given me some training on security issues at La Tourelle, it was his ever-present guidance that became my saving grace.

One day Mother made a statement that was both startling and comforting: Archangel Michael told her that he would manifest physically if necessary to protect her. Her love for him as an emissary of God was so great that she would gladly lay down her life 10,000 times for him.

Therefore, it became our job to decree to Archangel Michael to protect her and not allow energies of malintent to cycle into the physical. She explained that energy cycles into the four quadrants in this order: the etheric, the mental, the emotional and the physical.

"Archangel Michael, Help!"

I was no stranger to the intercession of Archangel Michael. I will never forget the first incident. It happened in Colorado Springs and I had just recently come on staff. On a wintry day I was driving down a steep hill turned to a sheet of ice in a VW with Cordell S., another staff member. On both sides lay deep chasms. Suddenly the car swerved dangerously toward one of them. Seeing the imminent danger, I cried out at the top of my lungs, "Archangel Michael! Help!" Then the miracle . . .

As though guided by an unseen hand, the VW moved to the center of the road and we slowly proceeded down to the bottom of the icy hill without incident. Cordell's mouth dropped open and his eyes were as big as saucers. We were stunned! We couldn't believe what had just happened. We agreed that this miracle must have been the intercession of God through Archangel Michael in response to the call. There was just no other explanation for it. This near mishap made a firm believer out of me in the power of Archangel Michael and his protection. And it's happened since—both times in the dead of winter.

Once on top of the Tetons (elev. 13,000 ft.+) I started skidding down the mountain in my Honda. Another time outside Dillon, Montana, I was taking a shortcut on a narrow dirt road along a gorge and a large rig barely missed hitting me. Both times I survived without a scratch to my vehicle or me. I was grateful for Archangel Michael's intercession and glad I had remembered to make my calls for his protection beforehand. I know of others who have had similar experiences with the same results. Try it for yourself. If you find yourself in danger, remember, "Archangel Michael! Help!" You'll be glad you did.

Like Joshua and the Battle of Jericho

During a conference in Pasadena, Mother was preparing to deliver a dictation in the auditorium. At the same time, right next door, a group was praying against her and the service. Disgruntled fundamentalists plagued us. They were determined to block the release of light. Mother said that because of their prayers of malintent, she had to deal with a great deal of virulent energy. They were angry because we recognized there were many Ascended Masters and they recognized only Jesus. The answer Mother gave me concerning their accusation against her was that Jesus never said that he was the only Son of God.

There came a day when an angry group of agitators decided they had had enough of us and that we must go. So they organized themselves in the manner of Joshua of old and marched around our campus, praying and shouting with trumpets for six days. They were determined that on the last day our movement would be destroyed, as Joshua had taken Jericho.

And the LORD said unto Joshua, See, I have given into thine hand Jericho, and the king thereof, and the mighty men of valour.

And ye shall compass the city, all ye men of war, and go round about the city once. Thus shalt thou do six days.

And seven priests shall bear before the ark seven trumpets of rams' horns: and the seventh day ye shall compass the city seven times, and the priests shall blow with the trumpets. . . .

So the people shouted when the priests blew with the trumpets: and it came to pass, when the people heard the sound of the trumpet, and the people shouted with a great shout, that the wall fell down flat, so that the people went up into the city, every man straight before him, and they took the city.

(Joshua 6:2–4, 20)

Because of the hatred of these agitators, their prayers were turned into darkness and a great heaviness rained down on our campus and staff. Mother bore the greatest brunt of this darkness physically in her body. It amazed me to see how centered Mother was throughout this entire time. She had absolute faith in Almighty God that he would see us through this trial and that we would have our victory.

On the seventh day, the light of God bore witness to the Truth of our movement. By the power of the spoken Word, darkness was transmuted into light and when their trumpets sounded, instead of destruction peace rained down.

Lanello Saves the Day

Mother's presentation on the science of sound[1] in September 1980 at Philadelphia, Pennsylvania, was a real eye-opener. This fascinating lecture and accompanying slide show demonstrated the effects of sound on molecular structure. Afterward everyone was dismissed for a lunch break. Walking out into the foyer, we were still pondering the amazing lecture we had just heard. But when we approached the doors to leave, we were in for a surprise. Hostile Christian fundamentalists had blocked all the exits. They were just itching to engage us in argumentation and prevent us from leaving.

With split-second timing, Lanello inspired upon me to start singing, "I AM the Violet Flame!" to the tune of "Santa Lucia" (70.11 in our decree book). Soon everyone caught the flame and joined in, expanding the action of the violet flame like a mighty crescendo, rolling back the darkness and replacing it with light. And it worked! The agitators gave up and moved aside and the conferees were able to

---

[1] *The Liberating Power of the Word*, 7 Steps to Precipitation by the Command of the Word and *The Science of Sound*, September 12, 1980

get their lunch. This was the closest I have come to seeing the re-enactment of the parting of the Red Sea.

Everyone enjoyed their lunch that day, unaware of the true miracle that had transpired through the consciousness of our ever-present Guru, Lanello. I was grateful for his intercession, as close as heartbeat, constant protector and comfort in time of need. All we have to do is to remember to make the call, "Lanello, help!"

Seraphim Guarded the Entrances

Mother said she was able to see with her inner sight a Seraph as a great being of light standing guard at each entrance to some churches as a result of the devotion of the people. This was also true during our conferences because of the light released and everyone's deep love for Mother and the Masters..

During dictations, a staff member would decree outside the entrance to protect the forcefield. However during one conference, Mother suddenly stopped her dictation. It seemed that he was decreeing so loud that it broke her attunement. She waited quietly while I ran outside to handle this situation. She then resumed right where she left off and completed her dictation.

During services, people who were unbalanced sometimes became more unbalanced in the presence of so much light released and would do some odd things. Occasionally someone in the audience would think they heard voices and start walking toward the platform when Mother was giving a dictation. To safeguard the delivery of the Word through the Messenger, an usher would escort the person out. It took only one person to become an open door to compromise the forcefield and allow astral energies into the room. For that reason the Masters requested that staff and conferees not fast during conferences.

At one fall conference, a man walked into the auditorium while Mother was on the platform lecturing.

A few of us noticed he was carrying a large briefcase and acting strange. Checking further, we found he was unbalanced and was carrying a gun in his briefcase, so he was asked to leave.

Quick Obedience Saves the Day

In the winter of 1985, Mother went on a month-long tour with her stump team contacting thousands, traveling from the Philippines to Australia and Hawaii. She had come with Saint Germain's message for the Coming Revolution in Higher Consciousness and the Lost Arts of Healing. She delivered her address to enthusiastic and record-breaking audiences all along her trip. She then went about sealing several thousand as the servants of God in their foreheads with the Emerald Matrix. The stump team followed up with lectures.

> *And I saw another angel ascending from the east, having the seal of the living God: and he cried with a loud voice to the four angels, to whom it was given to hurt the earth and the sea,*
>
> *Saying, Hurt not the earth, neither the sea, nor the trees, till we have sealed the servants of our God in their foreheads.* (Revelation 7:2–3)

Being driven through heavy traffic in Manila, Mother was on her way to conduct a conference. Seated in the back, she suddenly got a premonition of impending danger. She quickly darted to the other side—just in time! A few moments later, her vehicle was hit broadside right where she had been sitting. Unharmed, she did the necessary spiritual work on this attack against her and the mission and went on to deliver her talk.

When she returned to the United States, she relayed this story to staff at La Tourelle and used it as an object lesson. She made the strong appeal to always listen and obey the voice within. She said this is the voice of God giving the warning and that it could literally be a case of life and death.

She realized only too well that had she not been obedient, she could have been the victim of a plot from the sinister force to try to take her out of embodiment.

She shared another experience she had while riding with Mark years before. Once again she received a warning of impending danger to her and quickly rolled up the window. Right afterward, some kids threw red tomatoes at her window. She realized they would have hit her had she not obeyed immediately.

Chelaship before Her Safety

One afternoon Mother needed to get an important message to her husband. So she gave it to E.J., a staff member, saying where he could be found. When E.J. returned without delivering the message, she decided he had not tried hard enough. So she sent him out again, reiterating where her husband could be found. This time he succeeded.

She then determined this staff member needed to develop the "I AM the Guard consciousness." So she assigned him the job of guarding her—not for her protection, but for his chelaship and to gain his self-mastery. She placed more importance on chelaship than even her own protection.

I want you to know that I ask God to judge my soul daily, and his angels to rebuke my errors, to teach me and to show me the way to do better. I give no power to the enemy's judgments of my life and work, but I do implore the Holy Spirit to analyze all constructive criticism, of friend and foe alike, and set before me the Will of God for necessary change and progress in my soul and in our Church.

—Elizabeth Clare Prophet, September 18, 1983

King Arthur weds Guinevere

15

AN IDEA WHOSE TIME HAS COME
The Once and Future Mystery School
by Alex Reichardt

Let all, then, who have heard of Camelot, let them come. Let them come from the farthest shores, let them come again, let them hear the call and answer; for I would discipline and I would nourish and I would train chelas, and I would bestow the gift of knighthood and the flame of Mother to ladies of the flame. I would return you, then, to the jousting and to the tournament. I will return you to the holy quest.
—El Morya, *Pearls of Wisdom*, Vol. 20, No. 25

Roaring applause greeted Mother's announcement to devotees attending the Harvest Class "Soul Liberation" in 1977. Camelot was come again!

There had been many sacrifices to make this vision a reality. Saint Germain ordered a 24-hour, 10-man tag until the right property was secured. Members young and old had given their summer's earnings, their widow's mite and hard-earned cash and other possessions for the down payment. Mother expressed her deep gratitude to everyone who had made this happen—those who had set their alarms for 1 am, 2 am, 3 am, 4 am to participate in the tag, those who had sold their furniture and jewelry and those who had worked extra jobs.

As the midnight hour approached, an enormous seven-tier cake decorated with American flags and flowers was presented. Mother said, "This cake is not made of what you think it is. It's the alchemical cake, consecrated to Krishna, hence totally healthy!" Everyone laughed.

Mother explained the true mystical purpose of Camelot: it was to be the instrument of God in his chelas for the new Culture of the Age, the Culture of the Divine Mother. This was the Masters' alternative to the downward course of civilization, the place where the true teachings of Jesus and the Buddha could come forth.

Then Julia, a staff member, rushed to the stage and presented Mother with a bouquet she had been saving for her. This was the same bouquet Mother had received almost a year earlier at the New Year's pageant and ball—still fragrant and lovely. Mother thanked her and announced the flowers had become immortalized.

Over 1,000 devotees of Saint Germain pledged to support Camelot—the once and future mystery school of the Masters. This was the defining moment for each one who had made the commitment. These are the stalwart ones who shared the dream of Camelot and the vision of the Holy Grail. This would be a night we would long remember! I don't think there was a dry eye in the house.

We Claimed the Land for Saint Germain

Early morning on October 10, over 800 devotees packed chartered buses. Destination: Mulholland Highway and Las Virgenes in Calabasas—future headquarters of Church Universal and Triumphant, home of Summit University, Montessori International and Summit University Press.

We gathered at the majestic wrought iron gates with the gold crown to get a first glimpse of our new home, "Camelot." After the ribbon-cutting ceremony, the gates opened wide, and the excited crowd hurried along in fast procession, with Mother in the lead, breathing in the sweet air of expectation. The early morning mist gave way to skies of azure blue and lacy white, as we proceeded past graceful eucalyptus trees creating a cathedral above.

This idyllic picturesque setting in so many ways seemed ready-made for us by some majestic power. Purple foothills rising from the mists of the valley stood guard in the background. We were struck by the early morning light and the dew-kissed meadows winding past the stables. Up ahead we crossed over Swan Lake with white swans gliding. Beyond loomed the white stucco mansion with its arched plaza. A statue of Saint Thérèse of Lisieux with roses in her arms stood at the foot of the steps leading down to the lake. We caught sight of the formal courtyard and fountain. Across the sweeping lawn stood the Holy Grail building with its hand-carved vaulted ceiling.

Mother was elated to finally have a real chapel as a fitting place for the Masters to give their dictations. Quite a contrast to the dark auditorium with concrete floor and no windows at the Pasadena campus.

Mother named it the "Chapel of the Holy Grail" for the knights and ladies of the flame come again as the mystical experience of disciple and Master. This 500-seat chapel was modeled after a Roman temple, with its imposing marble columns and ornate altar. The four apostles of Christ—Matthew, Mark, Luke and John—depicted in the stained glass windows, looked down upon the congregation below. Colorful reflections played across the wall, adding to the sense of reverence and awe.

The atmosphere was charged with excitement as we offered our gratitude and gave Archangel Michael's battle cry, "Charge, charge, charge! And let Victory be proclaimed!"

A full-sized white statue of Jesus with arms outstretched greeted us as we left the Grail building. Nearby was a smaller chapel that Mother named the "Chapel of the Holy Family."

Outside the mansion was a swimming pool shaped like a double-edged razor blade. A reminder that this had been the estate of "King" Gillette, the razor-blade baron. More recently it had been the campus of Thomas Aquinas College. And now it was ours.

Mother asked that the creche in the Chapel of the Holy Grail remain a permanent focus until we were successful in stopping abortion.

Welcome
to
Camelot!

Mother carries the oil
of spiknard to the chapel

The High Altar in the
Chapel of the Holy Grail

Conferees gathering in front of the Holy Grail

Easter 1978

Sunday afternoon at Camelot

16

ATLANTIS RISING
Camelot Come Again
by Alex Reichardt

Camelot is won! Camelot is here! And yet that winning must be reaffirmed month by month as the demands to retain the victory come at every level—spiritually, morally—through constancy and through the offering of that special and sacred supply upon the altar. —Lanello

July Fourth, 1978, will go down in history as the day that El Morya realized his dream of Camelot, the once and future mystery school come again. The Masters and their disciples gathered under the banner of Maitreya, Morya and Saint Germain.

We came to claim our land in Calabasas, California, just over the hill from Malibu. Students from around the world made their trek to this site. All were in great expectation for what was about to take place. This was the fulfillment of the dream held in the hearts of the Masters for the rekindling of the flame of freedom for a planet and its people. Today the dream of bringing Camelot to America was to come true. From here we would expand our worldwide outreach. And all was in readiness.

For this grand opening celebration, I had presented Mother a scroll with sketches for the festivities in keeping with the theme of King Arthur and the knights of the Round Table. Mother gave the go-ahead, saying "they recaptured the spirit of the original Camelot." Festive flags representing the Age of Arthur lined the drive from the entrance to the statue of Jesus facing the Grail building. A miniature castle with turrets was set up over the road fording a stream.

The Name of God "I AM THAT I AM"

Reminiscent of the pilgrims of old, we were carrying sacred relics and focuses for the altar in the Chapel of the Holy Grail. Mother led the procession to the Grail as we came carrying portraits of the Ascended Masters—of Jesus and Saint Germain, El Morya and Kuthumi, Lanello and Godfre, and statues of saints of East and West.

Chanting the name of God "I AM THAT I AM!" we processioned along the drive, over the bridge across Swan Lake, through the arch and up the white marble steps to our final destination in the chapel.

Once we were assembled, in gratitude for all God had given us that day, Mother made an invocation to the flame of the Holy Grail, igniting the hearts of the congregation. After placing the spiritual focuses on the altar, we partook of Holy Communion and waited upon the Word of the Lord from Gabriel, the Archangel of Purity, and his dedication of the Chapel.

Following the dictation by Gabriel, we relaxed at an old-fashioned Fourth of July picnic with fun, food, camaraderie and a trio of accordionists serenading the high-spirited crowd encamped along Swan Lake. This was the first of many such gatherings on the lawns of our beautiful property.

The Message from the Middle of the Lake

That evening Mother appeared in a royal blue hooded cloak, ready to give the landmark address. Over 1,000 had gathered around Swan Lake. All eyes were upon her as two knights escorted her by boat across the lake to the small island to give the final dictation from El Morya. The boat stopped as Mother reached into the water and grasped the sword Excalibur from the "lady in the lake." When she raised her arm high brandishing the sword glistening in the moonlight, she was greeted by resounding applause. The silhouette of the white stucco mansion and arches provided a stunning backdrop. She got out of the boat and proceeded to the white-canopied tent set with El Morya's regal chair. It was time for the dictation.

El Morya spoke about the original Camelot and revealed that Guinevere and Lancelot had been betrayed by witchcraft determined to destroy that original mystery school. Morya said without all of the "once and future knights and ladies of the flame," there would be no Camelot come again. He bid us tell the story of Camelot, the story of the search for the Holy Grail enshrined within our hearts. He said eons ago, there had been an ancient focus of light on this very spot.

Fireworks and the circle of the AUM, followed by dancing and folk singing, completed the event. Late into the night we all gathered, holding hands as we stood around the lake. When the circle was complete and unbroken, Mother concluded the conference and sealed the light within our hearts.

All had gone according to plan. The flags remained long after opening day. Mother liked the castle and wanted to keep it, but there was a concern it might hinder fire trucks from coming onto the property due to limited clearance.

Mother Gets a New Home

Our move from Pasadena to Camelot was carried out with swiftness and enthusiasm. However, it was quite a challenge to go from 17 buildings to 7. By this time there were 400 staff, all needing a place to live and do the Masters' work.

Like Pasadena, once again no place had been set aside for Mother. She had planned to occupy a small house on the property but unfortunately her cottage had been given away to a staff couple. Not wanting to displace them, Mother rented a house a few miles away.

Eventually we were able to carve out a limited space for her. On 218 acres in the country, Mother could now be with her chelas and fulfill her daily mission and raison d'être, but it would require a sweeping transformation.

The top floor of the former Gillette mansion was converted into living quarters for Mother and her family. Cutting through the two-foot-thick stucco wall, a closet became a kitchen. By hard work Richard (who owned a cabinet shop before staff) was able to transform this area into a galley kitchen. Mother loved it and thanked him for his fine work. For her upstairs office and residence, we pulled out donated furniture from a cargo container. But when she saw her office, she thought it looked like a furniture showroom, so half was removed.

In setting up her office, Mother was very specific on how she wanted it arranged to maximize her spiritual forcefield. Her desk was to be centered in the room with a crystal chandelier overhead to reflect the light and energy from the Great Central Sun. As the finishing touch, portraits of the Ascended Masters were placed on the walls to focus their Electronic Presence. When purchasing furnishings, she preferred French, saying this was the style she remembered seeing in the retreats of the Brotherhood after traveling there at night in her finer body.

When staff asked to meet with Mother on thorny issues, she would often tell them to first sit outside her office and give their decrees to the Elohim Astrea. It was amazing how these powerful decrees got immediate results! She would not meet with anyone who was disgruntled or angry. In fact, she said she couldn't even be in the presence of someone with that vibration.

Exploding the Boundaries of the Heavens

Everything had to be done to exact specifications. To maximize the light in the room, Mother transformed the Chapel of the Holy Grail according to Ascended Master standards. She changed the drab walls to "Archangel Michael blue," so named because this hue focused the Electronic Presence of the Archangel. Horizontal bands around the perimeter matched the gold of the crown above the main altar. A seven-foot-high painting of the I AM Presence Chart was hung above the high altar. Mother loved the large portraits of the Masters Jesus and Saint Germain painted by Charles Sindelar that hung on either side of the Chart. She said the Masters had appeared to this artist, who saw them with his inner sight. Mother said having the larger pictures also increased the light.

When the Masters' pictures were hung, their eyes were to be above the eye level of the congregation out of respect for their spiritual office. The frames were to be gold with no antiquing. Crystal chandeliers with brass fittings completed the setting.

Mother asked me to get other focuses for the high altar, including miniature statues of Western saints and Eastern deities. One of them was carved from ebony so she told me to have it gold-leafed to hold more light. Mother wanted a velvet altar skirt made for the high altar. But when it was ready to be hung, it was too heavy and couldn't be supported. Without another word, she had it replaced with something lighter.

Ark of the Covenant

Mother also requested an exact replica of the Ark of the Covenant be built and placed on the altar. Reading from the Bible, she said that the Ark of the Covenant was where God manifested his presence on Earth and went ahead of the Israelites wherever they traveled. She said it had to be fabricated according to Biblical references beginning with Exodus 25. The box was made of acacia wood, gold-leafed, and was 2.5 cubits long and 1.5 cubits wide and high (45"x 27"). Two gilded cherubim facing each other stood on the lid with their wings covering the "Mercy Seat." Spiritual treasures were placed inside, including the Ten Commandments, symbolizing God's covenant with his people.

Focus for the Unborn

At the foot of the platform was a crèche with baby Jesus, Mary and Saint Joseph, along with the shepherds, as a focus for the unborn child. It was placed there one Christmas, and Mother asked that it remain until we were successful in stopping abortion. Of all challenges that America faces, she said this one is the most serious and makes us vulnerable to cataclysm and economic debacle. Pictures of the saints of the Self-Realization Fellowship were placed in the back of the chapel to focus the light each had internalized. Votive candleholders were added for those wishing to pray for loved ones in need.

Next we tackled the Chapel of the Holy Family, starting with the "right violet" to maximize the action of the violet flame for our decrees. Once again pure hue was a must. Burnt umber and lampblack were out. If the color was muddied or toned down, it was not acceptable. She said this was the vibration of misqualified energy and was incapable of containing the light as a proper forcefield for the Masters.

To augment the life-size statues of Mother Mary, Jesus and Saint Joseph, Mother wanted the 14 Stations of the Cross in bas-relief placed around the walls. This was a reminder that we too must follow the same path as our Lord and Saviour Jesus Christ. As he said, *Whosoever will come after me, let him deny himself, and take up his cross, and follow me.* (Mark 8:34)

We still needed furnishings for the altars, when we learned that a wholesale furniture warehouse was going out of business. Mother and a few Board members were flying up to San Francisco and she asked me along.

The Importance of Reading the Masters' Words

Once airborne, Mother took out her *Pearls of Wisdom* and gave me five to read. Hot off the press, she wanted to share them. She always encouraged staff to use their time wisely and keep abreast of the Masters' words in their latest releases.

She said this was our daily bread, the engrafted Word, as the pure river of life that was able to save our souls. She explained that there are many tracks to these messages. Each time we review them, we will find new keys to help us on our spiritual journey. As we read the Masters' releases, we are raised in vibration and the Master becomes aware of our attention upon him. As we begin internalizing a portion of his flame, he can overshadow us and sometimes he even stands in our aura, depending upon our devotion. It never ceased to amaze me.

Finally at our destination, we felt like we were walking into a treasure chest. It seemed as though everything we needed was there. Besides furniture, there were hand-painted Italian statues of Archangel Gabriel and Raphael for the altar in the small chapel, and a life-size white marble statue of Jesus. Mother got everyone's input before purchasing this statue, to be sure it was the right one and that it conveyed the presence of Jesus. Mother was pleased how well the purchases filled our needs.

Mother shared an incident that took place when the owner of the warehouse invited her out for lunch. Although initially cordial, when she began speaking about Saint Francis, he became visibly upset and she started to experience some hostility. Still Mother felt the need to defend Saint Francis because this man was maligning his character. Seeing how devoted she was to the saint, the man regained his composure. Mother gave Kuthumi's explanation about the aura turning inside out and exposing itself. She said the man revealed his deep-seated rebellion against God and his representative, and it surfaced because of Mother's light that exposed this aspect of the man's consciousness.

Recording the Rosary from Mother Mary

The forcefield now set, Mother had staff and S.U. students assemble in the Chapel of the Holy Family to record *A Child's Rosary to Mother Mary*.[1] We were told that when we participate in the recording of a devotion, whether a song or a decree, a mantra or the Rosary, we merit good karma as people use the recording to augment their devotions. After practicing the cadences in unison, we were ready.

Mother gave us the profound teaching from the heart of Mother Mary that, although we may have sinned, we should not accept the condemnation of being sinners. So the last two lines of the Hail Mary were modified for Mother Mary's Rosary. The word "sinners" was replaced with "sons and daughters of God," and "at the hour of our death" was replaced with "at the hour of our victory over sin, disease and death." Thus we are affirming Life and not death.

> Hail Mary, full of grace
> The Lord is with thee.
> Blessed art thou among women
>   And blessed is the fruit of thy womb, Jesus.
> Holy Mary, Mother of God
> Pray for us, sons and daughters of God
> Now and at the hour of our victory over sin,
>   disease and death.

---

[1] Mother Mary said she prefers we give the long version of the Rosary, *Mother Mary's Scriptural Rosary for the New Age* which is about 45 minutes. But if we don't have time, then we can give the Child's Rosary.

Mother Mary has asked us to give her rosary daily. The Child's Rosary which is for devotees of all ages takes only 15 minutes and can be purchased on CD from The Summit Lighthouse.

I commend you now to the giving of my rosaries, for through those rosaries I can multiply many million times over the light released to you. —Mother Mary

Another
joyous day
at Camelot

17
STOP AND SMELL THE ROSES
"What Do You Think of God Now?"
by Alex Reichardt

Pain, beloved, is not something to be avoided but to be welcomed. Pain, sorrow, the sense of one's own impurity that precedes the sense of one's purity, the dark night of the soul and the Dark Night of the Spirit—these are the elements of life that let you know that your feet are planted firmly on the Path of the adepts and the Ascended Masters who sponsor you.
— Gautama Buddha, Pearls of Wisdom, *Vol. 37, No. 22*

While meeting with Mother one afternoon in 1978, she suddenly turned to me and gave me a very fierce chastisement. The intensity of the unexpected, stern rebuke shook me to the core. This fiery initiation left me feeling my soul was stripped raw. I was still chafing when she exhorted, "Well, what do you think of God now?"

Until then, our conversation had been very congenial and I wondered what I had done to bring this upon me. Yet all I could feel was the great love of God through her and I responded, "God has many faces!"

I realized that this must be the "trial by fire" she had spoken about. She said this fire is the very essence of the love of her heart for each person. We must bank our own fire in our heart, thus meeting fire with fire. Some who did not understand this railed against their chastisement instead of letting the fire pass through them.

Ever the compassionate Guru, in a loving yet firm voice, she said, "Maybe next time I'll be able to give you a better message."

Some years later during a casual exchange, Mother disclosed to me that El Morya had chastised her for treating me more as friend than chela. She wanted me to know that my chelaship was at the Master's direction and that she herself was answerable to the Master and could make karma if she withheld the admonishment—and therefore the fire. I had no idea that Mother continued receiving chastisement from her own Guru. Then I realized that all the Masters up the ladder are accountable to those just above them in Hierarchy.

Shopping at Bargain Prices

Noticing an ad for a going-out-of-business sale, Mother decided to take advantage of the savings. So I drove her and her daughter to a ladies' boutique in Beverly Hills on Rodeo Drive.

Loud rock music greeted us as we entered the store. Mother walked over to the clerk and told her she would have to turn the music off if they expected her to shop in their store. That dispensed with, she was able to get a few nice outfits in Ascended Master colors at bargain prices. I enjoyed her enthusiasm as she got my input on some of her choices, which she paid for with her own money.

This incident became fodder for the gossip mill as rumors began to circulate, suggesting Mother was extravagant. If they had only known how thrifty she was, not only with her own funds but also with the Church's, they would have had nothing to say. Even growing up, she seldom wore store-bought clothes. Usually her mother made her clothing.

This reminded me of the flak Mark used to get when he bought his clothes. He started out with a $19 suit from

Hecht's Department Store. Some said, "He's the Messenger and shouldn't be wearing such cheap clothes." Later when some students gave him money for custom-made suits, the gossip started again. "How can he spend so much money on his clothes?" As Mark said, "You're damned if you do and you're damned if you don't, so you may as well do the thing that you get the most good out of."

When her parents passed away, Mother inherited their house in Red Bank, New Jersey. She asked me to help spruce it up to make it more saleable. After a fresh coat of paint and new light fixtures, it was put on the market. She said she was using the proceeds from the sale to help the Church.

The Camelot Rose

I was working in my office one afternoon when Mother called. She wanted to share the beauty she had just experienced. "You should see the beautiful rose that I have in my office!" Her soul was always touched by beauty, and she especially loved pink roses.

When we first moved to Camelot, Mother had a rose garden planted along the front of the Holy Grail building. Each time we went to services, bright blooms in pastel hues greeted us. She said she wanted to focus the love of Lady Master Venus from the planet Venus. We were told the life-waves on Venus live in a higher octave (the seventh level of the etheric) than those on Earth. Therefore their presence cannot be revealed through any scientific probing.

One time I shared with Mother a visualization I got after doing my decrees. I saw misqualified energy cycle out of my heart to my I AM Presence and back again as pure light on the return current in a figure eight flow. She told me that was correct and asked me to share this instruction with others during the next staff meeting, which I did. She explained that placing our attention on our I AM Presence, and surrendering our human substance while visualizing this action, was very powerful.

Darshan Ends in a Chastisement

At the Camelot mansion, several rooms opened onto a central courtyard and fountain. Shortly after we moved to the property, Mother transformed one of the rooms into El Morya's Room. Morya's blue velvet chair sat next to an imposing limestone fireplace with crackling embers. On the floor was an inviting thick white wool rug on Mexican pavers. The scene was set, ready for the Darshan[1] to begin.

Following one Darshan with staff and students, Mother walked up to a Board member and me and chastised us for not responding to an important need she had during her talk. She explained that she had given us "a certain look" that we should have recognized that meant she needed assistance. I felt embarrassed to tell her I had forgotten my glasses and therefore did not respond to that look, which I understood to be that of El Morya.

Another time Mother gave me some direction on a project I couldn't quite hear. As a result she told me that I needed to have my ears cleaned out. She said she really meant it, and not just figuratively. I found out she was right!

Mother not only brought forth the engrafted Word of everlasting life, but she also made sure staff and students received good home-cooked meals that she oversaw. One time we had vegetable lasagna along with strawberry short-cake—her favorite dessert—on the outside terrace. Mother shared a happy memory of a time when she was young.

---

[1] **Darshan:** The Hindi word *darshan* comes from the Sanskrit *darshana*, meaning "seeing" or "looking at." According to the *Encyclopedia of Eastern Philosophy and Religion,* every encounter with a guru or holy person can be regarded as darshan. The Ascended Masters teach that darshan is the holy sight of the guru, through whom the light of God flows. It is communion with the Ascended masters through the Messenger's "mantle," which brings blessings of holiness, purification and the transfer of light and the initiation of spirals of God consciousness within the chakras. A dictation from an Ascended Master is the highest form of darshan. (From *Pearls of Wisdom* Vol. 37, No. 30, Jesus Christ, July 24, 1994, notes)

She went up to New England one summer with some friends. After venturing out in the fields to pick the fruit, she learned how to make great strawberry shortcake from the pros, New England style.

Dazzling Spectacles

Marriage ceremonies were special. The Chapel of the Holy Grail was all decked out for the impressive service. The organ in the loft sounded the sure note announcing the ceremony was about to begin, followed by the angel voice of the soprano. The beautiful bride, ready to tie the knot, proceeded toward the altar to the strains of the *Wedding March* by Mendelssohn. Mother officiated at the altar most of the time. Experiencing this ritual was like mounting the initiations for the marriage of the Lamb and the Lamb's wife. This was a reminder to all that we should be putting on skeins of immortality—exchanging the human for the divine.

One memorable wedding ceremony took place on the lawn above Swan Lake. Afterward there was a reception at the outer courtyard in front of the mansion and along the Lake. Three troubadours—Werner, John and Peter—played polkas and waltzes on their accordions, as the bride and groom and guests toasted and danced into the night. Many events like this made us realize how magical Camelot was, and what a joy it was serving the Lord each day. How blessed we were with such a rare opportunity.

Empowered from On High

Mother had an aura about her of one empowered from on high with a vital mission, and she was very intent on fulfilling it to the best of her ability. In order to do this, she said that she needed to reside in the etheric octave 90 percent of the time and in the physical octave only 10 percent.

Occasionally this might have given the impression that she was absentminded, when in fact she was very much engaged in communicating with the Masters. Mark was the same way. I always knew when I could speak to him and when to remain silent. This developed over time as sensitivity to the needs of both Messengers and out of respect for their office. Dictating through Mother, Lanello brought up this point to reaffirm the need of the Messenger to remain in the etheric to be able to fulfill the duties of her spiritual office. He even admitted that he would appear to be absentminded at times in his last embodiment.

One afternoon a few staff and I were riding with Mother when she went into a high meditation. After a few minutes, turning to us she said, "If you could see what I can [referring to the etheric octave], you would never sin again." The beauty of what she had just experienced was so transcendent, it had touched her soul!

On a more sobering note, in the early '90s she could see scenes of impending disaster but was told she had to remain silent. It was during this time that she received a number of dictations from the Ascended Masters warning about the possibility of impending economic debacle, cataclysm or even nuclear war. This reading was based on the returning karma of the people—especially because of abortion. Mother said these things could be averted if the people would turn around and face the light. The prophecies were in no way set in stone. The righteous can be instrumental in earning dispensations of grace.

18

SLEEPLESS IN MALIBU
More Friendship than Chelaship
by Alex Reichardt

The Guru is like a wish-fulfilling jewel granting all the qualities of realization. He is a father and mother giving their love equally to all sentient beings. He is a great river of compassion, a mountain rising above worldly concerns unshaken by the winds of emotions. And he is a great cloud filled with rain to soothe the torments of the passions.

In brief, the Guru is the equal of all the Buddhas. To make any connection with him, whether through seeing him, hearing his voice, remembering him, or being touched by his hand, will lead us toward liberation. To have full confidence in him is the sure way to progress toward enlightenment. The warmth of his wisdom and compassion will melt the ore of our being and release the gold of the Buddha-nature within.

—Tibetan Lama Dilgo Khyentse, *The Wish-Fulfilling Jewel*

I was in Mother's office at Camelot in 1979. For a split second I happened to look into Mother's eyes and felt as though I had seen the beauty of her soul. I had never seen anything more beautiful in my life. Reflecting back on this event, I realized that I had experienced the greatest love I had ever felt. The love of God was radiating through Mother. This was confirmed when the Lord God dictated

121

at a later time. He revealed that it was He who often spoke through the Messenger. He said that some, thinking that the rebuke came from Mother, criticized her, not knowing the true source. He reminded us that there is a price to be paid to enter into the Kingdom and retreats of the Brotherhood. Other times He lavished upon us the greatest love. Others having similar profound experiences kept it in their hearts.

Meetings on the Go

Meetings with Mother were frequently on the fly. Area heads would line up waiting to get her input on jobs in progress. Sometimes these meetings extended into the night.

One time I had a very intricate design to present to her. Like a puzzle, I had all the parts lined up in a row in her office, fully prepared to make a well-organized presentation. But when her time ran out, she told me to gather everything together and jump into the back of her car and present it there. The Suburban was packed with people, each one taking a turn with their own assignments.

As I interjected various pieces of information on my project, Mother was conducting business with others on separate topics. Riding over bumpy roads and winding around steep curves, parts of my proposal were scattered everywhere, falling off the seat onto the floor. My sense of organization was tried to the nth. Through all this I marveled that somehow she was able to keep everything straight and like a conductor of a symphony, she didn't miss a beat.

The wisdom of Gautama consoled me as I remembered his words to be non-attached to the fruit of action. The humor of it all melted my concerns, and the project went ahead with God-direction.

I'll never forget another meeting with Mother conducted in the back of her vehicle. It happened on the Pacific Coast Highway in Santa Monica. I couldn't recall the exact dimensions for an important design project. They had just slipped my mind. Mother's response was both direct and final—and she said it came from Lanello: either I would remember this vital information right then or I would be let out on the side of the highway. Now this was no small matter, as we were on our way back to Camelot, over an hour away. It was amazing how fast my memory came back to me!

How Did Mother Know the Status of My Inbox?

At Pasadena and Camelot, I sometimes ended up doing three jobs. I would look around and see a need that had to be filled, and I would take it on. Once someone made that move, the responsibility became theirs.

One time Mother phoned and said my inbox was too high—and if I didn't know how to do something, I should ask a Board member to find out. Of course, she was right. Since she had never been in my office, I realized she was either using her inner sight or a Master had told her.

Mini-blind Fiasco

Mother called me over to the S.U. Classroom in the Grail building and pointed out the bare windows. At night the casement windows looked like black holes. She said they were a point of vulnerability and told me to have mini-blinds made and installed.

But there was one problem. Handles protruded from the windows into the room. Not sure how to measure for them, I decided to check with a Board member. For the handles to clear he suggested having the blinds cut two inches above the sill. So that's how I measured for them.

When Mother saw the blinds installed she told me they looked ridiculous, and I would have to pay to have them re-cut to the full length. She explained that it was not because she was cheap, but that I had to learn to do the job right. There were a lot of windows so this lesson cost me $350. After this I decided to get a pro in on the job up front. In retrospect, I might have had idolatry for the Board member, thinking he was the final authority.

The Backlash

The day after any conference was always the most difficult due to the backlash we experienced to the light released and our fatigue level. Maitreya has said that we often get tested when we are at our weakest point.

After one conference the backlash was exceptionally intense. Two other staff and I went to Mother's house to keep a decree vigil. Our job was to make sure nothing disturbed her rest. She was living with her family in a rented cottage in Malibu on a high bluff above the Pacific. Everyone was very tired after supporting the conference. So I let the other two staff members sleep while I took the watch. My mistake was not waking one of them when I took a brief restroom break.

At that exact minute, the dog next door started barking and wouldn't stop, waking Mother up from a much-needed deep sleep. Unable to get back to sleep, she ran on the beach and returned with a message from El Morya. The three of us were suspended from staff for one week for letting down our guard and for not protecting the forcefield. So I stayed at the White Cube, a staff residence not far from Camelot, to do some soul-searching. We felt terrible for letting Mother down and were relieved when we received a letter of forgiveness from Mother afterward.

Getting in the Driver's Seat

Mother often needed a driver to take her to appointments and to campus for teaching S.U. and leading services. My job was to see that the driver was there when she needed him. It was expected that this person would decree for her protection until she was ready to leave. When he saw Mother rushing out the door, he would jump in the driver's seat, ready to go. Then he was to focus on his driving and allow Mother to give her decrees undisturbed. She did this to maintain her attunement with the Masters and help hold the balance for her chelas and world karma.

One time a driver started to decree along with her, but she told him to remain silent and focus on his driving. She was very diligent in giving these decrees. When she had finished, she would ask if there was anything she should know. This was an opportunity to bring up important matters requiring her input—someone in need, Church matters or world events for her calls.

At the onset of one conference, I received a phone call from Mother asking where her driver was. I had waited too long to send out the driver, making her late for the start of the conference. She was very unhappy and asked, "Did you ever see me come out late on the platform for a conference?" She then fined me $75 as a reminder to be more diligent.

Another time, I was driving Mother from Malibu to L.A. via the Pacific Coast Highway. We were running late for an appointment. Approaching a major intersection, the light was just turning yellow. Mother yelled, "Step on it and get through that light!" Putting the pedal to the metal, I gave it my best shot. Smiling, she said, "Good, you passed your test," as we sailed along. She told me the importance of being on time for appointments, explaining that it was not only out of politeness, but "it puts you in the driver's seat!"

Morya Finally Accepts Me

Dictating through Mother, Jesus counseled us to pray without ceasing. (1 Thess. 5:17) This simple statement had a great impact on me. One summer in 1986 at Camelot I was inspired to give a certain mantra by El Morya continuously. After three days I had built up such a momentum that this world meant less and less to me. At the end of the third day, Mother, looking very much as one on a mission, walked over and spoke to me. I was surprised by her comments, because they told me she knew my innermost thoughts and desires. She knew what I had been doing and what I was going through. She then told me something I will never forget. She said that after 23 years El Morya had finally taken me on as a Chela. I was very grateful and thanked her and El Morya and determined not to let my Master down.

If Mother had not given me this message, I might not have known what had just transpired. I realized that others might also have experienced this same initiation by El Morya and not know it on the outer. I wanted to share this story in case others have felt the closeness to this blue-ray Master with his strict discipline and great fiery heart of love—truly a man for all seasons! This is something we should all be striving for. Once achieved, you will never want to go back to your former self. This world with all its temptations is just not worth it.

If you could just let me in a little bit every day, I could give you a lot of information, a lot of understanding, a lot of love and a lot of assistance, whether it's regarding health problems or other situations.
    —El Morya, July 4, 1997

19

ALL IN A DAY'S WORK
Mother's Prediction Comes True
by Alex Reichardt

If one sees the teacher merely as an ordinary being, then one will only receive the "blessings" of ordinary beings. If one sees him as an arhat, then one will receive the corresponding blessings. If one sees the teacher as a bodhisattva, one will receive the blessing of the bodhisattvas. If, however, one can see the teacher as a Buddha, then one will receive the blessings of the Buddhas.
— Tibetan Lama Dilgo Khyentse

One evening Mother asked me to drive her two daughters back to Camelot from her home in Malibu. She then gave me a stern warning from the Master: If any dogs should try to attack the vehicle, keep going and do not swerve to avoid hitting them, thereby jeopardizing the lives of her daughters.

After just a short time driving along the Pacific Coast Highway, suddenly the loud barking of a pack of vicious dogs enveloped the car. Remembering Mother's warning, I kept steering straight ahead with the dogs yelping on all sides and the girls screaming in the back seat.

After the sounds subsided, one of the girls pleaded that we go back and make sure the dogs were OK, saying she would feel awful if anything had happened to them. I turned the car around and when we returned to the same spot, we were relieved to find no sign of them or any evidence they had ever been there.

These were astral energies that Mother had anticipated were going to attack us. Had I not heeded her warning, I might have fallen into the trap and an accident could have taken place.

Walking the Fine Line

Providing security for Mother was a delicate matter. On the one hand she didn't want security personnel around her infringing on her privacy, yet she appreciated the decree work they did for her protection. So security personnel tried to be invisible, yet still be in the vicinity should she need them — usually to run an errand or to find someone.

After Iraq invaded Iran in September 1980, Mother gave a Freedom Rally at the Shriners' Auditorium in L.A. Security at such a large event was a real challenge. Widely advertised, there were over 4,500 spectators. Fortifying ourselves with calls to Archangel Michael, the best security we could provide was a human shield alongside her to and from the stage. When this event came off without a hitch, we all breathed a sigh of relief in gratitude for the assistance from above. Mother always affirmed the canopy of protection from the Brotherhood in such matters, so long as we were right with God and did not compromise the honor flame.

After threats on Mother's life were received, a clear lexan shield was installed in front of the altar in the Chapel of the Holy Grail for her protection. However, it was removed a few months later because Mother didn't like being separated from her staff and students. Videotaping her was also difficult because of the reflections from the screen.

In time, Mother was not able to sleep at Camelot because so many people had their attention on her. She began to feel that the only place she could survive was directly on the sea. This began a series of moves along the Pacific Coast in Malibu with beach rentals. Being right on the surf helped her sleep because the negative ions helped nullify the energy directed against her.

She also recommended this to others. As a protection, she suggested taking a shower or bath to immerse yourself in water, since water can insulate you from negative energies. She recommended doing this at night before retiring to wash off the effluvia of the day. You can also give the violet flame—either invoking the flame or singing it. This invites the joyous response of the elemental beings of fire, air, water and earth.

Even so, additional spiritual work was needed and she required tags for her 24/7 to roll back the energies of witchcraft and black magic. She even received phone calls at Camelot from practitioners of witchcraft warning her to "stop whatever you are doing" because it interfered with their work.

Snow White and the Seven Dwarfs
by Paul Grondin

My staff assignment at Camelot was installing carpet. Just before the New Year's conference in 1979, Mother asked me to put down some aqua carpet over the travertine floor in the sacristy. To get it done in time for her to use her office, I began working early morning with a few others. We wanted to finish so we could hear Mother's lecture later that afternoon. She was giving it in the Holy Grail on the other side of the wall.

I still remember the scene. It was really quite amusing! When the project was finally wrapped up, we cracked open the door, huddled near the inside and all lined up like Snow White and the Seven Dwarfs to listen to her lecture. We must have looked quite a sight from the audience.

Called on the Carpet

One time Mother commented that the sacristy seemed dark and wondered what could possibly be done to lighten it up. Thinking it would help, I had the California oaks outside her window trimmed to let in more light.

Next morning Mother called me into her office and wanted to know why I had the trees trimmed without her permission. She was very upset, saying they had provided a shield between her and Mulholland Highway and that I had compromised her security. Though the highway was quite a distance away, nevertheless she felt vulnerable. So the Gold Bus was parked there as a screen and private retreat. I felt bad that although my motive was right, the result was not.

Decree As Though Your Life Depends on It!

Nightly decree sessions for Mother were often quite a challenge. During one particularly difficult time, she came into the tag room and asked, "Who are you decreeing to, entities?" She admonished us to "give it more fire and decree as though your life depends on it!" We always knew we had done a good job when she would come in early in the morning smiling and thank us for our work.

Do not react when I send my Messenger to rebuke you, for I will not allow the fire to be withheld from you any longer lest you be totally unprepared for the day of the spiritual trial by fire that is indeed far greater than the fire that comes to bring you the suffering of physical loss. Yes, beloved, I seek the ones who are tired of waiting to become the adepts on the Path and who will now set aside their garments for the higher way.
  —Gautama Buddha, *Pearls of Wisdom*, Vol. 36, No. 4

20

LIGHTEN UP
The Only Way Out Is Up
by Alex Reichardt

My bridal garment, which I wear before you, is an image and a vision impressed upon your soul, that you might have remembrance that you, too, stepped forth from the altar of God in that bridal garment and you will wear it once again. The vision of yourself as the crowning rose and the bride of light must establish that self-worth that enables you to strive and overcome and keep pressing back and pressing back every attempt to take from you your space to be the bride.
—Lady Kristine, *Pearls of Wisdom*, Vol. 25, No. 34

Florence Miller's passion was to get out the Teachings and she worked tirelessly to accomplish this. Rising early each day, she often worked late into the night. Being in charge of the Graphics Department, she gave her all and expected as much from her staff. Her raison d'être was to support the mission of the Two Witnesses, and she meant business.

She became a role model for others. More than anything, however, was her great love for God and her striving, walking on the path of the saints. In fact, she was a saint. As Saint Teresa of Ávila, she was often described as having a "robust spirituality and vibrant personality."

Florence's sudden passing at the age of 43 was difficult to bear for many of us, but most especially for Mother. Florence had been a special friend. Mother said she could not have made it without her support. Following Mark's transition, Mother tended to lean on Florence, both in publications and as a Board member. Her sensitivity and intuition proved invaluable.

When Florence passed on, her husband, Tom, became very distraught. Some thought one of the reasons he had married her was her resemblance to his own twin flame, the Ascended Lady Master Nada. Mother was concerned about Tom and his great grief. Therefore, she asked me to stay with him to comfort him. A few days later, when he was still disconsolate, Mother gave the following counsel: She had made the calls for him that should have cleared up any remaining grief. He was now dealing with grieving entities that he would have to work on himself. A few days later, he snapped out of it by God's grace and Mother's intercession.

Lady Kristine's Causal Body

Mother revealed that Florence, knighted Lady Kristine by Saint Germain, was finally able to attend Summit University after her transition. She couldn't find time when she was on staff because she was too busy getting out the Teachings.

One day Mother asked me to get an urn for Florence's ashes.[1] She wanted them on the high altar as a focus of light and for the presence of her Causal Body in the Church. I found a nice alabaster box with bands of turquoise and gold that Mother really loved. To protect the "Holy of Holies," Mother allowed very few people on the high altar so that the forcefield would not be disturbed.

[1]**Cremation:** The Ascended Masters recommend cremation at the end of an embodiment. This frees the soul to go to her rightful place in other octaves.

Reflections on Lady Kristine
by Margaret Reichardt

Florence gave 110 percent to the mission of the two Messengers. For over 8½ years we worked long hours together. She was my mentor. She took me under her wing and taught me everything she could. Her favorite adage to those burdened or bowed down was "You're taking yourself too seriously. Lighten up!"

When we were in Pasadena, we were on the "number one diet"—raw vegetables, fruit and nuts.[2] Often late at night after everyone had retired, we went upstairs to the kitchen, found a chunk of cheese, and cut off a big hunk. This gave us the boost to keep working. Occasionally we went shopping—usually for shoes. Florence's feet hurt and she was always looking for something comfortable. She liked ice cream and could eat a triple-decker.

Florence seldom took any leisure. If she had any spare time, she used it to catch up on sleep. Often at night she would lie down on the couch in her office and conk out to wait for the next interruption instead of going to her room. If Mother was not available, Florence would make decisions on her own. She would just do it and take the fire from Mother afterward. She had an amazing connection with the Mind of God and would catch errors overlooked by everyone else, even right after she woke from a deep sleep.

Florence was singularly interested in and intent upon making her ascension. Nothing much distracted her from this objective.

When it was close to her time, Mother told her to pass the work on to someone else and train others to run the department. Mother insisted she take a break and not work. Florence was distressed with this request. She halfheartedly passed the work along to me and a few more. We were only too happy to let her continue making the decisions because we weren't inclined to get into the hot seat.

---

[2]**Number one diet:** This diet was followed as a means of purification.

Toward the end Florence started having violent headaches. Still she had the discernment to make correct decisions and keep the presses rolling. Mother would call her up and yell at her. This was fierceness like the fire of an Ascended Master. I didn't know what to make of it. Florence was out of her mind in pain and could hardly speak. She would hang up and look at me and say, "The only way out is up!" I have since realized that Mother had the soul-knowing that Florence was going to take her leave and wanted to give her all the fire she could take.

On September 19, 1979, Florence was taken to the hospital. Mother, of course, was by her side. The next day, September 20, she passed away and went on to her ascension in the light as the Lady Master Kristine.

Florence and Tom

21
A Good Time Was Had by All
Fireworks!
by Alex Reichardt

There is nothing more invigorating than to take a deep breath and say, "This day I have lived for love and for God and I have expanded that breath of life to the fullest extent possible to me in my present evolution. Therefore on the morrow I will accelerate, I will have a greater evolution and more life will flow through me." This is the exciting, ongoing nature of life whereby you are a witness to God's perfect stream through you. This is the fulfillment of right effort—being mindful of right effort and then being satisfied in the Lord's effort through you.
—Elizabeth Clare Prophet, May 2, 1980

Though some may say that life on staff was all work and no play, such was not the case. We had many fun times and exciting presentations. Each one contained a message. The M.I. (Montessori International) students frequently put on performances for attendees at conferences. They were both entertaining and instructive. The staff also staged a number of plays and musicals. These fun times were a balance to our hard work and gave us the opportunity to get to know each other in a more personal way. Putting our hearts into these productions lifted our spirits and inspired the audience. And we had a great time doing it!

A Musical Skit for Mother's Birthday

In honor of Mother's 38th birthday in 1977, several of us decided to put on a musical skit, which I emceed. Knowing how much she loved Switzerland, we chose it as our theme. We built a little Swiss chalet with hearts and flowers, dressed in peasant garb and sang some favorites from *The Sound of Music*. Playing their parts on stage were about 20 staff, including Florence Miller (now Lady Kristine) and Tom, Anita, Alexia, Eileen, Jewel, Theresa, Philip, and my wife, Margaret. We had tried extra hard to get it right this time. The year before, her birthday celebration fell short.

After the last note sounded, Mother smiled sweetly and said how very pleased she was. Our little skit had reminded her of La Tourelle and she remarked, "I can almost see the snow falling!" She then reminisced about being in the bosom of Abraham and the great love we shared for Mark. She went on to talk about the joint mission we had come together to fulfill. Many of us are part of the 144,000 who came with Sanat Kumara and Mother.

"The Call of Camelot"

For Freedom 1980 as a special treat for conferees, some staff and M.I. students put on a lively musical extravaganza directed by Tani, and composed by Tom Miller. This rousing piece was commissioned by Mother. Tom said before he composed any music he first made his contact with his Presence and prayed to God to inspire him.

For this production the script called for five Lanellos. Players included Kenneth McNeel, some of Mother's children—and me. Travis did an impressive job playing the fire-breathing dragon.

Riding white horses and wearing Lanello's blue cape, we galloped up the drive through the archway to the front of the Holy Grail building. Dismounting, we were ready to vanquish this fearsome creature that was glaring at us with red fire flashing and steam belching from its mouth. Swords drawn, we remained undaunted—while the audience howled and the children tried to get a closer look at this beast!

Mother explained that the dragon represents the not-self (also termed "the dweller") and all that would attack our Real Self on the path of discipleship. Although we took our roles seriously and really meant business, we enjoyed this sport and had a lot of fun performing it. Perhaps one day this gem will be discovered and grace Broadway with its wit and charm!

Fireworks! Stirs the Soul of America

Uncle Sam steps through the veil! He's concerned about America. People are having too many problems with not enough answers. They're losing the vision and the spirit of freedom. He's wondering how he can inspire someone to take action. Suddenly, Andy gets the idea to do a play on freedom. Uncle Sam becomes the guiding influence for Andy and his friends as they produce and perform this show.

There were many foot-stomping songs from America's past, beginning with "The Battle Cry of Freedom." Shouts of "Dump the tea!" and "Give me liberty or give me death!" moved us with the overwhelming sense of the spirit of America. Audience after audience applauded these enthusiastic students with standing ovations. The spirit of America was rekindled!

It all began in spring 1979 with an M.I. Senior High field trip to Washington, D.C., and Williamsburg. The students had set out from Camelot to see the historical sites of America's past. They interviewed senators and congressmen and realized what's missing is the real spirit of freedom.

Invigorated from their trip, the students began practicing famous speeches of great American patriots. The 42

"Camelot Players" first performed *Fireworks!* before an audience of 1,200 that July in a grassy meadow behind their school. The grand finale brought down the house with thunderous applause. *Fireworks!* was born.

M.I. moved on to bigger performances, and with each one *Fireworks!* took on new dimensions. When the Iranians seized control of the U.S. embassy in Iran, taking many American citizens hostage, M.I. accepted an invitation to perform *Fireworks!* at a freedom rally staged at the Los Angeles Convention Center that November. M.I. students made the evening news.

Two weeks later, they were called to another freedom rally — this time at the L.A. Coliseum. In December, *Fireworks!* was performed before a crowd of 6,000. The students realized if they were ever to really get their message to the heart of America, they would have to do something big. So they decided to produce a video.

Meanwhile, the Bob Hope Hollywood USO packed its clubhouse to capacity with veterans eager to see the M.I. performance in March 1980. Navy bases began calling for the production of *Fireworks!* on their own home ground. After the enormous response at the Port Hueneme naval base, the commanding officer made M.I.'s next performance mandatory for all personnel on base! The following month officers at Naval Air Station North Island in San Diego were so impressed that they offered financial backing to M.I. for the dramatic arts.

Filming for Video

When they weren't performing, the students were filming the play for video on location at Knott's Berry Farm, California's replica of Independence Hall — complete with Liberty Bell.

Afterward the M.I. students were invited to perform in Larne, Northern Ireland. Irish students had accepted M.I.'s offer to stage their drama of American freedom. The audience was delighted. In appreciation the mayor presented them with a plaque depicting the Larne coat of arms.

From the western coast of America to the shores of the British Isles, M.I. students carried their inspiring love for freedom in *Fireworks!* The well-known actor Keenan Wynn was so moved by their efforts that he agreed to add narration to the video.

The students' incredible determination inspired an L.A. video production company to videotape their performance as a half-hour TV special, with the students themselves as part of the production team. The flame of freedom has since made its way into the hearts of millions across the country on cable TV stations serving tens of millions of viewers.

"When you kids put on a show, sparks of freedom fly right out of your hearts!" someone responded enthusiastically. "They've actually captured the feeling when we were becoming an independent nation. They've captured freedom!"

"I AM the Guard" by Our M.I. Students

On April 11, 1982 Archangel Michael, dictating through Mother during the Easter Conclave at Camelot, explained the great need to protect this nation and announced that there must be an "I AM the Guard" consciousness.

He then urged us to take to our hearts a fifteen minute salute to the National Guard by our students. They had given the credo of the National Guard in a military marching drill exercise against the musical backdrop, "Victory at Sea" by Richard Rogers. He said, "By their voices performing this in the Chapel of the Holy Grail, it carries both the devotion of the heart of Saint Germain and the flame of the altar. This ought to ring from the students' altars daily, even if no one is present. It is a call to the angels, a dedication of life, and a rededication of each one's heart." He exhorted us to use the mantra, "I AM the Guard in Archangel Michael's name!" and to stand as the guard for well-meaning people, so that the standard of The Lord Our Righteousness be not lost. Otherwise it will be very difficult for the Darjeeling Council to restore the guardianship of right hearts in this nation.

Call Upon the Lord
Withhold Nothing from Him
And He Will Withhold
Nothing from You

22

FIERY BAPTISM
Another Day Another Miracle
by Alex Reichardt

*The fire within the heart is the Allness of God. It is not a rep-
lica of God; it is not a focus of God. It is God. It is not a reflection of
God nor even an image. But the Threefold Flame in the heart is God
Himself, condensed there that you might have the Consciousness
of God and expand it. Think, then, of the great progress that can be
yours and can be mankind's if you will apply with diligence all the
teaching that has been given. Let there be balance in all pursuits.
Let not the children of the light lose themselves to darkness through
loss of perspective, loss of their God Consciousness.*
—Sanat Kumara, *Pearls of Wisdom*, Vol. 17, No. 18

The devastating fire of 1980 swept through Malibu
Canyon and threatened to cross Mulholland Highway. Like
harbingers of doom, crimson flames engulfing the surrounding hills eyed our property, ready to devour it on
several fronts. On its heels, the loudspeaker boomed, echo-
ing through the hills as a police car swung into our gates
warning everyone to evacuate immediately. But El Morya
had the last word.

"Dig in or suffer the consequences," El Morya told
Mother, "Otherwise everything will be destroyed!" So she

rallied staff to stand and fight to save our property. Every able-bodied man and woman went to the front line, while the elderly and infirm assembled in the chapel to reverse the tide[1] on the oncoming blaze.

Mother's assurance that the mantle of the Brotherhood would protect us strengthened us in the battle. And fight we did as she made intense calls at the altar. Wearing protective gear, we stood 400 strong along our property line. We battled the encroaching flames before they could jump the road. By nightfall, we finally saw the light of a dawning triumph and the end of the siege. The flames were stopped in their tracks, the property and buildings were saved, and our victory was secured. Miraculously, no one was hurt.

How Long, O Lord!

Michael Kaufmann, a devoted church member, was out of town when he heard the news. His house in Malibu was directly in the path of the threatening inferno, and the fire was moving fast. He rushed to a phone and called Mother for help. Then Mother directed me to find some men and run out to his house to protect his property. The entire inventory for his jewelry business was stored there. Mother was willing to help him because a number of staff worked for Michael in his jewelry business. Fortunately I had been out to his home before and knew the way.

I grabbed two guys, jumped in a van and took off — but not for long. All roads were blocked, so we cut through Pepperdine University to the Pacific Coast Highway. Looming menacingly on both sides, fiery California oaks going up like matchsticks were a constant reminder of our solemn mission. Drawing near the property, we couldn't see Michael's house. Our vehicle had become totally engulfed in thick smoke. We hosed down the roof and tossed boxes

---

[1]**Reverse the tide**, number 7.05 in *Prayers, Meditations, Dynamic Decrees for the Coming Revolution in Higher Consciousness*. This decree is given for the purpose of rolling back negative energies.

of jewelry into the pool—just in time! By God's grace and Mother's calls, the mission was successful.

Afterward Michael asked Mother for my help designing his jewelry kiosks and ladies' boutiques. Realizing this would be good training for me, she agreed to this as my staff assignment. Unbeknownst to either my wife Margaret or myself (and perhaps even to Mother), this assignment, that was supposed to last several months, stretched into years. This venture would eventually take me to Georgetown, Washington, D.C., San Francisco, then on to Oahu.

This arrangement became a big burden for both Margaret and me. Finally one day Mother told Michael, "You just can't keep Alex indefinitely. He needs to return to staff." This was music to my ears! So finally, after four years, Margaret and I were reunited at the Ranch. It's probably a good thing that neither of us could foresee how long this separation would last. If we had had a crystal ball, we might not have passed our test of endurance.

How Morya Saved My Chelaship and My Mission
by Margaret Reichardt

When Mother and the Masters determined that Alex was to go out into the world to get some experience for 10 months, we decided that wasn't too long. We were busy and didn't see that much of each other anyway. However, after Alex got another assignment and another, I was distressed and in a bad vibration.

Every day I was working on publications with Mother, and I thought she must know how I felt. I actually resolved that this separation was too difficult and I would have to leave staff. I got on Mother's appointment list a few times to tell her that I was going to have to leave, but something always prevented me. Sometimes she wouldn't see me and sometimes she changed the subject. Once, though, I determined to discuss my problem with her. I was driving her home and she was a captive, if reluctant, audience. She seemed not to understand and perhaps not even be interested in my plight. It was then that I realized that our separation wasn't really Mother's doing or even her idea. It was actually out of her hands. Some dictate from On High was guiding our destiny.

One year went by, then two, and then three! One day we received a wonderful dictation from El Morya. I was missing Alex and I was sad that he couldn't be by my side to hear the dictation too. So I called to El Morya and poured my heart out to him, "I miss Alex so much! Can you please help me?" Then I walked to my room. And on the way I was amazed. El Morya came to me and gave me a great big pink hug! I didn't see it but I really felt it. I had already realized that this matter was out of Mother's hands and now it looked like even El Morya could not interfere with this trial.

Things changed after that. Whenever I started feeling lonely and homesick for Alex, I remembered El Morya's hug and how much he and Alex loved me. This big hug of El Morya stayed with me for one more year. After four long years of separation, except for a few short visits when Alex had business at Camelot, we were finally able to be together.

This actually turned out to be a good thing, although at the time it didn't feel so good. Because Mother held the line and supported us while we went through this initiation, we did not turn our back on our mission, as I was tempted to do. This whole experience actually resulted in strengthening our inner tie, with each other and with our Guru. Like that ancient saying, "What does not kill me strengthens me."

What I learned from this is that the Masters do know when we are suffering. They care about us and want to help us if we will just pray to them, lean on them and tug on their heartstrings. Thank you from the bottom of my heart, dear El Morya! Invaluable lesson!

One Chance in Nine Million!

More powerful than the most sophisticated spyware was the ability of Mother's calls to locate a person on the globe and get an immediate response. That's what I learned from this incredible experience.

Michael and I were walking down Fifth Avenue in New York near the Plaza Hotel, when to my surprise I recognized Gilbert, a former staff member, walking away in the thick crowd.

The odds of this happening were one in nine million—the population of the city at that time. Amazed at this seeming coincidence, I pointed him out to Michael, who was about to call Mother. Twenty minutes later, he returned with an important message for me. Mother had just prayed to God for someone to find Gilbert because she urgently needed to speak with him. I was to find him and tell him it was important for him to call her. End of message.

Now the conundrum: to figure out where he had gone. Noticing he had walked toward a 60-story office building, I determined to give it my best shot. Following a hunch, I went into a salon and learned he had just been there. The stylist assured me that he would give him the message and I left.

I was amazed that Mother's call had resulted in this little miracle and that our paths had crossed in such a remarkable way.

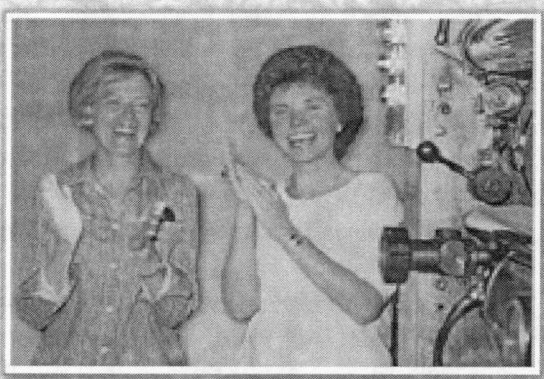

Mother and Florence are overjoyed as the Miehle press is moved into its new home at Camelot

Mother and Margaret celebrate the purchase of our 2-color printing press, our biggest press ever. This made it possible to publish the historic first editions of *Lost Years of Jesus* and *Lost Teachings of Jesus I & II*.

23

A HANDFUL OF HOPE
Maitreya's Mystery School
by Margaret Reichardt

It is required that there be a mystery school in the physical octave in this century, teaching the path of the ascension, where the only graduates from that school are Ascended Masters.

It is required that the Path be set, that there not be a mincing of words or indulgences, paid or unpaid, but there be the pure and simple Path demonstrated by ourselves and yourselves to keep this Earth in its cosmic spin. We are proud in the true, humble sense of the word as we rejoice that there is indeed a school in this time and space.

–Kuthumi, *Pearls of Wisdom*, Vol. 28, No. 9

When we moved to Camelot in 1978, we planned for the many additional facilities that were greatly needed. These buildings were to be laid out according to the four quadrants of the Cosmic Clock–etheric, mental, emotional and physical. Included was "Victory's Temple"–large enough for the quarterly conferences that had grown to include thousands. No more tents! On the third floor of this three-story circular building was to be the "Ascension Temple." Only those chelas receiving the highest initiations and disciplines for their ascension would have access to this area. Once the temple was completed, the Masters had promised to step through the veil and assist their most faithful chelas in the ritual of their final victory, the ascension.

Starting with a larger cafeteria and more dorm space, we repeatedly applied for building permits and were repeatedly denied. The National Park Service had their plans. They wanted to acquire this beautiful estate for a park. It's no wonder they wanted this property. Besides the magnificent beauty, it was located adjacent to the Malibu Creek State Park. The only obstacle to taking our property by eminent domain was lack of funds. This was by the grace of God. Otherwise, we would most likely not have received the true worth of what was called one of the most stunning locales in the Santa Monica Mountains.

As we have been told, we will know the Will of God by the outplaying of events. We had to come to terms with what other steps the Masters might wish us to take. Realizing that Camelot is more than a place, it is the people of God coming together, the dream of a self-sufficient, new-age community was in need of adjustment. Our time at Camelot in Malibu had to end.

"The Trek Upward Is Worth the Inconvenience"

Our new home was to be the Royal Teton Ranch. We also called it the place prepared by God, the Inner Retreat, "the place of great encounters." It was a very large property (12,000 acres) in a remote part of Montana. This was a bold, dramatic step—and expensive. Another mountain to climb, another river to cross, another giant leap of faith.

The staff who could were asked to contribute $1,000 each toward the purchase. For some this meant getting an outside job. This was to be seed money to bring about the alchemy for the full purchase price. With everybody pitching in and people in the field giving their all, this venture soon became a reality. On this property, there was a restaurant with bakery and a country store where organic produce grown on our land was sold. Cottage industries were a big part of our lives—sawmill, solar power, wind power, food dehydration, livestock. You get the picture: self-sufficient! Oh, and yes, we even had our very own mountain—"Maitreya's Mountain." Then there was Devil's Slide, so named because it was believed to be the place where the angels fell from the heavenworld. We renamed it Angel's Ascent.

One of the most holy and heavenly spots on the property was the Heart of the Inner Retreat. Such a pristine place to have our summer conferences we had never had before. Mother said she bought the land at the Royal Teton Ranch for the Inner Retreat because of the Heart. The stream that runs down from the Heart flowing into the Yellowstone River serves a valuable purpose. Mother explained that the undines in the water use the spiritual light from the decrees and devotion of the students to bless the surrounding land and the people. The Yellowstone River carries this light all the way to where it empties into the Missouri River.

The very first gathering in the Heart of the Inner Retreat was the Retreat of the Seven Chohans of the Rays in August 1982, followed by a survival seminar and wilderness trek. Attendance was not open to the public but was by personal invitation only—to those who had given their fervent decrees and hard-earned dollars to make the Inner Retreat a reality. No new seekers were allowed to attend this first conference at the Royal Teton Ranch.

The task of preparing the Heart was gigantic and required many experts. Creating and improving the one-lane road up the mountain, the sites for camping, the cafeteria/kitchen for eating, bathroom/shower conveniences, health care facilities and all that was necessary to make the pilgrims comfortable was a task beyond our comprehension. Only God and His Emissaries got this done, through the many hands and hearts who volunteered. It took just over a year to accomplish this feat. The Masters sent the right souls with the exact expertise needed at the right time. We realized by this wondrous timing that we were on the right track and being sponsored.

Establishing Maitreya's Mystery School

In a dictation given May 31, 1984, Jesus announced Maitreya had dedicated the Heart of the Inner Retreat and the entire Ranch as his mystery school. This Mystery School was allowed by reason of a dispensation from the Great Karmic Board. Not since the Garden of Eden had Maitreya's Mystery School been established on this planet.

The other mystery schools, in addition to the Garden of Eden–Atlantis, Lemuria, the Essene Community at Qumran, Pythagoras' school at Crotona, among the best known–had all been destroyed or disbanded. We couldn't completely realize the magnitude of this cosmic event but listened in awe as Jesus explained in this same dictation:

> *The planetary body, therefore, has gained a new status midst all of the planetary bodies, midst all of the evolutionary homes. For once again it may be said that Maitreya is physically present, not as it was in the first Eden but by the extension of ourselves in form through the Messenger and the Keepers of the Flame.*

Camelot Is Sold!

Morya heralded the sale of Camelot on July 3, 1986. The giant gold and white tent in the parking lot beside the Chapel of the Holy Grail was filled to capacity. All were captivated to hear the story of this alchemy unfold. Some were cheering, some were crying. Mother looked radiant and happy in her lovely pink chiffon dress.

Camelot was not listed for sale in the beginning of June when the call came in asking if the property could be looked at by representatives of Soka University. Soka is a Japanese university that was searching for a location in the

United States. When they saw the property, they liked it and negotiations began. Just two weeks later the papers were signed and the deal was closed. The final sale price was $15,500,000 cash, a tidy sum considering Camelot had been purchased nearly nine years before for $5.6 million.

Edward (the business manager) admitted that this whole transaction took him by surprise. To him the way the events unfolded made it clear that the hand of Morya was acting. Just a few months before, at the Easter Class, Edward had announced that it seemed almost impossible to relocate to Montana by January 1, 1987. This important date had been mentioned in several dictations, beginning on April 11, 1982, by Archangel Michael.

The Archangel announced that it was important for each one to find himself "exactly and precisely at the right place" on January 1, 1987. "I ask you to call to me personally for the protection of your life, your soul, and your family, that you are found in the right place on that date and that all things moving in your life in this hour will move toward your oneness with our bands in that hour. I do not say that place for you personally is the Inner Retreat. But I do say you have a right place, and you have a right to know what that place is when God desires to reveal it to you."

During the 1986 Easter conference, the Great Divine Director had made this decisive statement: "This altar and this room that is called the Sanctuary of the Holy Grail is the most important room on the planet. . . .Until, therefore, the church at the Inner Retreat is built and ready to immediately receive all that can be accomplished here in that place, we cannot approve the leaving of Camelot. We cannot pull up stakes. For this is the vessel whence the Light proceeds." Fortunately by the time Camelot was sold "Saint Germain's food barn" was almost completed, so this became the place for the chapel, though we thought we were building it to manage the food that was to be grown on the Ranch.

One big issue was that Soka wanted immediate possession of the property. But we needed at least a year or more to find a new home for our school and other departments. The final agreement stated that by September 1 Soka would take possession of the Grail building and by December 15 we would be completely vacated from Camelot. Those of us involved in meeting these timelines were stunned. But Mother's attitude was "Is anything too hard for the Lord?" So, buoyed up by her confidence, we set about an almost impossible task.

We Finally Pulled Out of Camelot

We were at Camelot for five years after the Royal Teton Ranch was purchased. Only the staff needed to run the Ranch were sent to Montana. Summit University, S.U. Press, Montessori International, Mail Processing and Graphics stayed behind.

Now we have all read stories of the initiations that must be passed before one can enter a mystery school of the Brotherhood. And the Inner Retreat was no exception. There were tests to be passed, and those who were to be allowed to join the staff at this "place of great encounters" would be required to be one-pointed in their goal of reunion with the God Presence in the ritual of the ascension. So not everyone was allowed to go to the Inner Retreat.

Some were sent out to make their way in the world. Each one had to be recommended or not by their department head. However, the final decision—to go or not—was in the hands of Mother and the Masters. Department by department we gathered and waited outside Mother's office with the department heads and Mother interviewing each person. On the spot each one's fate was sealed.

Some weeks before this final review, Mother told me, "Unless you put on the Christ Mind, you won't be going to the Inner Retreat." This really distressed me. Alex was already there. We had been separated for four years and I was really looking forward to being a part of his life again.

It was during these years I learned from Mother that Alex and I are twin flames. She revealed that Alex's imposter was a man on staff. This man, she said, had placed black wedges in my heart hundreds of years before and he leaned on me, still, when things got difficult for him. I couldn't believe my ears. I had no rapport with this person. There was nothing of any connection in my outer mind. He might as well have been the man in the moon. I was instructed to work hard to remove the wedges and cut the ties. Besides decree work, I had to drink clay each morning and do a physical as well as psychic cleansing.

Our Initiations Intensified As the Days Rolled By

The Graphics Department was the last department to leave Camelot. We were working on a couple of books and Mother was determined we were going to finish before we pulled the plug on the equipment. Since I was one of the department heads, I had to make very certain that every part of these books was finished and ready for the printer. Once the equipment was down it would be many weeks before we were up and going again. Just as I breathed a sigh that the last of the edits Mother had given us were complete, she would call me and give me another change. This happened so many times I lost count and eventually surrendered ever seeing the end of the drama. It was a challenge to juggle between the need to get the work done and the Board members' demands. They were urging us to let them finish loading the moving van that was overdue to leave. Finally, I guess I passed my test sufficiently for Mother to say, "Pull the plug, all systems go!"

I breathed a sigh of relief to be setting up home in Montana with Alex once again. We really learned that it was the depth of our love for each other, the Masters and the Guru that helped sustain us through all of this. We never cease to thank God for each day we have together.

We Made It, but Just Barely!

The Church met the timeline of January 1, 1987 with everything from Camelot relocated to Montana—and then we found out from Saint Germain what this initiation was all about: "The significance of this day of January 1, 1987, is the coming of the golden sphere of light—of which it was not known if it would be possible until a certain proving, then, of yourselves in your initiations—and the very certain coming of the dark sphere of planetary karma.

"The significance of the hour is that the Four Horsemen move on and intensify in their delivery of karma and that many will suffer. The significance of the hour is that the base must be prepared and continue to be prepared and that all of you who have responsibilities around the world must know that unless this place be prepared for and by yourselves it will be too late to get ready when the time comes."

24

THE WISDOM OF THE AGES
Mother's Psychology
by Margaret Reichardt

Your victory must be won! And this wrestling, as the spiritual work, must be accompanied by a true examination of the components of the psyche, hence the psychology. When you know yourself and know exactly why you have the behavior patterns that you have, I know that you will systematically go after them. You will be an observer from the center of the Eighth Ray chakra of the heart. You will watch yourself and your emotions and your conversations. You will listen to yourself speaking and reacting. And you will be in the heart of the Teacher.
—Mother Mary, *Pearls of Wisdom*, Vol. 32 No. 44

One day Mother was in Livingston and dropped by the Graphics Department to have a bite to eat. Being on the macrobiotic diet, she carried her food when she went out. Close to my office was a kitchenette where she could heat it up. There were only a few minutes before she had to leave for an appointment and so she sat down with Theresa and me. She asked her usual question: "Do you have anything to tell me?" This was the open door to allow us to speak with her about anything and everything.

Now this invitation was for our sake, not for Mother's education. It was our test to speak to her about what was going on in the department. It was necessary for us to recognize she was the one in charge and we must be willing to allow her the opportunity to give us direction. It should have been an easy task. But for me it was anything but. There were so many decisions to be made on a daily and hourly basis that I just got used to acting independently. And when I had to face this initiation, my human got in the way. It was very difficult to decide what to tell her and what to let go. I had to force myself to open up to Mother. I didn't always do it right. I felt at a soul level that this was an aspect of rebellion. And I was determined to conquer it.

As I said, the invitation from Mother to share with her was not for her edification. She already knew. This was proven by the many times she would call with a directive that was the answer to a challenge Theresa and I had just discussed. After a while I began to get the idea that Mother was actually there in my office, observing everything that was going on.

It Is Necessary to Heal Your Psychology

On this particular day, Theresa and I went over a few departmental matters and then ended up talking about psychology. Mother Mary gave two dictations in 1989 admonishing us to work on healing our psychology. She explained that this is necessary for us to make the greatest progress. Mother never considered herself an exception to the requests from the Masters. Therefore she diligently worked on her own psychology, even to the extent of seeing a professional. She had suggested from time to time that she had some issues to work out as a result of her difficult childhood.[1]

During this intimate time with her, Mother told us how over the years people have idolized her, thinking that

---

[1]**Mother's childhood:** Read about this in her autobiography In My Own Words: Memoirs of a Twentieth-Century Mystic by Elizabeth Clare Prophet, published by Summit University Press.

she's a Guru and therefore she's perfect, particularly since she had balanced 100 percent of her karma. They think everything she does should be perfect. She explained that no matter who you are, if you are in embodiment, you carry your human psychology.

One of her challenges was what to give people for presents. She very much wanted to give the perfect gift but didn't seem to have the knack of determining just what that might be. She always felt that she'd never get the right thing and this made her feel sad. Even with her kids, she sometimes couldn't figure out what to get them.

She realized this dated back to her childhood. Her father never once gave her a gift during all the years she was growing up and even after she left home. When she was young she would make him gifts. She put a great deal of effort into these presents because she very much wanted to please him. But when Christmas came around her father wouldn't even open her gift or when he finally did open it, he would say he didn't need it. This had a great impact on her young mind, because it happened a number of times. Since the gift was coming from her, she thought this meant he didn't want her. Now when she gave a gift, the record of her pain would surface.

She told us she had some unreasonable fears. Here she is with 100 percent of her karma balanced and she still has some issues to resolve. One was she was afraid of heights. She discovered this fear stemmed from a past embodiment when she was a temple virgin and was thrown over a cliff as a sacrifice. She explained that there could be a deep spiritual life but while in a human form, our records from the past are still there to be dealt with.

Over the 27 years I interacted with her, there were not more than a handful of times that she talked about herself in a very personal way. This is why I still remember so vividly this heart to heart chat. It lasted only a short time but opened up unexpected and even, to a certain extent, unrealized vistas for me. How fortunate my life has been to be given the opportunity for such close contact with a person in physical embodiment who has so much light and so much attainment, and yet is so humble and approachable. No one really knows just how much light Elizabeth, Mother, Guru Ma really has. We can only look at all her accomplishments with awe and realize what a wonder she is!

Mark enjoys a Trio performance during a conference. Mother listens to a delightful duo perform on flute and cello during a musical interlude. Colorado Springs, Colorado

25

THE DREAM GOES ON
Life at the Ranch
by Alex and Margaret Reichardt

I have said, I say, and I will say, "Help build My Country."
And remember this Our request not in warmth and abundance,
but in the cold and in moments of hardship.

It has been told that there will be instances which require
courage, that there will be sharp precipices which can be crossed
only in the Name of the Teacher.

They will say, "It is warm by the fire." You will answer,
"I hasten into the cold."

They will say, "Fine is the fur coat." You will answer, "Too
long for walking."

They will say, "Close the eyes." You will answer,
"Forbidden on watch."

—Morya, Leaves of Morya's Garden, 1925

Mother defined the Royal Teton Ranch in 1984: "So
great a gift has not been given in 10,000 years. This land
is our parchment. Now the Masters say, 'Write upon this
parchment.'" So began the adventure that topped them all.

Life at the Ranch in Montana was very different
from life at Camelot in Malibu, as you can imagine. From
the Golden State to Big Sky Country. From near sea level to
mile high. From smog, fog and congestion to good, clean air

and lots of open spaces. Montana has been identified as the epitome of unspoiled lands. It's also referred to as the "Land of Shining Mountains," for the sun glittering on the snow atop the Rocky Mountains that run along western Montana where the Ranch is located.

Our property is located in Paradise Valley, which extends from the Yellowstone gateway community of Gardiner at the south end to historic Livingston on the north. This region is appropriately named "paradise." It provides a unique backdrop of snowcapped peaks against expansive ranch lands, flowing rivers, spring creeks and abundant wildlife. Bounded by the majestic Absaroka-Beartooth mountains on the east and the Gallatin Range on the west, the valley follows the meandering waters of the Yellowstone River. The Ranch is located next to Yellowstone National Park.

Many times we remarked how time seemed to have slowed down since our arrival in Montana. Instead of 5 minutes walking between departments at Camelot it could take 10 to 45 minutes by vehicle to get from one part of the Ranch to another. For company we had cows, horses, bighorn sheep, elk, deer, bears, coyotes and each other, of course. We were filled with a great sense of anticipation and enthusiasm as we went about making this land our own.

Mother said the thing that made her happiest about our new home in Montana was the presence of a geothermal well (called La Duke Hot Springs) that "the Elohim had formed for us since they formed the Earth." About 50 feet above the Yellowstone, right on the river, is this wonderful healing mineral water. We called it Mother Mary's healing waters and planned to create a series of pools and spas for the health of our membership and the people we would minister to. As of this writing these plans have not yet been realized.

The Initiations Were Unique

Initiations at the Ranch were remarkably different from those of past years. The tests in Montana were far more physically demanding than we had ever experienced during our time on staff. There was also the descent of the physical karma of 25,800 years past, beginning on April 23, 1990. The severe winter weather for some was stressful and for others exhilarating.

On August 25, 1981, El Morya said,

I do not summon all, but only those who have the understanding and an inner fiery furnace whereby a heat is generated. The snows are cold in winter, and the winds that blow. And those who love the winter are those who have the internal fire. And in the snow and the wind they see not the cold but the fire itself. To them, the snow is sacred fire and the inner heat is a source of warmth and the burning lamp of light.

Thus, you see, God made a rugged clime for pilgrims. Rugged lands of Tibet and of other centuries and continents have summoned those who are not the lazy serpents sunning in the tropical heat, for they have no heartbeat to provide them with the inner glow. You must therefore understand that fallen ones tend to gather where the life is easy. And the individuals who are looking for something else than more and more materialism come apart and find in nature that which the greatest technology of all ages—which you have not even seen in this century—could not afford.

Our tests followed the four quadrants of the Cosmic Clock, beginning with La Tourelle, the Etheric Quadrant. Here was four-and-a-half acres of heaven with daily interaction with the Messengers. We lived in their aura and therefore were more aware that the Masters walked the halls and the angels took up residence. Some would call it the "honeymoon phase." The Divine Mother and Father were very much a part of our experience and we felt protected, loved and taken care of. Yes, we had tests and initiations but they were a small part of our life, yet it required a leap of faith and a willingness to accept correction.

At the Pasadena College campus in California our testing seemed more in the Mental Quadrant. The challenge was maintaining our contact with the Masters and the Guru while dealing with the minds of the millions who occupied the second-largest urban area in the country. Another factor was the elevation, living near sea level rather than a mile high at La Tourelle. As we have been told, it is more difficult to maintain the same light at sea level because the weight of the human effluvia is heavier there.

Camelot, in the Santa Monica Mountains, brought us to a higher consciousness. Our life was lived in the Emotional Quadrant, where there was the highest hope for our salvation and the salvation of the planet. Through some of the greatest difficulties, we had a firmly established, tightly woven community, a gathering of hundreds of like-minded seekers who wanted most to find God and serve the Masters.

The Ranch, then, is primarily the testing in the Physical Quadrant.

Not in My Back Yard

When the activity first moved to Montana there was considerable negative publicity. This was generated by the fact that we were unknown, with over 500 staff (just 200 less than the nearby town). To stir the pot, an unhappy camper from California had spread tall tales against us. So the deck was stacked before we set foot in Montana. Mother met this challenge with her usual levelheadedness and dynamism. She decided if folks really knew what kind of people we are, it would allay their fears.

She made herself available to talk at gatherings and had "town hall" meetings to give everyone the opportunity to ask questions. We also had social events–picnics and dances–and a Shakespearean play, *The Taming of the Shrew*.

The Ranch Kitchen was a great place where the locals and Church members could get some good home cookin' and be entertained by the Paradise Players, a group of staff members who put on a foot-stomping country-western dinner show. All her life Mother loved dancing. She also loved our get-togethers and parties where she would take the mike and sing. We all enjoyed ourselves during these fun occasions. This was the other side of Mother–quite different from the fiery disciplinarian she became as the Guru.

Mother Would Not Take No for An Answer

When someone's life was on the line, Mother spared no effort to roll back the dark energies and draw down God's Will for the situation. She put all the fervor of her heart into winning the victory. We remember one very serious situation when a young man had his head crushed while helping out at the Ranch. She summoned all of us to the altar and we gave non-stop, fervent calls until he was out of danger and on the mend. By the grace of God, he recovered completely!

During the hottest part of the summer of 1988 the largest wildfire in the history of Yellowstone Park burned approximately 1,240 square miles of the parkland. Fanned by a combination of drought, heat and strong winds, the smoke spread down Paradise Valley for some 40 miles. When this out-of-control fire threatened the Heart, Mother was on the front lines, defending our turf with fiery decrees. She shared with us her feelings at the possibility that we might lose the Heart for a hundred years. We, staff and Keepers, were called to the Heart and stayed there, sitting on hay bales, adding our energies to Mother's for days. This fire came within a mile of our property before the danger was over. Even the locals acknowledged that it was our prayers that turned the fire back.

Then there was the Persian Gulf War in Iraq in 1991 (U.S. involvement was called "Operation Desert Storm").

Again, Mother led fiery decrees by the hour for the protection of our troops. The coalition forces, led by the U.S. general, won this war in 100 hours. These four days were said to be the four most bloody and courageous days of our nation's history.

How Mother Coped with Trial and Tribulation

At times our Church and Mother came under a great barrage of energy–including legal battles. Mother reminded us that when you have the Christ Light, you will be persecuted. Have the courage to let your Light (your Christhood) shine, knowing that "men shall revile you and persecute you and shall say all manner of evil against you falsely for my sake." (Matthew 5:11)

On October 8, 1995, Jesus said, "Remember, beloved, it is not you that they hate: it is the Light (my Light), which you embody, that they hate. Thus, you can 'rejoice and be exceeding glad, for great is your reward in heaven; for so persecuted they the prophets which were before you.'" (Matthew 5:12)

One night during a difficult legal battle Mother took time out to watch *Disorder in the Court*, a Three Stooges comedy, to help lighten up an otherwise seemingly serious situation. On her way to meet the press she quoted the comedian Jimmy Durante: "What a revolting development this is!" Through all seeming troubles, we witnessed Mother remain centered, with an unwavering faith in God.

Reflecting on the challenges of the Church, she remarked that God had always seen her through them. So she decided to no longer be concerned, to put these weighty matters in God's hands and just do the spiritual work.

No One Said It Was Going to Be Easy

Mother realized she might have mistakenly given the impression that this Path is easy when, in fact, it requires hard work. She reminded us that to win the highest prize requires all our effort. She was never one to give a half-hearted attempt at any undertaking. She worked relentlessly to bring the Teachings to those hungry for Truth and the light. She led us by example to do likewise. She empowered us by teaching on the Indwelling Presence of God.

Mother engendered much hope and joyous expectation. We have all the tools we need to win at whatever we set out to do that is God's Will. We have the Masters, we have the Teachings and the knowledge of the Law, we have decrees and the Messengers' example of giving fiats and invocations—the power to move mountains.

Many caught the flame and attendance at the services and quarterly conferences grew steadily. The annual July Freedom conference in the Heart became the highlight of the year, with thousands in attendance from around the world. The tents were pitched and excited seekers flocked to be there for this feast of light, punctuated by many dictations and lectures. How different to be in the Heart for 10 days, away from the density and effluvia of the world with its downward pull. Once there you never wanted to leave.

Weekly Services and Other Special Events

Weekly services and special events were held at the South Ranch in King Arthur's Court.[1] We have fond memories of many late nights at our "Western Shambhala," with hundreds of pilgrims leaving a late night service. Headlights over a mile long breaking the darkness in procession

---

[1] **King Arthur's Court.** In a dictation given Christmas Day 1987, Lanello named the sanctuary at the Royal Teton Ranch "King Arthur's Court" in honor of El Morya. In the fifth century, El Morya was embodied as Arthur, King of the Britons and Guru of the mystery school at Camelot. Lanello said: "May you understand that Camelot has returned once again and you are called, each and every one, because of all past service to the Holy Grail. . . .Let this new Camelot . . . be seen on the inner planes by all the world. And let all the world have in this hour a mighty zest for a return . . . to King Arthur's Court as it is this day in the etheric octave—the gift of Morya over this very place to be lowered, then, day by day into this building as each one does embody that very spirit, that very diamond heart and that very fire and fervor of Love that does produce the living fountain of Victory." See *1987 Pearls of Wisdom*, pp. 625–26.

reminded us of the pilgrims with their torches lit in the movie *Lost Horizon*[2] as they made their trek up the mountain.

During the years at the Ranch there were a number of students who graduated from Earth's schoolroom and made their ascension, including:

Mary Lou Majerus balanced 61 percent of her karma.
Warren Carter balanced 54 percent of his karma.
Alice Boscoe balanced 78 percent of her karma.
Ruth Hawkins balanced 61 percent of her karma.
Ruth Farnam balanced 79 percent of her karma.
Patricia Johnson balanced 54 percent of her karma.
Ella Amber balanced 55 percent of her karma.
Helen Ries balanced 60 percent of her karma.

How many would have made it without their Guru, our Mother? Like others who preceded them, we have the opportunity to call to them to assist us on our own path to the ascension.

It's hard to end our section of this book. The story is not finished. Mother's influence is still very apparent. She is still changing lives, like she changed our lives and thousands of others. We invite you to read the stories of other devotees that follow in Part 2. The ripples she started continue out into the great sea of existence and lift humanity heavenward. We will never stop missing our angel from Mercury. Her strength fills the souls of those who know her with an indescribable grace and peace. The light from her angel wings will show us the way back Home.

---

[2] *Lost Horizon* (1939 version) was one of Mark Prophet's favorite films, which he recommended the staff watch.

Her Many Accomplishments Were Unprecedented
by Alex Reichardt

Mother had a get-together for staff at The Ranch Kitchen in 1986 and invited me to sit at her table. During the luncheon, she asked staff to speak and turning to me exclaimed, "Why, Alex, you're the longest-serving staff member here!"

Being in the hot seat as all eyes turned on me, I realized it was actually Mother who had served the longest on staff. I took the mike and the opportunity to recognize her many accomplishments. Since joining Mark in 1961, just three years after he began the movement, she turned everything around. She encouraged individual initiative and involvement, typed the Pearls, cleaned the house, cooked the meals for staff, and even printed the publications. All this while raising four children, taking thousands of dictations, giving lectures and stumping across the globe. This turned out to be a very warm and loving exchange.

Helen Ries

Mary Lou Majerus dancing with her friend Robert

The Master El Morya

Mother's guru and mentor in this life, and many
other lives, is the Ascended Master El Morya.
Some of El Morya's best known embodiments
were Thomas Becket and Sir Thomas More.

Thomas Becket

Twelfth-century saint and archbishop of Canterbury, Thomas Becket was murdered in his cathedral by order of his "friend" King Henry II, who had said: "Will no one rid me of this troublesome priest!" Becket had learned that you cannot come to terms with evil, so he became a strong churchman, martyr and saint. Becket remains a hero-saint down to our own times.

Henry II did penance at Thomas's tomb. But later, reembodied as Henry VIII, he despoiled that tomb and scattered the saint's relics, then outlawed all veneration or mention of the saint.

Sir Thomas More

It has been said that few saints are more relevant to the 20th century than Sir Thomas More. In 2000 Pope John Paul II officially declared Sir Thomas More the patron saint of politicians.

Thomas More was a remarkable statesman, witty and a hero. Supreme diplomat, counselor and chancellor, he did not compromise his own moral values in order to please the king, knowing that true allegiance to authority is not blind acceptance of everything that authority wants.

King Henry VIII desperately sought Thomas More's approval of his divorce and remarriage. He also wanted his endorsement of Henry as supreme head of the Church in England, because no one questioned More's personal integrity. Thomas knew to do so would have meant denying the Pope as the head of the Church. Unable to accommodate Henry's wishes, More resigned as chancellor. Thereupon the king decided to get rid of him. More was accused of treason and committed to the Tower of London. Upon conviction, More declared he had all the councils of

Christendom, and not just the council of one realm, to support him in the decision of his conscience. He was beheaded on Tower Hill, London, on July 6, 1535.

But Thomas had the last laugh. He is now the Ascended Master El Morya, Lord of the First Ray. Whereas those who sought to save themselves by their silence, more interested in their power and paltry positions than defending the truth, are still on the treadmill of samsara.

When Mother stumped England in 1985, she knelt in prayer before Sir Thomas More's statue. Later she visited the Tower of London, where he was incarcerated prior to his beheading. She recounted that she had been one of his daughters, Margaret, in that embodiment.

Saint Thomas More, by Hans Holbein 1527

Part Two

Amazing Grace
with
Elizabeth Clare Prophet

by Her Devotees

Mother with Mark,
devotees and
friends of the
Ascended Masters
in the early years
of The Summit
Lighthouse.

26

ON A CLEAR DAY YOU CAN SEE FOREVER
My Great Joy of Knowing the Messengers
by Virginia Fellows

*Hear me now, if you have never heard me before. Sense—
if you can still sense the vibration of Light and divide it from
Darkness—that I am here, that I have stepped into the very human
level of the Messenger that you might see my aura around her and
you might respect that presence in yourselves and you might get
on with your original purposes for which you came out from the
world to sit at the feet of the Ascended Masters, to sit at the feet of
your Mighty I AM Presence.*
—Jesus Christ, *Pearls of Wisdom*, Vol. 36, No. 72

My memories of Mother go way back to the first
picture I ever saw of her. It held me spellbound—I couldn't
take my eyes off it. Mother and Mark had just moved to La
Tourelle from Washington, D.C., when I received notice of
an Easter conference to be held there. I knew I had to go,
although I had never heard of The Summit Lighthouse.

So all alone I drove nearly 1,500 miles to look up
La Tourelle. When I located the beautiful home near the
Broadmoor Hotel, I remember walking up to the door.
Instead of feeling apprehensive and shy as would have
been typical of me, I felt totally at ease as though I were
coming home.

When I was met by Elizabeth and Mark inside (we called them by their first names at that time), I was graciously welcomed as though I were an old friend. Later I went back to my hotel room excited by what I had learned about them and the Masters.

As I was lying on my bed thinking of it all, suddenly my forehead seemed to catch on fire. A searing bright light flashed through my head. I remember thinking it was hotter than a stove burner on high. I took it as a confirmation of my deep feeling that this was the place I was meant to be.

Since that time I have been to one or two, sometimes three, conferences a year and have gone on a few trips with the Messengers. I have watched the many changes that have taken place, and of course, there have been endless miracles along the way.

Impressions of Mother in the Early Days

At that first conference Elizabeth (Mother) told me to go home to Michigan and start the first "study group" of Flint. I hadn't the slightest idea how to start one but bungled along as best I knew. It did catch on and is still going.

I do, of course, have wonderful memories of events and marvels that have taken place over the years, but what I want to do now is leave a little picture of what Mother was like in those early days.

Elizabeth was in her late twenties when I first met her, a young matron always with a tiny child on her back or in her arms. She was so pretty—still is, of course—with her lovely complexion and abundance of dark auburn hair. She dressed her hair in many different ways. I remember reading that the empress Elisabeth of Austria (one of Mother's past embodiments) had the same lovely hair. Once for a dictation she wore a little clear vinyl decoration in her hair that looked like a crown—it made her look like the princess that she is.

She confided to me that she always felt the need to dress appropriately for her office as Messenger and representative for the Masters. When I was with her in India, she invited me to go shopping for saris with her. What a privilege to help this charming young woman choose the lovely silk and gold robes that she wore so many times for her dictations. She always looked as beautiful on the outside as she was on the inner.

I think part of Mother's mission was to appear to be a typical, attractive young American mother who could laugh and sympathize and understand human foibles, but could rise to the heights of the Masters when she was called upon. People could relate to her. But along with it were her great spiritual abilities.

The Messengers' Clearances

I particularly remember being invited with a few other chelas to watch a "clearance" she and Mark were giving at La Tourelle in the Tower. This is where she did her private decrees and meditations and where Mother Mary gave her the new rosaries.[1]

Mother sat at one end of a long table and Mark at the other. Mark would "see" forms of entities and problems that needed to be exorcised. He would describe them to Elizabeth and she would make the calls to dissolve them. He described one great dark form that had its head in the Gulf of Mexico and its feet in Nampa, Idaho. It was dissolved by their calls. I was intrigued because I had once lived in Nampa and knew that its name meant "Big Feet." That amused Mark. He also removed a huge black malignant, although invisible, "spider" that had attached itself to the neck of one of the members present. You can imagine her gratitude. Our Messengers do hold enormous spiritual power that we only get glimpses of!

---

[1]**Rosaries:** Mother Mary's intercession is immediate through the giving of her New Age Rosary, which she dictated to the Messenger in 1972. This new rosary includes a modified version of the Hail Mary and the Our Father.

Elizabeth Earned Many Mantles

As the years flew by, I have watched as she grew from "Elizabeth" to "Mother" to "Guru Ma" (Teacher as Mother) as her service and responsibilities increased. She is not as available for personal contact as she was in the beginning when, as she has laughed, she kept her membership cards in a shoebox instead of on a computer. In the early days we could invite her out to lunch and have a wonderful private visit.

But I know she is still a warm and personal friend to me as well as my spiritual mentor. This she is to every one of her students, even to those who have come and gone.

My feeling about Mother's present state of health is this: it is a way—and maybe the only way—that she can be kept "in the world but not of it." We need her so badly but she can't function properly with such a burden on her shoulders. God bless her. I'll never, ever be able to express my gratitude and deep love for this wonderful soul who transformed my world and that of so many others.

Mother Couldn't Have Favorites
by Celeste Miller

Ma gave me earrings one year for my birthday. Then she came back to say she was disciplined by Mark because if she gave me a birthday gift, she would have to give everyone a present. When you're the guru, you don't have favorites. She was visibly upset, but had to do what the Master wanted.

She could not think of us as friends—only as disciples. She would not have any human sympathy. Later, she could have friends. But not in the early days.

After I left staff, I went to conferences and I would usually get to see Ma once or twice in passing. But I knew about this discipline and knew that I wasn't supposed to be her friend. At one conference, I decided her time was better spent with others who had problems. So I didn't ask to see her. I went home and Mother called me up and asked, "Why didn't you come to see me?" I responded, "My family is fine. I didn't need to see you."

Mother said, "I needed to see you!"

27

I AND MY FATHER ARE ONE
Lanello Is Closer Than You Think
by Paula Zarzycki

The master lives within you this day. Let him live! Give him room! Open the windows of the soul, the chakras, and let the precious air of the Holy Spirit flow for the increase of fire! The fire must have the air of the Holy Spirit to burn. Therefore open consciousness, open the way in the four lower bodies, open the way for the fire to flow. —Lanello, *Pearls of Wisdom*, Vol. 19, No. 51

I didn't want any part of New York City. I wouldn't have anything to do with it. I had bad experiences there and never wanted to go back. However, I loved San Francisco and decided I would move there. So I put everything I had into storage and went to Saint Germain's quarter of S.U. Then Morya gave a dictation saying a Teaching Center was needed in New York City, but I was looking forward to going back to San Francisco.

That night at 9 pm Edward came knocking at my door. Although I didn't know why he had come, I decided that I was not about to get out of the bathtub and told him I couldn't talk to him. So Edward said he would wait. He said that he had come with a message from Mother for me.

So I put on my bathrobe and he gave me the message. It was short and hit me to the quick. "This message is from Morya. If you don't go to New York City to start a teaching Center, there will be no teaching center in that city." Edward said, "Mother wants your answer now." But I was so unsettled on this issue. What was I to do! I decided to sleep on it. I laid down that night but I couldn't sleep. Finally I got up in the morning and gave Mother my reply. It too was short and to the point. I said "Okay, I'll go!" and surrendered my own desires to God.

We gathered together on January 1, 1976, at the Excelsior Hotel, which is where the teaching center began. Davies Anderson, Maureen Macchio and I were a triumvirate set up as the leadership of the New York Teaching Center.

We were neophytes to the Ascended Masters' teachings, except for Davies, who shared a lot about the "I AM" Activity since he had been a member. He taught us a great deal about Godfre and Lotus. One ritual that the "I AM" Activity followed was to have a formal place setting at the dinner table for a Master—Godfre, Lotus, Saint Germain, and others. The Masters' pictures were displayed to remind everyone that they were our guests.

We wanted to know more about the Masters, so Maureen suggested that instead of talking about the trivia of the day, we invite a Master of the week to the teaching center dinner table. Each chela took turns choosing the Master of the week, reading their dictations, and their past lives and sharing this information for our discussion during the meals.

Of course, Davies chose Saint Germain, Godfre, and Lotus. Others chose Cyclopea and Archangel Michael and Joseph Macchio chose Jesus. There are many pictures of Jesus, so he placed a picture everywhere—on the door of the refrigerator, the freezer, inside the kitchen cabinets, and on the bathroom mirror. Wherever you looked, you would be reminded of the presence of that Master. Maureen chose the Maha Chohan. Since we did not have any of his pictures at that time, she bought white doves and hung them all around.

I chose Lanello. We had Mark's picture, and I played a tape of Terry Canady's song "I Shook Lanello's Hand" constantly. Immediately we began to notice that the morale of the chelas was very high during Lanello's week. It was a joyous teaching center, and we laughed a lot. Two weeks later, I spoke to Mother on the phone and gave a report of what was happening in our teaching center. We did not discuss the master of the week. We were about to hang up when Mother said, "Oh, one more thing before you go. I have a message from Lanello. He said that "He thoroughly enjoyed his stay at the New York Teaching Center and he hopes you would invite him back!"

Mother Saved My Life

One time I was very sick. I had a blood clot in my leg and was hospitalized. And the clot was getting worse. In fact the doctor said I wasn't expected to live through the night.

So I called the church to ask for Ma's help. She was doing a seminar in Pasadena at the time. Sigrid called me right back and then notified Mother who went straight to the altar to give invocations. She stopped the seminar and asked everyone to start making intense calls for the healing of my condition. She said that this had to be turned around and not to take no for an answer. She then continued her calls at the altar until she got the inner confirmation the necessary spiritual work had been done. As a result I made a full recovery.

Yes, Lanello Is Very Close!
by Dorothy Lee Fulton, Messenger of Music

After our Messenger Mark's ascension, the Church leased a tourist court in Colorado Springs for staff housing. This is where I lived. Early one morning there was a loud, persistent knock at my door. It was my dear friend Emilie standing there, very excited and tearful. Emilie was a retired schoolteacher and we were real good buddies.

"What is it, Emilie?"

"Mark (Lanello) came to me and said, 'Emilie, go and buy a globe of the world and have it placed at the altar. I wasn't sure what he wanted. So he told me to go and find you—you would show me the one to buy."

I suggested she should go alone and just be led by God. But she insisted, "Oh, no! You must come!"

So we found ourselves going from store to store with absolutely no decision. Noticing there was still one shop left we went in. Suddenly it dawned on me. "Do you have a globe that is lighted from within?"

The sales lady obliged and the world became all light. We knew we had found Lanello's globe and bought it. I told Emilie to take it to those in charge during Mother's absence and tell them of Lanello's request. So she did. But much later, to her surprise, she found the globe was left on the floor and forgotten.

When she recounted her sad tale to me, I told her to find out why the globe was not placed at the altar. Returning, she said with a heavy heart, "They said they would rather have the money than the globe." So I told her to return the globe to the store and take the money to those that asked for it.

The Heavens Lighted Up
Now it came time to hear a dictation from Lanello in the chapel. Suddenly we heard the Master proclaim, "Go purchase a lighted globe of the world and place it at the altar." Afterward those that had rejected the globe rushed to our beloved Emilie and pleaded, "Please get the globe and bring it back!" This time I told her to get the larger, brightest one and take it to the altar.

28
A LIVING TEACHING
Traveling Life's Journey with Mother
by Theresa Yui

*Choose to be what you really are. And when you really
choose what you really are, you will be on the path of freedom and
you will find me there.*   –Saint Germain

My experiences with Elizabeth Clare Prophet,
respectfully known as Mother, were a profound part of
the continuum of my life and just one of the many unique
experiences of the individuals in the spiritual community
surrounding her. She played many roles during the time I
shared with her. The most profound was as a fellow traveler
in this journey of life. For several decades she shared her
own spiritual revelations and her life with me, along with
thousands of others. Our multifaceted community stretched
around the globe and welcomed dedicated seekers from
every country, background and pathway. Their personal
experiences would likely compose a fascinating mosaic of
life on the spiritual path.

I came to the Teachings of the Ascended Masters
wholeheartedly because of my belief that spiritual adeptship could be had by all. I had been devotional as a child and
had remembered detailed experiences of past lives. When I
was very young and acutely ill, a most beautiful lady came

to comfort me. Unlike many traditional images of angels or saints, she was inexplicably radiant—lovely in a garment of a sparkling blue-green, her hair bright as sunshine and her eyes blazing light. I sensed she was the queen of the angels. Many years later I saw a painting by Ruth Hawkins of Mother Mary and recognized the lady who had been at my bedside.

In the Teachings of the Masters, I found an affinity for my beliefs. There was a resonance in my heart. In our unique community, I found a vibrant teaching and a living teacher who would mentor me. I myself experienced walking and talking with the Masters. Mother was often their spokesperson and many of us were given glimpses of the Masters. We were truly in the living presence of Love! And I believe we still live in that presence through our individual spiritual awareness and continuing transformation.

Little Moments at La Tourelle

La Tourelle was very special for me because it was both an inner and an outer experience in community living. We were a relatively small staff, and we were one big family. If there was work, everybody pitched in. We got to do a little bit of everything, and I learned a great deal about a wide variety of people, jobs and skills. We came to know one another, almost like brothers and sisters. Most of all, I experienced the Masters and their Teachings in an interactive and everyday-life way.

La Tourelle was also special because Mark had been there and was still present as Lanello. Various staff members would see or feel him around—and could distinctly smell his fragrance whenever Lanello was in his dressing room, which was now the computer terminal room. Both Lanello and Mother were truly keeping a very personal eye on all of us.

A good part of the time when I was at La Tourelle, Mother was in Santa Barbara teaching at Ascended Master

University (later known as Summit University) or traveling to various locations for conferences. Yet, when she was home, Mother was very approachable. I might be in the kitchen cooking when Mother would come in and say, "Oh, can I have a burner? I want to make my breakfast." And we would talk—little conversations about anything and everything. A lot of times Mother would speak about how her day was going or what was happening with her children. We'd talk about our work, how I found the Teachings or various other things. Often we'd be laughing about this or that and have fun chopping a vegetable, like juicy tomatoes that squirted. (Mother liked to fry up fresh tomatoes with herbs.) Sometimes we would share our food. It wasn't always a long time by the clock—it was simply a pleasant, memorable time.

Early in my staff service, Mother and I were discussing various spiritual principles. She asked me if I had read a number of esoteric books. To all of her inquiries I said no. Mother then named a few titles that she suggested I might want to read along with my monthly Keepers of the Flame Lessons. Since our lives were incredibly busy and I was a slow reader, she suggested I take five or ten minutes each day during mealtime and read. I was amazed that after a year, I had read a remarkable number of books and all the Keepers Lessons published at the time. I am very grateful for Mother's mentorship, which encouraged me to gain a broader understanding of various spiritual truths and teachings so that I would have a fuller spiritual foundation.

At one point, I found a book about Mother Cabrini. The book was very moving for me, and I thought, *Oh, I wonder if Mother has a copy.* Walking along with the book in hand, I met Mother on the way and was able to ask her if she had the book and tell her how much it meant to me. Mother looked at Mother Cabrini's picture and told me that Mother Cabrini was likely the first Mother of the Flame. She had been the first American woman to ascend. Mother was musing on this as we walked and talked. I didn't have to ask her whether she wanted the copy. She took the book, cradled it in her arms and smiled.

During the first year of my staff service, we were discouraged from traveling home and visiting our families. We had plenty to keep us busy. Also, some staff had difficult relationships with their families. At one point, my parents requested I come home to organize and pack up the belongings I had hastily left when I had gone to A.M.U., thinking I would be gone for just three months. Mother was not available to ask, so I asked a few of the Board members who were in charge of my department. They decided I could not go because it was the "rule." I was flabbergasted. It was not just my request; it was a simple request of my parents. I explained my situation to Florence Miller. She went into immediate action and told me, "They have to say yes to you. You obviously have to go." She proceeded to walk with me to each member of the Board involved and convinced each of them to allow me to go home. Florence lived by love and her spiritual attunement, which led her back to her heavenly home a few years later.

I remember once we were having a special event and cookies were being served. I ran into Mother as I was headed to get a cookie. She was talking with some people. I was thinking, *Oh, Mother, would you like a cookie?* She turned and looked straight at me. It seemed like she heard what I had thought. *Oh dear*, I realized, *she can read my mind!* When I returned with a cookie for her, I had to search for her down the hall. "Oh, you found me," she exclaimed with a hearty laugh.

Love Is the Key!

La Tourelle was also the place I experienced a profound teaching. I was on phone duty and there was a very important message for Mother so I had to find her. La Tourelle was a big place, and she could be anywhere. I headed toward the kitchen and noticed Ruth Jones relaxing in the rotunda. At that very moment, Mother came bolting through the kitchen door into the rotunda, heading right for Ruth. Mother was wearing an ankle-length dress of vibrant electric blue—El Morya blue. Mother spoke to Ruth with the greatest fervor and fire. I could not hear the words, yet I could feel the fire. It felt searing. And then I heard, "You have to do this if you want to make your ascension." I was kind of shaking because I had not felt this much spiritual fire through Mother directed toward any one person.

Somehow, I knew that this was not a discipline or a rebuke. I felt that Morya or another master was over-shadowing Mother to deliver this urgent message to Ruth. *I wonder if Ruthie's all right,* I thought. *She's in her late seventies and I wonder how she is taking this.* When I looked at Ruth, I saw how she was looking at Mother and her eyes were shining with exquisite love. Ruth was totally open and gracious. Ruth sighed and calmly said, "Alright, Mother, yes, Mother." And I was thinking, Wow! What an amazing moment!

I was then a little nervous to give Mother her mes-sage. *What if she does the same to me—would I be able to bear it?* Mother was walking up the spiral staircase in the rotunda. When I called her name, she gracefully turned and she gave me the sweetest smile. I gave her the message, and she sim-ply said, "Thank you." I knew then that Mother had deliv-ered the fiery message to Ruth directly from a Master.

Ruth carried her immense love right until the end. When she went to the hospital, the staff rotated around the clock to be with her. She was having incredible visions of healing centers and was constantly saying, *Love is the key, Love is the key.* During the time of her transition, Mother encouraged us to go see her. All of sudden her skin had turned totally clear, smooth and translucent. No more wrinkles or aged skin. It was almost as if you could see through her body. And I'll always remember riding on our staff bus to La Tourelle one morning after Ruth passed. I saw an incredibly brilliant, enormous cylinder of pulsating golden light coming from the sun to the Earth a little above the horizon. At that moment, I knew Ruth Jones had made her ascension! Hallelujah! Her memorial service followed shortly afterward, and her ascension was announced. What a victory for her! And what an incredible experience for me!

Laughter as Transformation

One time I was counseling with Mother about a personal burden that I was unable to shake. We were sitting in the family room at La Tourelle and Mother was seated in what I came to know as the violet flame Saint Germain chair. Out of the blue, Mother started laughing a deep, happy laugh. She laughed on and on for a very long time, at least ten minutes or even longer. I was definitely thrown off and didn't know what to make of this. Well, after the good laugh, and with a twinkle in her eyes, Mother said that Saint Germain had laughed through her because he wanted to share with me how these human burdens could be laughed away. And it was important not to take oneself in the human condition too seriously because the divine was happy and joyous. As I was leaving I noticed how I had almost completely forgotten the problems I had come in with. What power had been in that laugh!

Mother Was Very Brave

On the first anniversary of Mark's ascension, Mother gave a special service and a dictation from him. I thought Mother was very brave to be at the podium publicly, connecting so personally with her beloved Mark, who she missed so very much. I remember her vividly in her beautiful long white gown with bright green velvet ribbons that ran the entire length of the dress. She began speaking about Fearlessness Flame, and I believed the dress was her Fearlessness Flame mantle. During the service, tears started to slowly trickle down Mother's face and continued during the dictation. Afterward, she talked about Mark and how much he had done. My heart melted as she shared precious moments from their time together.

Work Hard, Pray Hard and Play Hard Together

When the community was larger in size and number, often the amount of time we spent working seemed to shift us away from remembering our true purpose to serve the Masters joyfully. Sometimes when we would have very challenging situations at work, Mother would come and listen and then give the directive that we needed to go to the beach or get out and run. As she put it, we needed to work hard together, pray hard together and play hard together. After an afternoon or a day away, doing something like playing volleyball, we would find some of our rough edges smoothed and we were able to get back to the work at hand.

One dedicated and highly creative staff member was counseled by Mother to work from 8 am to 5 pm, rather than the often elongated schedules we were keeping at that time. He was to get out and exercise and enjoy his time after work in some physical activity. Decades later, I can still see his ear-to-ear, purely delighted grin as he got on his bicycle, waved and rode off on a beautiful sunny day at 5 pm outside my office window.

One absolutely gorgeous day I had this incredible desire to go to the beach. We were about an hour's drive from the beach and without a car this seemed quite impossible. After the Sunday service, a friend of mine joined me in figuring out how we could get a ride. A third friend greeted us and asked what was going on. I told her we wanted to go to the beach and had no way to get there. She said she would be most happy to drop us off and pick us up. Perfect! We were ready and on our way in a flash.

We got to the highway along the beach and soon were surprised to see Mother's gold travel bus parked alongside the road. I remember the compelling impulse I had to go see her and I asked our driver to stop and park behind the bus. I jumped out of the car with the others following closely behind, raced to the door of the bus and knocked. Mother herself answered the door as if she were expecting us. She smiled warmly and said that she had made a call to the Holy Spirit to bring my friend and me to her today. She thanked our driver for bringing us to her and said we would be able to go back home with her. We spent many hours on the beach and in the bus talking with Mother about many things.

Mother mentioned that we needed to include the Lords of Form, Lords of Individuality, Lords of Mind and Lords of Wisdom in our preamble for our daily department decrees to bring the answer to our requests into the physical. We were amazed that somehow she knew we had been working on the right wording for the decree preamble. She explained that the Masters had just told her to tell us.

We had so many inspirational moments like this during our time with her that day. As we were driving back to campus, I remember Mother was talking about Mark and asked us to read the old advertisements for the services and lectures and the original materials Mark had written. She said lots of it might seem corny, yet this is what had brought many precious people into contact with the Teachings.

Saint Germain Shows Mother the Microchip of the Future

In Pasadena, we acquired the new computer, "Apollo." A special room had been prepared for it. During the 1970s computers were housed in large mainframes with disks that might have measured a foot across, each storing only a limited amount of data. Computer terminals were just robotic arms of the main computer where information was input. Mother came in to bless the new computer. These blessings were a regular part of her job as Messenger. She opened her palm with a giggle and told us Saint Germain was showing her that in the Cave of Symbols he held something no bigger than a small spot on the palm of her hand that would one day be more powerful than the large cumbersome new computer we were now installing.

Learn by the Holy Spirit

Mother often told me that when you have the Holy Spirit, you don't need any rules. To Mother our goal was to become a community of seekers who lived by the Holy Spirit. We were individuals who had unique needs and spiritual gifts to develop. We were also a community family learning how to live and serve together to create our own personal path to the summit of being. I believe the rules were guidelines until we matured enough to live fully by our Spirit.

One rule in the staff code of conduct was that you could only talk with somebody of the opposite sex alone for ten minutes. In the beginning I liked this rule because it kept me from being too personally involved with any one man. However, when we were given assignments to go out two-by-two to spread the Teachings, I was asked to visit various sacred temples and do some research into other religious practices with only one other person, a man. Oh great, now what? What about the rules?

When I talked with Mother about it, she said, "Rules are made to help you on the spiritual path. But they aren't your life. You have to learn by the Holy Spirit. You have to be guided by your Christ Self. The rules are your beginning because you need some help, some guidelines. They become guides for you to become who you really are and then you know what to do." This was an important lesson for me because it came at a time on my path when I was becoming less flexible and somewhat rigid. I wanted to follow all the rules, do everything right, so I could be more "holy"—thinking that following the rules was the way to go. Mother asked me if I had any romantic interest in the gentleman involved. I told her I did not, and she said, "Then what is the problem?"

As time went on, I began to flow with the rules a little bit and understand what Mother meant. For example, our weekly devotional services were often considered mandatory to attend, yet we also had work that had to get done in a timely manner, which precluded going to those services. I was in a quandary. I was working in a room above the chapel, and I would hear the heavenly music from below. I would be so moved that I would run downstairs and drink in the devotion of the service. My heart and my work were more filled with love and devotion afterward. Whether the attendance was "mandatory" or not was not the issue: I had discovered that both the need for work and the need for services could be fulfilled.

Many precious teachings came to us while serving on staff. In the early days, we had no tape recorders and often no time for recording in our journals. We were engaged fully in the mission of the Messengers with little time to spare. We worked hard and were dedicated to service. Yet, we also played at the beach and had waltzes and parties and other fun activities. Sometimes staff would decide on their own to skip the fun activity, thinking they could accomplish more work   .

On one such occasion, Mother asked me to make sure another staff member was coming to an event. He claimed he had too much work and would not attend, even at Mother's special invitation. I believe that incident allowed this staff person to see how he had come to a point where he was losing sight of his reason for serving on staff. Soon after, he made a choice to leave staff service and pursue a different career path. I remember asking him, "Why are you leaving? We have everything here. We have a Living Teaching." Despite my own devotion to staff service at the time, I believe he made a wise choice for himself. He recognized his right path without having to

be told and went on to become a very successful business-
man using spiritual and self-growth principles. Perhaps
Mother's personal invitation, which I delivered, even
propelled him into making his decision. And, some time
later, Mother was delighted to hear of his success.

The Way of the Guru and the Guru Within

Mother's real teaching was to show us how to
connect with our own guru within. It was not just about
being on staff or following every rule or living by the letter
of the law. One time Mother asked me how I was doing and
I told her of something that was a burden to me. Mother
explained that she could make the calls for me and lift the
burden, and she would earn some good karma for assisting me. However, if I made those calls and did the spiritual
work myself, I would have the gift of self-mastery.

I remember George Lancaster. I called him "blue
eyes" because his blue eyes sparkled when he came to conferences. He was a classic example of someone who was
always tied to Mother, always following the guiding light
of the Guru. He would say, "I come to every conference.
I want to find out what's current that I should be praying for.
I want to find out from Mother what is next." That was his
mission, his goal in life. He made his ascension by his heart's
love and service.

Personal Words from the Masters

Sometimes, I wanted to be alone when we would
have a special dictation from a Master. So I would find a
quiet place to listen to the live service over an audio feed
somewhere other than the chapel. During a dictation from
Archangel Gabriel, I was sitting in a library office with the
door closed and heard a distinct voice saying, "You are
closer than you think." I got up and looked all around the
room and saw no one. I was not hearing the words of the
dictation that was coming over the feed, I was hearing
again, "You are closer than you think." I grabbed a piece of

paper and wrote the words down wondering what or who I was hearing. Sometime later when I mentioned what happened to Mother, her comment was that when a Master dictated there were many levels the Master might be speaking on. She thought that at that moment I was able to access another level and hear the Master speak to me directly.

A special gift that I received in the mid-1990s was foreshadowed by my having profound experiences of going to El Morya's Darjeeling retreat. I vividly remember entering a vast room covered in the most luscious soft white carpet that was like no carpet I had walked on before. A large fire was roaring in the fireplace, keeping the room just the right temperature even as I looked out the many large windows revealing the cold Himalayan snows. Morya stood to greet me as I was making my way to him. His arms were outstretched as I ran the last little distance into his arms. He had me sit on the carpet as he sat in his armless chair. I put my head into his lap, and I felt his warm hand as he softly stroked my hair. I was bathed in the greatest love and comfort.

For a number of nights this event took place. I told no one because it was so special to me. I wanted to retain the memories without diluting the experience by trying to put it into words. I felt no words could truly describe the fullness of the actual event. Less than two weeks later, Mother gave me a message from Morya that "each night as you rest your head upon your pillow, know that it is my lap that you are resting upon." Mother told me how sweet she thought the message was. She did not know why such a unique message was given—only I knew.

Alone and All One

I always loved a popular science fiction series story about the investigation into an incident on a starship where various crew members had completely different stories as to what they had witnessed. Each of their stories was from their unique viewpoint and could be construed as true based on their own individual vantage point. However, when all the stories were matched with images of the event from the ship's computer, you saw how the individual stories were just a portion of the whole. In some cases, the interpretation was congruent and augmented the whole; in others the interpretation diverged from the whole. Life in the community reflected this story. We were all on the same mission of spiritual growth and understanding. Yet we were all individuals on our separate paths, with different backgrounds, experiences and stories to tell as the community grew and evolved.

Mother always emphasized to me that when we get to the dais at the end of our life, we are all alone, no one is with us—no Master, no Guru, no twin flame. We are alone in the review of who we are and what we have accomplished on our individual paths.

Mother has been and continues to be my mentor, allowing me to share in her journey of self-mastery and in the deepness of her love and her giving me the gift of doing it myself. I am deeply grateful for all that I have learned and become in the process. I continue my work of self-transformation, spiritual growth and rejuvenation because for me, as well as for you who are reading this, the journey is ongoing.

A Postscript May 2009

Today, many years after the events of my story, when I was praying to find just the right little message and inspiration to be published with my story. I found this in the book *MORYA*. I marveled when I realized that I most likely had never read it before.

We cherish you each one. We cherish all life. We cherish the Christ of all. We hold all close to good will—to God's will. May the breath, then, of Darjeeling's splendor be conveyed to you and may you feel the softness of our carpet here. May you walk without sandals in our tower room upon the white, soft carpeting. May you stand in my presence and may you feel my love in greater intensity still, in time to come. —El Morya

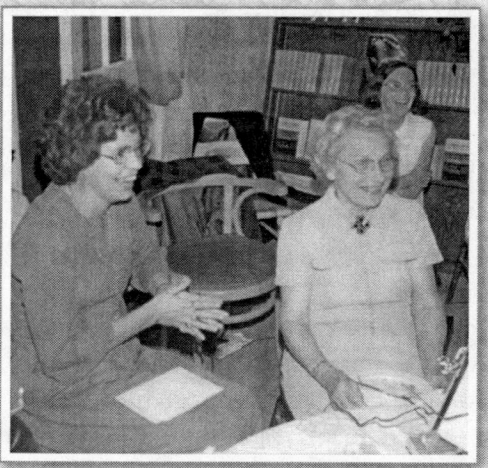

Mother, Ruth Jones and
Celeste Miller enjoy a
hearty laugh

Mary Lou Majerus shares
a confidence with Mother

29

THE LAST HURRAH
Witnessing the Ascension Coil!
by Timothy Connor

Victory then is the cry of Love! Victory is the call of the hour! And I, Serapis, have come to make the ascension as a goal more tangible than your very existence itself. I give to you to drink, to quaff, substance of ascension's flame that you might taste the glory of victory and never forget that taste, that you might pursue it unto the end against all odds, against all adversaries of the carnal mind posing as everything else but the carnal mind.
–Serapis Bey, *Pearls of Wisdom*, Vol. 16, No. 26

I was impressed by what Ruth Jones, a devoted staff member, had done with Sunday school and during a number of interactions with her. What a fiery soul and such a loving heart!

She had come from a fundamentalist Baptist background. It fascinated me that she made such a seamless transition from a strict religious interpretation to the Masters' Teachings. I believe this was possible because she had a deep and abiding love for Jesus. She was a true seeker of Truth and a real bonfire of spiritual energy.

Ruth had a reputation for fierceness and being very stern. She was really about God's business and it did not pay to get in the way. Not that she would treat a person unkindly—she wouldn't—but let's just say she would not suffer a foolish moment patiently.

The greatest experience I had with Ruth was in connection with her transition. Mother was at the care center with Ruth when she called and said, "Come down here. You must experience this." So all the staff got into the staff bus and lined up and down the hall outside the door.

When we entered the room, Ruth had already made her transition. Mother asked us to kneel so that we could feel the ascension coil. The ascension flame was very tangible and a very intense experience I will never forget.

A few days later, her ascension service was held in the chapel at a mausoleum in Colorado Springs. The chapel was situated up on a little plateau facing the front range of the Rocky Mountains. It was gray and overcast that morning as we walked into the service all dressed in white. There had been little snow that winter and on all sides was a rather bleak and colorless landscape generally as far as the eye could see.

It was an enormous service of Light, and we were in there singing and doing decrees as the cremation proceeded. Mother was leading the entire service and it went on for hours. Then there was a final benediction, and we were all dismissed.

A number of oversized bronze double doors to the outside were swung open. To our collective amazement, a blanket of snow covered all things near and far—the parking area and cars, the trees, houses and fields, and of course, the towering peaks in the distance. The shimmering sun lit all the visible world in a glistening whiteness. The experience of our spiritual work coupled so intimately with this elemental white shower of light, set every person to an inner contemplation. All these many years later, I can recall us, perhaps a hundred or more, standing there silently, in that magic setting, basking in the ascension spiral.

30

THE KING'S ENGLISH
More than Fun and Games
by Terry Canady

Steadfastness to holy purpose on the part of the Messenger, knowing full well that holding of the balance of the planet is the sole and certain cause for being, has led her to not let down, to not give up, to not turn aside, but to remember that to withdraw or to slacken or to lessen the holding of this burden would mean certain calamity to many lifestreams—especially the innocent, especially the holy ones who themselves could not bear it until they should come of age.

I am sure that you realize that the holding of this balance could only be to that point where the Messenger could sustain life in embodiment. And therefore, where there has been war and loss of life and others bearing the burden, and death itself has come more as a reality than an illusion to many homes, it has been because we have chosen to preserve her life and allow others to pay a certain karmic accountability for debts they owed to life in many past centuries.
–The Goddess of Liberty, *Pearls of Wisdom,* Vol. 25, No. 39

Over the years I've sung my song about Mark and other songs right at the lectern with Mother by my side. She and I have been best of friends for over 30 years. She's worked with me, and guided and counseled me in some of the most personal, precious ways. She has been to me a sister, friend and Guru. She has laughed and at times shared with me like her brother. Other times she's counseled me as a holy teacher would a trusting student. Occasionally she has been the chastising voice of the Master, completely unafraid of offending the carnal mind in me, knowing that my test, or initiation, would be to learn how to differentiate between the Messenger and the Master.

Thank God that Mother knew how to dole out "tough love" to those of us who desired to be chelas of the Masters. Thank God that the Masters loved us enough to require us to traverse these coals of chastisement. Of what value the summit without the pain of the climb? As Master El Morya has said, "The trek upward is worth the inconvenience." How grateful I am for all the testings I've received.

Preparing the Way for the Seventh Root Race

In December 1973 I went to South America with Mother and that time with her was absolutely wonderful. As I recall there were about 56 students of the Ascended Masters on that journey. We went through six countries in 16 days. It was a real whirlwind trip.

Our mission was to support the Messenger as she traversed the continent, making all the calls necessary for the clearing of ancient negative records. This paved the way for the incoming seventh root race, a karma-less group of souls that was to incarnate, unencumbered.

On one of our long train rides we were all crammed into one car, instead of the two that we had been promised through travel arrangements. Now, this was a 12-hour ride. So to be fair to everyone, we would all switch positions from time to time between sitting in a seat and standing or sitting in the aisle.

After we had been rolling along for a few hours and immediate topics of interest had all been discussed, things got quiet. All of a sudden Mother looked at me and said,

"Terry, how'd that song go that you recorded in Nashville? Could you play it for us?" My first thought was, *Gee, I don't think this song is going to be proper for this church group.* So I said, "Oh, Mother, I don't think you would be interested in hearing it. It's kind of a worldly song." To which Mother responded, "No, I'd like to hear it. Play it for us."

I responded, "Oh, gosh, Mother, I really don't think you'll want to hear it." At this point, our dear sweet Messenger, who I was sure was not used to having people tell her no, looked directly at me with the sternness of a commanding officer and simply said, "Terry, sing the song!"

Well, needless to say, I opened my guitar case with the reluctant obedience of a child. I tuned up my guitar and said to myself, *Well, here goes, God!* Then I proceeded to plow into the first few lines of "Mama Bear."

> "I know Goldilocks is just a children's story,
> And fairy tales, they never do come true
> But, I found footprints on my windowsill this mornin'
> And Goldilocks don't wear that big a shoe!
> "So, woman, who's been eatin' at my table?
> Who's been . . . "
>
> (Copyright Green Grass Music [BMI]. Lyrics by Wiley J. Smith)

As quickly as the whole thing started, it just as quickly came to an end when Mother, with a slight smile on her face, interrupted with, "Uh, that'll be enough, Terry. Thank you very much."

I did a lot of really neat things with Mother back in the '70s and '80s. Traveling with her all over South America was one of those things. When I went to South America with her, I became a new participant in one of the chapters of her life, fighting the spiritual battle of light versus dark. I feel deeply honored to have been there with her and to have been able to work alongside her at various times ever since.

Getting Serious about My Fiery Destiny

In the fall of 1974 I chose to go to my first quarter of Summit University (Ascended Master University). A.M.U. was a 12-week course, held at the Motherhouse in Santa Barbara, California. For that period of time I withdrew from the entertainment circuit. That was a major decision for me. I took this time to study spiritual matters in a serious way. I realized that life is more than fun and games.

During this period of study my relationship with Mother went to a new level. I transcended the friendship level and ours was now a guru-chela relationship.

I chose of my own free will to subject myself to the initiations of all that would be involved with being on this Path of spiritual teaching. The Path and Teachings were what I needed and it was what I wanted. And I knew it at the very core of my being. No one dragged me to the feet of these Masters and their Teachings, and by the same token no one was going to drag me away. And it seemed the more the subtle forces of darkness opposing my decision tried to keep me from the Path, the more determined I became to stay the course. I finally got to thinking, *If so much is trying to keep me from studying these Teachings and make them an integral part of my life, what is it about this Teaching that is such a threat?*

As time went on, I began to realize just how very special this Messenger, Elizabeth Clare Prophet, really is. She committed herself to keeping these Teachings alive on this planet. When I began to understand what a noble soul she is for having taken on such an arduous task, I began to see my role with her in a completely different light. No longer were little initiations that I may have gone through with her simply personal interactions, but my soul's testing being conducted by those Masters on the other side of the veil, to see whether or not I could take the heat.

Holding the Balance for Planet Earth

She did her job as she was entreated. I saw that firsthand. Never did I sense her shirk from her responsibilities as a Messenger. I was very close to her in those earlier years and was privileged to witness up close the mettle of this female warrior. I know now why this job of holding the balance for planet Earth and her evolutions at that time was given to one Elizabeth Clare Prophet and her twin flame Mark L. Prophet.

Watching Mother steer the ship of these Teachings through the treacherous waters of this planet made me want to be not only a student of these Teachings, but also a spiritual soldier fighting alongside her. I am honored to have been involved in many a battle she has fought on behalf of Saint Germain, the Brotherhood, and the many souls just trying to evolve on this planet. I can say that I am truly honored to be considered a friend of hers.

For what I saw in our Messenger was a most shining example of a devotee of the Will of God in its most fiery manifestation. Oh, how she loved her Master El Morya, Chohan (Lord) of the Will of God! Defending those of us who took up this path of initiation and studied these Teachings, she was like a lioness defending her cubs. She was absolutely fierce in her determination to see that these Teachings got dictated and published, and that they got translated and distributed to the very farthest corners of the Earth.

Oh, How Fortunate I Am!

My gratitude goes out to the Universe for having given me the opportunity to know Mark even for a brief period, just long enough for his heart to have been anchored within my own. Second of all, I shall be eternally grateful for having been given the opportunity to know and to work so closely with Elizabeth Clare Prophet, our precious Mother.

Mother gives the blessing while
Mark makes the invocation.

Mother and
Terry at the
Motherhouse,
Santa Barbara,
California

Mother blesses Anita Buchanan with the oil
of spikenard in 1973 after Mark made his
transition. Colorado Springs, Colorado

31

SHE MADE MY DAY
Her Answer Hit Me Square in My Soul
by Jean Allison

Have you thought, blessed hearts, that there is nowhere that you can go and not receive the comfort of the Mother and the comfort of the Father? Whether here or in the next octave, wherever you are and wherever you go, you will have the comfort of the Messengers. Those who tarry and those who go—both are received in the arms of their love.
—Serapis Bey, Pearls of Wisdom, Vol. 16, No. 26

I worked in hospitals for about 18 years, for which I am truly grateful. Then one day I decided to go to Ascended Master University and took a leave of absence. I had found a greater calling. After completing A.M.U. at the Motherhouse, I hadn't made up my mind about returning to my home and my job at the hospital in Colorado. So I took a temporary job answering phones for The Summit Lighthouse.

At that time I had an Oldsmobile in very good condition. Mother would ask me to drive her around occasionally. What an opportunity. She had her office downtown in a quiet area because the Motherhouse wasn't big enough with A.M.U. in session. There she was able to do her writing as well as take dictations. This was an excellent solution for her to do the work required of her as a Messenger of the Great White Brotherhood in addition to teaching.

One day Mother needed to go downtown to an antique shop and asked me to drive her. When we arrived, there were no available parking places and it was definitely not in the nicer area of town. So I dropped Mother off, thinking I would find a spot and get right back to the store. I had to drive several blocks before I finally parked. I got out of the car just in time to see her walking toward me. I began to feel guilty leaving her by herself in this rougher part of town. So I apologized, explaining I couldn't find a parking space.

She looked at me and immediately responded, "Don't you think these people need my light too?" The impact of her simple statement of who she is and what she represents hit me square in my soul. She is the Mother who holds all to her heart, for the victory of each lightbearer.

Whenever I had the opportunity to drive Mother, her main thrust was to give powerful affirmations while moving about the streets of Santa Barbara. There were no conversations because she took every moment to use the science of the Word.

Remember Gautama Buddha!

One day after dropping Mother off at her home I said, "May I ask you a question on a subject that is weighing on my mind?"

She smiled and said, "Of course!"

I told her that I was torn between remaining on staff and returning home. So I asked her, "Do I need to go back to my family?" When I went to A.M.U. I left my husband and two great ladies, his mother and my mother. None of them were too happy that I had left for this occasion.

Mother said three words that changed my life, "Remember Gautama Buddha."

I remembered he left his family to follow the Path. She knew that I was very close to Gautama and was reminding me of something important for my life. Relieved, I responded, "Thank you, Mother."

I remained on staff that spring of 1974. I am still on staff and it is now nearing 2007. Although I have been with the phone system all these years, I was also head of personnel, housing, tags and decree leaders. Often I worked on social events, which is a wonderful responsibility, bringing people together in a congenial manner.

Balancing Telephone Karma

Annice B. assigned me to answer the phones. She also placed me in the kitchen, temporarily, one time for some mistake I needed to clean up. This was due to some karma I had accrued over an assignment.

I take my jobs seriously. One day while cleaning up the kitchen, I looked pretty messy and had to catch the front doorbell. Of course I ran into Annice and she looked at me and said, "What have I done to you!" We both laughed and I got back to my original job.

Therese Baures, Jean Allison and Leola Bergeson

Jean talks with Mother.

32
I'LL KEEP MY EYE ON YOU
Mother Captured My Heart
by Ruth Bolton

*It's not necessarily the physical contact with the chela,
though I would dearly love to figure out how that physical contact
could take place. But it is the contact with the Inner Christ that you
feel from my Inner Christ, my I AM Presence or my mantle, so that all
you have to do is think of me and you have access to my mantle.*
—The Messenger, Elizabeth Clare Prophet, March 26, 1997

Shasta! The name was magic to my ears. I was
driving to Mount Shasta in northern California on a blissful
sunny day in June 1975. On the way posters proclaiming a
gathering led by a prophet, Elizabeth Clare Prophet, caught
my eye. Yes, she was the magnet that drew me and my
friend to a four-day conference at the foot of Mount Shasta,
the snow-topped beauty of California. For a month now I
had been climbing a small hill in Arizona every day to build
up my strength in order to climb the mountain. I was able at
last to fulfill a two-year dream—that of going to a Summit
Lighthouse conference!

We drove into the town and went to the motel. As
a Keeper of the Flame for several years, I had been instructed
to go to a pre-gathering that evening. It was my first time
in a large group of Keepers and I was overwhelmed by the

sound and vibration of the decree given to Archangel Michael. I just sat there in awe listening to the thunder of the voices pealing out the words. The words were poetic and the action powerful! I was in bliss as I remained silently absorbing the vibration of the decrees, verse after verse.

The next morning I went to the conference site. As I rounded a curve, in the valley below lay a large white tent surrounded by smaller tents. A fresh-faced young girl registered us and directed us to the main tent. The tent was filling up fast. We found seats toward the back. I later learned that 2,300 people were in attendance.

Finally a beautiful young woman appeared, walking toward the front of the tent. She stood on the platform in a filmy, flowing dress. A lovely voice floated through the tent — half singing, half chanting. Elizabeth Clare Prophet seemed to dance as she chanted the verses. The voice and the words were intoxicating! The young girl beside me whispered, "I've never seen her like this before." (I learned later that she was on the staff of the Church.) The words thrilled me and raised my consciousness. I was in another world.

My heart was overwhelmed by this lovely woman, who seemed so much a part of God. Love for her swelled up in my heart. I knew she was a Messenger of God and I was ready to be her chela. My first dictation was from the Ascended Master Godfre, the ascended Messenger of the "I AM" Activity. That piqued my interest, since I had been a member of that organization for two years before I went to Shasta.

The most awesome dictation for me was that of Cosmos. He came to give us a discipline. With his coming the tent darkened and the "word-spanking" he gave was fearful and awesome, reminding us of our shortcomings and negligence in following the laws of God.

I was especially moved when Alpha dictated. Elizabeth knelt for a long, long time after his last words. She was weeping. The story I heard later was that before she was ever embodied on Earth, she went before Alpha and begged permission to come to Earth. It was after Lucifer had rebelled against God and had been cast into Earth with his fallen angels. She wanted to go to those who had been cast out and persuade them to return to God. It is my understanding that she was personally acquainted with some of them.

So, for all these centuries Mother has been re-embodying, working with the fallen angels to persuade them to be obedient to the laws of God and to turn and serve Him. But now Alpha said that the time and opportunity to repent for those angels who had rebelled is over. Their punishment is due. It was heartbreaking for her to hear this. And, of course, to have her Heavenly Father come to her was overwhelming.

There were many wonderful and inspiring dictations during the conference, including one from Mother Mary. The book called The Great White Brotherhood[1] is an account of the wonderful happenings at the Mount Shasta Conference.

It was a great joy to meet Elizabeth Clare Prophet and shake her hand. Of course, we had fireworks over the lake on the Fourth of July! I met many chelas of the Ascended Masters, including a couple from Scottsdale, Arizona, where I lived. When we returned home together, we were able to form a small group and meet once a week at their home.

The Grand Finale

The story does not end there. The prophet and Messenger of God had captured my heart and in the fall of 1976 I entered Summit University. After a three-month course at S.U. in Pasadena, California, I applied for staff. I had found the Ascended Masters, their Teachings and their Messenger and there is where I wanted to stay!

---

[1] The Great White Brotherhood in the Culture History and Religion of America by Elizabeth Clare Prophet is published by The Summit Lighthouse.

In January of 1977 I was accepted on the Summit University staff and resigned my position with the Edgar Cayce Association of Research and Enlightenment run by the Drs. McGary, where I had worked for seven years. This was just the beginning of 22 years of many wonderful and exciting experiences, which also contained disciplines through Mother that stripped me of human nonsense, ignorance and pride.

Becoming a chela of Guru Ma who divinely prepares us for the ascension is an essential experience, which I shall always treasure.

Mother signed my book *Kabbalah: Key to Your Inner Power:*

> To my Beloved Ruth,
> Forever we are one!
> Mother

Ruth Bolton, Esta Buckland and Mother with fragrant lavendar lilacs in full bloom against the snowcapped Absarokas. Paradise Valley, Montana

33
MOMENT OF GLORY
My Heart's Calling
by Michael McCann

If you acknowledge something, some love or sweetness of the Light in your Messenger, then have it! Have it yourself, beloved, for all things of God can be thine if you will but be one-pointed.

If you will rest your heart on kindness, I guarantee that you will acquire many other virtues in the process.

In order to be kind you must be practical, you must be thoughtful, you must be about the business of your Father-Mother God. You must not waste time or energy. You must not be self-indulgent or subject to highs and lows.

—Kuthumi, *Pearls of Wisdom*, Vol. 34, No. 33

I was on the spiritual path trying to find my connection to God for a long time. I had been involved in hippie things and knew I was spinning my wheels. I wanted to find my calling in life so I decided to go back to college and get a degree. In the summer of '75, my whole life changed.

While attending the University of Maryland I bumped into Marilyn and Patrick K. doing laundry. I was out of soap so I went to the Laundromat and got more than I bargained for—a whole explanation of the Teachings. Wow, just what I was looking for! Marilyn had just made the call to contact anyone who was meant to go to Shasta '75, an upcoming spiritual conference. But how could I get to Shasta, California, in three days with no money and no transportation?

Testing the Waters

With no time to lose, I decided to hitchhike across the country. I borrowed $35 and started thumbing a ride. Almost immediately I was stopped by the Highway Patrol. What should I do now? I thought. Why not start praying to Saint Germain and his gift of the violet flame that I just learned about to test the waters!

Within minutes I got a ride. Later that day I found myself stranded in a cowboy town. Once more I cried out to Saint Germain, "I don't know who you are, but the only way I can get to Shasta in time, is if someone comes along and gives me a ride driving 100 miles per hour!" And that's exactly what happened. Right away some college kids picked me up and were going at jet speed.

The conference was sheer bliss. I saw Mother and heard the dictations. There was something so familiar about her—almost as though I somehow knew her before I ever saw her. Then I remembered my out-of-the-body experience two years earlier.

I was living up in Vermont with an old guy. One night I had a dream. It was more than a dream—it was a vision. I woke up with a start. My body was up in the air, filled with light! Then I heard my name being called. It was the most beautiful voice! Suddenly I was brought down to earth by the old guy's snoring.

I didn't know what I had experienced. This was the first time I had ever known such a spiritual love. It wouldn't be until later, after Shasta and Summit University, that I would make the connection.

The White Light

Now, I'm a sensitive person and can pick up on people's vibrations, but I don't pick up on auras. Nonetheless at Shasta I saw a white light over a whole group of people. Then I saw Mother step out and the light moved with her. I realized she was the one with the light. After the conference I went to Summit University and had an interview with Mother. I wanted to ask her what I should do with my life.

She looked at my picture and asked, "Is this a photograph of you from three months ago? That's a wonderful transformation!" She was acknowledging my striving and the light I invoked through the power of the spoken Word in giving decrees.

Afterward, while attending the University of Maryland, I was living at the Teaching Center in Washington, D.C. As I was about to walk out from a meeting with Mother, she called my name. I had an instant recall. It was her voice that was amplified in my heart as a tie with me two years earlier in Vermont. It was her! She was the voice in my vision calling me. This was the answer to my efforts to find my connection to God. She had come for me. I was so grateful to finally be able to come into the light—and so grateful to God that He had answered my call through Mother!

34

LITMUS TEST
Miracle Light Proves the Teachings Are Real
by a Devotee of the Mother

Do you see, then, that your most important role is first communion with the heavenly hosts, meditation, and invocation daily? Let us not be chary with the Lord! Let us be generous in our invocations, beloved hearts, for it is now in this hour when your energies are required for the victory of a planet!
—Portia, *Pearls of Wisdom*, Vol. 19, No. 24

I came into the Teachings during a conference in Spokane, Washington, called "Freedom 1974." At that time I was going to school there and I saw a poster with a picture of Mother standing on top of Pikes Peak and became interested in attending. The large auditorium was packed to the gills.

The conference ended with a powerful dictation from Archangel Michael. Someone came running in after this dictation and told everybody to go outside and look up at the sky. So we all rushed out, wondering what we would find. We were amazed! In the sky right above the auditorium were incredible lights. We saw an outline of a perfect angel, a big angel! It must have been about 100 feet high. The angel was kneeling and praying with his hands together. We could see his wings in perfect detail. And there

213

was a huge parabolic arc. It was distinct and looked like the St. Louis Gateway Arch.

And then there were circles of light, almost like a crown, maybe 500 feet high. Streamers of light were coming down all around where Archangel Michael had just given his dictation. And they were all connected to this hoop. It was so tangible that you could almost feel drops of light on your face, like a mist. There was a siren and policemen pulled up to see where this light was coming from. They didn't know what to make of it.

I was talking to Alan about it. He saw everything I saw. He told me that before the conference he had made calls to Saint Germain that everyone who was supposed to be in the Ascended Masters' activity would be cut free. He also prayed that there would be such a miracle light in the sky that there would be no doubt that the Teachings of the Ascended Masters were absolutely real! I told him thanks for making that call because what convinced me was all that manifestation of light afterward. I knew it was real.

Next day there were write-ups in the paper. They had all this rationale as an explanation of what this was, like it could have been the aurora borealis. It was very unusual that the northern lights could come down that close. There was no doubt in my mind that I was on the Path at that point. So in 1975 I joined the staff of The Summit Lighthouse.

This incident reminded some of a similar phenomenon at La Tourelle in Colorado Springs several years earlier. After a dictation through Mark by the Goddess of Liberty, the image of the Statue of Liberty, clearly defined, was visible in the sky above the chapel. At that time Mark explained that the sylphs of the air created this image as a witness to what had taken place inside the chapel by the spokesperson for the Great Karmic Board (see *All for the Love of God: Life with Mark Prophet, Modern Day Mystic*, page 76.) That night I returned to my small apartment about 25 miles away. Looking back on Spokane, I could still see this phenomenon of light. It was like ripples after dropping a pebble into a pool. The sky was full of this undulating light. It was physical. And I was in awe.

You Definitely Learned Things When Around Mother

I was driving Mother from Pasadena to the Ashram in downtown Los Angeles when a dog ran right out in front of us and I instinctively swerved. I then had to swerve back and counter correct. Mother really got after me and I learned my lesson. When I drove Mother, I had to call my own shots because she was not a driver and couldn't advise me. She didn't totally understand what a car could and could not do.

She would tell me to pass cars in Malibu Canyon. This canyon winds back and forth and has blind corners. If there was a red car in front of me, she would tell me to pass it. To her a red car was a red flag. I really got in trouble one time driving Mother on that road because I couldn't pass a red car. And I said, "Well, I just can't pass it, I can't see well enough in front." I just couldn't do it. I'm glad I didn't pass the car because, who knows, I might have had a wreck. I had to use my own Christ discrimination.

Mother was always giving me some kind of an initiation. One happened when I was driving her. I had to learn to turn on the radio the minute the news started so she didn't miss any information—not during the music or ads, only the news. When the news finished or an ad or music came on during the newsbreaks, I had to turn it down immediately so she didn't hear it. That meant I had to tune into when to turn the news on and when to turn it off, and drive the car at the same time. I thought, *No way! I'll never be able to do that.*

I asked, "Mother, why do I have to know how to do this?" At the time I thought, *This is silly, this doesn't make sense!* But she said, "This is an initiation from Sanat Kumara for you personally and you have to develop your attunement to be able to discern any vibration that is not right. Some day lives may depend upon your having this kind of attunement." So from that point on I took it seriously.

Mother didn't say anything when I did it right. But if I got it wrong, I got into trouble. And she would say, "You should be able to do that." But actually I got pretty good at it. It was amazing. After a while I got in sync and sensed when the ad was over, and I turned on the news. At first I got it right 90 percent of the time and then after a while 99 percent. To this day, I can't tell you how I did it.

One time she told me to do decrees to Archangel Michael. I made the mistake of doing a long invocation before I started giving the decrees and it was a case where the decrees needed to be done right away. As I was doing the invocation, the energy was starting to build up. I could feel the opposition to my call because the Messenger was there. And I was starting to get a little panicky. I had to drive and I felt all this energy come rushing in. Finally she stopped me and told me that I had to start decreeing to Archangel Michael to take care of the energy.

There were a lot of little things I learned from just being around her. For instance, I had to deal with the negative energy directed against her right away, and not try to tackle all the world energy. I learned a lot of inner things and had inner initiations, inner teachings that can't be explained to anyone. All those things propelled me on the Path and gave me insight I would never have had.

The Angel with the Sword

Sometimes when decreeing at night for Mother, I would actually see the angels. During a particularly difficult period, Mother had a lot of trouble sleeping. My job was to decree and I would decree all night long. The tag would be down below decreeing also. The angels would procession in a line, forming a cube around where she was sleeping. They walked very straight with their swords held up vertically in front of them, with their eyes closed. They were meditating.

Most of the time there was just one angel. I don't know if it was Mother's guardian angel or an angel from Archangel Michael's band. I didn't see a lot, but I did see that. I would see one angel on duty and nothing could cross his path. I remember how he looked. The angel was dressed in white with long blond hair. When this angel sensed any encroachment beyond the line he had set, he would move into action on the double. When more energy was involved, additional angels would come. It wasn't a figment of anyone's imagination. It was real!

At one point I saw a self-styled enemy of the Church trying to stick his astral head into the forcefield to attack Mother. At that very moment, the angel of the LORD, who was walking very meditatively, swiftly turned and with a ferociousness that was shocking, was right there in his face as if to say, "Do not cross this line!" It was truly amazing to see how these angels would come and protect Mother's space while she slept, so long as calls for her protection were continued. If we kept making the calls and giving the decrees, everything was fine—the angels would be there alert, awake. They would be walking their post, their guard post, with their sword, ready to do battle with anything trying to interfere with her sleep or work. But if we stopped giving decrees, nothing would happen. The light is so real. The Masters are real. The angels are real. It's a whole other world out there behind the scenes.

Mother's Inner Powers

One time I was decreeing in a car a few yards from where Mother was working in the Gold Bus and I felt Mother's mind. (The Gold Bus was a converted Trailways bus spray-painted gold, therefore its name.) She wanted to tell me something but there was no radio in the vehicle.

It was very cold outside, and she didn't want to send any of her staff out. I kept getting a very strong feeling that Mother wanted to talk to me *now!* She wanted me to go to the window of the Gold Bus.

When this happened, I rationalized that maybe it wasn't something I was actually sensing. Then an amazing thing happened. All of a sudden I saw her mental body. I saw her form actually come right out of the window of the Gold Bus to the car and she said, "Come to the window of the Gold Bus right now!"

And I thought, *OK, OK, this is enough! I'm moving.* Just as I opened the door to the car, I heard her physically yell my name. Mother had the ability to leave her body. She had the ability to project her consciousness anywhere she wanted to. And if she wanted to get your attention, she'd find a way to do it.

I was close to her and have always loved her a lot and still do. I was there to serve Mother. That was my reason for being. Whatever she needed and wanted me to do, I tried to do it. I didn't ask a lot of questions. I just did it. Some people might say that I was brainwashed. That was not the case at all. I did it out of love. I have a lot of love for the Masters. By serving Mother, I was serving Morya.

I was serving Mother because the light of El Morya was coming through her and she was a vessel for the Masters' consciousness. She had the mantle of Messenger. She was a mouthpiece for Morya and that was good enough for me. I had many experiences where I knew the Masters were working through Mother. That's why I followed my heart and served the Masters all those years. I was there about twenty years.

35

A MANY-SPLENDORED THING
Only Love
by Steven Love

Take a step forward this night; and consider that in taking that step you are stepping out of the skins of the former man and into the raiment of the Christ. And when you take that step as I shall direct at the close of my address, you shall have placed upon you my cape, my capuchon.

I say then, will you not stand with that cape, won't you stand then with that cape in this place in time and space as you would stand in the Consciousness of the Christ, your own Christ-identity? I want you to leave this meeting tonight in the consciousness that you are the Christ—not a lesser being evolving toward that stature of the Christ, but standing in the place of your Holy Christ Self to receive the Immaculate Word from the Heart of God. —Lanello, *Pearls of Wisdom*, Vol. 16, No. 32

I hadn't heard of The Summit Lighthouse before but after finding their teachings, everything else I knew was past tense. This included the Theosophical Society and the "I AM" teachings that I had been studying. My sister, who lived in California, received a circular from The Summit Lighthouse about their upcoming Easter conference. When

I saw it I said, "Look, these people are Messengers like Edna and Guy Ballard of the 'I AM' Activity!"

So I went to my first conference—"Only Love" in Pasadena, California. Kenneth M. was one of the first people I met when I arrived and he gave me a big slap on the back! I showed up in a rose pink shirt and wore sandals I got in India—all hearts and hand carved. I then went to registration and met Virginia. She pinned a tag on me, looked me over and said, "Let me see, Steven Love from St. Louis! Buddy, you're at the right place at the right time!" (I later found out that St. Louis is the spiritual focus of Chamuel and Charity, the Archangel and Archeia of Love!)

Padma Sambhava Places His Mantle on Mother
This was the conference where Padma Sambhava dictated and placed his mantle over Mother. Here she was given the appellation of "Guru Ma." Afterward she expressed her gratitude for what he had done for her. She told the audience that the intense love she was feeling was two-pronged: the love from the entire Spirit of the Great White Brotherhood and the love of everyone in the audience.

Still immersed in the presence of Padma Sambhava, she said, "I want to touch every one of you!" Then we filed by and I just wanted to touch her hand. She squeezed my hand and sent a current back to me that left me speechless from head to toe—way beyond anything I had ever felt. It was just a loving rush of light! One of the few interactions I ever had with her was when I went through that line. Much later she told me, "Oh, you've got a heart flame!"

After the big blessing Raymond took me to the cafeteria and I asked, "You mean I have to eat something?" I felt so full of light! He responded, "Yeah!"

The Church was asking for donations for their new headquarters in Calabasas. I had $800 in the bank, so I wrote them a check for the full amount.

When I decided to go to the October conference, I had no idea where I was going to get the funds. But amazingly I had just enough money by the time I flew out to "Soul Liberation" in 1977. Then the call went out for volunteers to do a decree work "tag" for Mother. Being a willing servant, I said I would be glad to help out.

Grace was leading decrees to the Elohim Astrea. This was the first experience I had doing real fiery decrees. I was keeping up for the first three stanzas. After that they took off and to me it sounded like they were going into cyberspace! As the decree session progressed I was real proud of myself. I could actually hear the words they were saying. But it took the whole conference before I was able to hear every word spoken. When I returned home I was stoked—really flying high!

After I had been back home working for about eight months, I signed up for the winter conference. That was the beginning of Mother Mary's S.U. quarter. I was making a huge sign at the Kirkland Sign Painting Company while listening to Mother's *Science of the Spoken Word* album. Wow, the science of the spoken Word! If I made the call on a problem, things were great! If not, nothing worked. This convinced me that I had to become more involved. I set my sights to go to S.U. and quit my job to join staff. I packed up everything I had and set out for California and had no intention of coming back to St. Louis. By this time Church headquarters had moved from Pasadena to Calabasas. The new property was called "Camelot."

When I arrived I was assigned to work in the bookstore, next to the swimming pool. It was halfway between the Chapel of the Holy Grail building and the cafeteria. So we got a lot of traffic.

I was assigned to the bookstore with Kenneth M., the person I met at my first conference. He told me he had just made a call to Lanello, "I need a little more love in the bookstore!" Then Mother phoned him saying, "I've got Steven *Love* to help you." Later on I worked in the Stump Department with Kenneth. I was supposed to organize everything, so I had to learn organization and I had to work hard! But all Kenneth had to do was to put his hand out and he got everything he wanted. He never had any trouble finding anything.

Mother Was One with Lanello's Heart

One time I was lamenting about not being able to maintain my harmony. It was a little thing but it hit me hard. I was in the Great Divine Director's Office and had just gotten blistered by three supervisors. I was sitting at a desk making the call to Lanello, telling him, "You know, Lanello, I don't want this substance in my life!"

All of a sudden Mother came into the room and said, "Hi, How are you? Don't you think this is just the greatest place to work in the world?" And she just took away my substance. My burden was completely gone. And I responded, "You're not just kidding!" I didn't have a great deal of contact with her, but when I did, Wow! I was getting supercharged and I got pummeled!

Mother's Incredible Presence and Vision

The way Mother was able to bring us from where we were in consciousness to such acceleration by her aura was truly amazing! And her incredible stump vision—the mission of saving the planet. I could feel the mission! So much intense training and so many details. And then there were the security training classes.

At the "Battle of Portland" an entire group rushed the stage. Ma was standing like a rock. Steven and Murray were holding the line against big 200-pound guys. This is why we had to keep up our decrees and keep the "I AM the Guard" consciousness. It was so important to hold the forcefield. The agitators jumped up, shouting. We felt absolutely sealed by Archangel Michael.

I remember going up to one guy and saying, "Come on outside, someone out there wants to talk to you." Surprisingly, he obeyed and followed me out. Then he went ballistic! The police were there in 10 minutes. The officer said, "I understand there has been some disturbance." I explained the problem. He took one look at the guy and pulled him out. The policeman then reprimanded him and said, "Look, you just can't disturb this talk. These people paid for this place to hold their lecture."

I had a sense of being in an army of light. Later on during the Labors of Hercules in King Arthur's Court at the Royal Teton Ranch, Ma was there telling us how many fallen ones were taken after our decrees were given. When we gave calls to Archangel Michael, we felt like he was right there. Those decree sessions were the most incredible releases of light!

An Unforgettable Era!

It was a lot of fun—a time I will never, ever forget. Experiences we had were so very special! Mother's ability to communicate the Teachings on the tapes was remarkable. And Mark! I rejoiced in his tapes all the time. He had such a wonderful heart flame. Even when he was disciplining someone, there was never a smidgeon of a doubt about the messengership or dictations. The vision was unmistakable! I could never understand how anyone could leave. When that happened, Ma would say, "They never had the vision!" Every dictation was such an experience. The light was so incredible you couldn't lift a finger.

It's astounding the closeness we developed on staff because of the intensity and camaraderie we felt. It was like the bond in the military. I can talk to people I haven't seen for years and I realize there is still an inner contact. The mandala was brought together at that particular time to hold the vision and to fulfill an important purpose. And so many miracles.

The Masters are still there. Mother did her job. The Teachings are still there and you can prove their validity.

I can still remember some of my experiences at the Royal Teton Ranch in Montana. One that was a real dilly! I got an assignment to put up a thermostat in a room in the Ranch Office and had to fish a wire through the floor, "nail through hole." It had to go through a one-inch hole from the attic down into the Business Office below. Problem was I couldn't see where to put it! So I made a call to Lanello, "Take her home!" And amazingly it dropped and the nail set right through the hole exactly where it was supposed to. If we didn't make the call, nothing happened!

Mother Mary's Promise: Her Cloak of Protection
In 1980 when we moved to the Ranch, I remember doing a tag for Ma with another staff member, Alex I. There was no Ranch Headquarters then. We made a lot of calls. Then I went to the Business Office to get a bowl of granola. All of a sudden I could sense exactly the energy that was hitting Mother.

When I returned, we did intense calls and decrees on the energy and continued on for 20 minutes. We then felt this release like Wow! It knocked out the tooth of the dragon and I knew we had nailed the dark forces.

I went over to the Blue House attic to sleep. When I got to my bed, I was on my knees and prayed to Mother Mary. I was afraid that I couldn't go to sleep because of the backlash. Then I felt the presence of Mother Mary. I remembered that she had said in a dictation that if we call to her, she would place her cloak of protection over us. I knew I had so much to do the next day to prepare for the upcoming conference so I made the call she had requested. Immediately I felt her place her cloak over me. That night I got the best night's sleep ever.

Next morning I saw my coworker and asked him how he slept. He told me that he had the worst night he'd ever had. So I asked him if he made the calls for the protection of his night's sleep. He said he didn't, so I reminded him of what Mother Mary had said.

These Experiences Were So Real!

It was Mother who filled us with the vision of our individual and collective goal to help save the world and rescue the lightbearers who were caught in maya and illusion. Mother was the lodestone for all of that and that's why we were all there. We came to support her and the mission.

This inspiration carried all of us through when we had our trials and had to look at our human substance. What an opportunity it was! It was really a major thrust that the Masters were able to pull off. They were able to raise us out of our daily grind, to set our karma aside to enable us to do our work. What a wonderful gift. If we could all just remember! *We've invested all too much in this to just let it go.*

Padma Sambhava

36
LIKE A KID IN THE CANDY STORE
How I Found True Bliss
by Christopher Allen

I say, you are all candidates for the ascension if you choose to be. And if you choose to be this night and in the coming weeks, then I will sponsor you and I will direct the Mother of the Flame to sponsor you also. There is no need to tarry; there is no need to go back to the old ways of the human consciousness. I say, your Christed awareness, your Christed Being, is the blazing Reality of your consciousness! It is the new day dawning within you! It is your potential of victory! It is your purity now!
–Lanello, Pearls of Wisdom, Vol. 16, No. 32

It is my hope to impart the deep gratitude I have for Mother, for the great wealth of teachings and for the community of our fellowship. This trinity is in the fabric of my soul, internalized, ever present and ever welcome. When I decree, I hear Mother's voice within my heart saying the words. In meditation she peeks out from visualizations to assist me in right absorption. I am always better for it. In spite of my many shortcomings she firmly, of her own will and in a beautiful manner established the golden thread of the guru-chela bond with me, and I will share this occasion with you as well as I can.

The Church had just moved its headquarters from Colorado Springs to Pasadena, so I also moved there. I rented a room a block away and attended everything. The Archangel quarters of Summit University were soon to start, beginning with Archangel Michael. There were a number of occasions where Mother would see me on campus and speak with me, asking if I would be attending S.U. I had my heart set on Zadkiel's[1] quarter, which was the seventh Archangel quarter and wouldn't be held for some time.

You see, for the past year and a half to two years I had been doing 8 to 10 hours daily of violet flame decrees, so I was slightly leaning toward Zadkiel's quarter. As circumstances would have it, Mother requested that I join staff, which I did, serving in the kitchen. After returning home from work at an engineering firm in town, I worked the salad bar and then dishes and mops until the cafeteria was buttoned up for the night. There were always more duties than personnel so we all had a multitude of responsibilities —no boring or lazy days!

Zadkiel's quarter would be the first one at Camelot and was expected to be the largest class to date. There was much preparation to be done. The S.U. classroom needed the theater-style seats put in, living quarters up the coast at Camp Victory needed much cleaning and the cabin heaters were in dire straits, etc., etc. A couple of days before the start of S.U., I received the OK to attend! But, being a staff member meant that duties and responsibility were still mine. I quickly became a bus driver for the students, usher or security at every service, and more!

No Blissing Out

Well, we lived through Zadkiel's quarter and now it was time for our graduation party at the Ashram of the World Mother in Los Angeles. I am a lover of Bliss; it is

---

[1] **Zadkiel** is the Archangel of the seventh ray, the ray of the violet flame.

in my nature. I thought that this would be my day of respite, euphoria, sweet simple bliss! After unloading my bus of students I strolled leisurely, quietly and happily to the courtyard. It was at this moment that someone approached me to request that I assist with security for the day's event ... ARGH! It is a privilege to serve, so I took up my position just inside the courtyard door near Saint Germain's office — resigned to duty and no blissing out!

Sometime later Mother descended the stairs and proceeded to my security position leading outside. Stopping in front of me she asked, "Christopher, are you happy?" Gathering myself a little I responded, "Yes, Mother, I'm happy." She went on out to where the students had gathered and were waiting for her appearance. Grand applause, kind words, book signing and a wonderful time for all. Everyone looked so blissful!

It may have been several hours later when Mother emerged from the group and came right to my door again to re-enter the Ashram. Stopping right in front of me and looking me straight in the eyes she asked, "Christopher, are you happy?" A bit more self-gathered than before, I answered, "Yes, Mother, I'm happy."

Like a Ball of Fire

She then went on into the Ashram and I thought to myself that the day's activities would be drawing to a close. Maybe 15 minutes later Mother once again approached my door, but this time she was wearing a shawl to keep warm, since the sun was beginning to lower in the sky. She stopped, stood squarely in front of me with a big grin on her face and asked for the third time, "Christopher, are you happy?"

With a little bewilderment but with a smile I answered, "Yes, Mother, I'm happy." Without hesitation she clenched her fist, raised her hand and hit me with a solid punch in the shoulder directly above the bicep. Inwardly I saw a ball of fire from her hand fly directly to my heart, where it exploded like watching the sun explode, filling me to overflowing. She grinned and her eyes danced as we looked at each other. She then proceeded on to her other guests. Needless to say, I was enveloped in such Bliss!

The Golden Cord

I remember little else from that day as my focus remained fixed upon the conflagration within, and the attendant enveloping love God shared with me at that moment through the blessing of Mother. This was the moment she affixed the guru-chela tie with me and I knew it. It is a golden cord between us.

I hope that as you read this you will remember your own special moments of your spiritual journey. They are as real as breathing, and they can define you or be left behind you. As for me, every kind word, every tough rebuke, every agonizing discipline given, every single moment in Mother's tutelage—I am grateful for them all and I cherish them all. There is not a single moment of any day that Mother is not a marvelous influence in my life.

37

NO GUTS, NO GLORY
The Master Was Speaking through Her
by Andrew Kramer

There are three classes of disciples. The third-class disciple
merely does the Guru's bidding. The second-class disciple does
not have to be told. He acts as soon as the thought arises in the
Guru's mind. But the first-class disciple acts even before the
Guru has had time to think.

—Swami Turiyananda

When I first joined staff in 1978, Mother assigned me
to be part of her personal staff at the Ashram. It was located
on a four-acre parcel in West Los Angeles on Country Club
Drive. Mother and her family lived there as well. When we
acquired Camelot, a 218-acre parcel in Calabasas, I moved
out there as a construction foreman.

I had a very special "elemental"[1]—a dog called Electra
—and I wanted to take her with me. But there was a rule of no
pets on campus. So I had to leave her behind with a friend.
After she was passed around for a while, it appeared that there
was no place for her and it burdened me. I was out of options.

---

[1] **Elementals:** Nature spirits who offer their selfless service to construct and maintain the physical plane so that we can evolve here. They do not have a Threefold Flame nor do they have the opportunity for personal immortality. There are
four trypes of elementals corresponding to the four elements: salamanders (fire),
sylphs (air), undines (water) and gnomes (earth). Some animals are ensouled by
an elemental.

The very day something had to be done, I was doing something at Mother's house. And she came up to me and asked what was bothering me. So I explained about Electra.

To my surprise, she told me that I could bring her. She became a mascot for the Graphics Department down at the converted stables and Florence Miller, who was in charge, "adopted" her. Electra was black and brown and used to jog with the guys in Graphics. This little story exemplifies Mother's heart tie to her chelas and how she so personally felt even our simple burdens.

Through the Fire I Became Totally in Sync with Her

It was a hot summer day in 1980 at Camelot. I learned that Mother was going to do a book signing after the meal following the Sunday service and I felt prompted to assist her. So I went ahead to try to anticipate her needs.

I looked for an umbrella to help shield her. But Nancy J. told me that wouldn't work because of the flow of people and the setup.

So I rigged up something out of pieces of pipe and tarps I found in the cafeteria. I ended up creating a makeshift sun block tent as a lean-to.

I was just putting the finishing touches on it when Mother came up and asked what I was doing. So I told her I knew the sun would be too much for her and rigged this up to protect her. She said, "I can't tell you how much I appreciate what you did for me!"

I said, "Ma, there is nothing I can ever do to pay you back for all you have done for me!" She then asked someone to bring a table and a couple of chairs. She told me that she wanted me to sit next to her while she signed her newest book on the teachings of Jesus and Kuthumi, *Prayer and Meditation*.

What I was supposed to do when each person came up, was to open their book to the front page, slide it over and tell her the person's name.

Suddenly Mother was really giving me the fire and said, "What are you, some kind of lumberjack? You're not wearing gloves. You're wasting my time!"

But alchemy took place, and I was almost getting telepathic, picking up subtle clues, and I became totally in sync with her.

Finally, we got to the end and it was getting dark. Now, the last person in line was Annette Z. Mother then asked, "Is that it?" So I said, "That's it, from A to Z!" She went into an intense belly laugh!

She looked at me and said, "Andrew, I want you to know that this is not the first time you've built things like this for me. More than once you've done this for me before."

I said, "It's been such a joy!" She responded, "God bless you. I can't tell you how much I appreciate your diligent service!"

Morya's Fire!

We built the S.U. classroom at Camelot. One day, shortly after it was opened, I walked into the front hall of the building when L.L. came up to me holding some kind of focus. She was in charge of S.U. and was the head teaching assistant. She said, "Mother wants someone to bring this into the S.U. classroom."

Now, I knew S.U. was in session and Mother was teaching and felt hesitant about going in there. So I asked her, "Why can't you do this?" She simply said, "No, I can't." I asked her again, "Are you sure?" She simply repeated her statement. But something just didn't feel right to me. I finally said that I would do it if it would help Mother.

I walked down the hall and went through the double doors into the front of the classroom. Mother was seated in her blue wing chair, her Guru chair, on the platform. Unbeknownst to me, she was in the middle of a teaching session by the Ascended Master El Morya to her students.

I was standing off to one side and blurted out, "I'm supposed to bring this to you." Not only had I interrupted her discourse, but I also broke her thread of contact with the Master who was overshadowing her.

She responded sternly, "How dare you disrupt this forcefield. You come over here right now!" and pointed to the front of the platform. So I immediately obeyed and stood in front of her while everyone in the class looked on in hushed silence. She then said, "Just who do you think you are?" I told her, "L.L. sent me in here."

She responded, "Are you talking back to the Guru?" Her look was so stern. Her words were chastising. She continued to read me the riot act with intense fire! "You have chosen to come here and disrupt the forcefield in the midst of the Master's presence. Is your chelaship rusty? You're not worthy to consider yourself a chela." I could really feel the fire descend! "Get out of my sight! I can't stand to look at you!"

I believe this rebuke came from the heart of Morya, since Mother was giving a teaching on him at the time. He was speaking through her with great intensity.

Overcoming My Fear

The very next day when I was in the construction office down by the pool, I overheard someone say that Mother was in the sacristy looking for a folding lawn chair. It was such a beautiful day and she wanted to sit outside.

Now I was familiar with the furniture that the Church had, which was stored in a trailer on the property. And I remembered there was a lawn chair made of PVC with yellow stripes that would work for her. And I even knew exactly where it was.

But I still felt stung from the day before and in one sense, I didn't feel like I wanted to be within 100 feet of her! But I felt a responsibility to bring her that chair. In fact, I felt a burning in my heart that she had a need and I could help.

So I overcame my fear, got the chair, rang the bell and knocked on her sacristy door. She called, "Who is it?"

"Andrew! I'm here because I heard you wanted a chaise lounge and I have it outside on the grass."

A couple of seconds later, the door flung open, she had a big smile and asked, "Where is it? I want to go out and read."

"Where would you like me to put this, Mother?" She pointed to a shady place and said she couldn't be in direct sun, because of her sensitive skin. So, after she sat down, she continued, "Well, come and sit here with me for a minute." So I sat down on the grass next to her chair.

"I want to talk to you about this thing that happened yesterday in the S.U. classroom."

"Yeah, I remember. I got a little down. I really feel bad about it."

"You don't work for L.L. You work for me directly. These people become tools and the force works through them to disrupt me, the Masters and the Teachings." She continued, "Andrew, I know you're devoted to me. And your bringing this chair proves how dedicated you are to me and my office as Guru. And I know you make calls for me all the time for my protection. But what you don't seem to understand is that you have an office too. And that office is Chela. You need to make calls daily to protect your office. And I want to tell you as a side note, Andrew, you need to share this teaching." (Many times, throughout my subsequent years of service, I had the opportunity to share this teaching at the right time.)

"Andrew, I want to take a few moments to explain what was happening yesterday when you were chastised in front of all those students. When the Master comes forth and is present, it is because of my office as Messenger. If he wants to speak, I'm the vessel for him to speak through. What happened yesterday, when you came in the room, was that I was giving a teaching on Morya. And because you came in . . ."

I responded, "I became a tool myself because of my lack of attunement and because I wasn't centered and I wasn't thinking."

She went on, "The Master realized he had to give me a teaching for you that moment—and it couldn't wait. Here is what took place when you were standing in that room.

"Your consciousness is like a latticework—diamond shaped. What happens through your embodiments is that substance gets into the latticework and clogs it up. What I am referring to by this is misqualification of energy. All misqualified substance gets encrusted and gets clogged up. So the clear stream of your Christ and higher consciousness cannot flow through it unimpeded.

"So here's what happened. The initiation of you in that room was the fire coming through me from the Master. The purpose of that fire was to burn through the substance and encrustations in that latticework so that light and fire can flood through. At the point when the fire comes through, a chela is at a crossroads. It's a basic choice whether to humbly accept the fire and let it pass through you, taking the substance with it.

"Some chelas, through pride, choose not to bend the knee and accept the fire. So what happens is that the fire can't pass through them and they hold it in, and it consumes them and causes them to spin off the Path because they can't contain it. There is nowhere for the fire to go. If you let the fire pass through you, the key is that it does its job. I can tell that your willingness to come here today is proof that you accepted the initiation. And I want to tell you that you passed a big test on your path!" Once again she asked me to please share this teaching where appropriate.

Teaching on How to Deal with the Dweller (the Not-self)

I was still a department head in the Construction Department and was having a problem with one of the staff. It was very big problem and I didn't know how to deal with it, even though I got my "Archangel Michael" sword[2] out and made calls on it. So I called up Mother and asked her, "What do you think I should do about this problem?" Mother responded, "You're the department head! Use your Christ discernment and deal with it."

I responded, "I don't know what to do. If I go to this person, he'll get all emotional and go ballistic!" She responded, "And therefore, what?"

"I don't know if I can handle this. It will be emotionally intense."

She then asked me a profound question, "Do you love the person? Do you love the soul? Are you willing to help the soul?" I answered, "Yes!"

She continued, "When you confront the dweller on the threshold of the person, the dweller is going to react. And here is the key and what comes down for you, Andrew. You have to love the soul enough to be willing to take the emotional onslaught of the dweller when you confront the out-of-alignment chela."

She went on to say, "What tends to happen after that encounter is you counsel the soul, once the initial barrage of energy takes place. Tell him you are doing it for his soul's own good and that you're not doing it to give him a hard time or because of arrogance. You are just doing it because you care enough for the person—you were fully aware that he was going to react and in spite of this you did what you did to help the person.

"In most cases, the person will feel the fire of your love and the end result will be that the person will thank

---

[2] **Archangel Michael sword.** The sword is of a medieval (falchion) design with a wooden-and-brass handle, 13-inch stainless steel blade, and leatherette scabbard. The blade is hand-engraved with "Archangel Michael." It is not sharpened and should not be sharpened. It is a ceremonial sword for altar use only. Once you consecrate it, Archangel Michael will place the focus of his sword over yours. You can then use it daily to cut yourself and your loved ones free from the energies and substance of the lower octaves.

you for caring enough to wrestle with their dweller, and therefore you will be a true leader to guide them."

Mother explained further, "We all know the soul is not evil. It's the dweller that we are dealing with. If the person is out of alignment, the dweller is acting. The true teacher takes the soul and person aside and gives the teaching of the Real Self and the not-self."

The decree "I Cast Out the Dweller-on-the-Threshold!," dictated by Jesus Christ, came out in 1983 and is the antidote to the out-of-alignment state.

I took her teachings to heart and went to talk to the person, and what took place was exactly as she had said. As a result, I became very close to this person and we developed a heart tie and a sense of camaraderie. I was extremely grateful for Mother's insight and teachings.

Personal Initiations: The Dark Night of the Soul

Several years later I was working on heavy equipment at the Inner Retreat. It was a time when I was having very intense projections. I knew these projections going through my consciousness were not mine. As Paul said, "The things that I should do, I do not; and the things I should not do, I do."

I called Mother and told her that I felt like I was being pushed up against the wall and I didn't understand it. Mother said, "I'll get back with you." In about three or four days she said, "I want to meet with you and your wife." My wife was there for the whole meeting because Mother wanted her to know what I was going through so she would be able to support me.

Mother proceeded to tell me that she did some inner work and what she tuned into was a previous lifetime. She told us that when she did the spiritual work all of my records came up. She told how during this one particular embodiment, had I been in the right state of consciousness, I could have prevented something that could have changed the whole course of history. She explained that instead of being at the right place at the right time and doing the right thing, I was outpicturing my dweller, and the dweller was in control of my life. She went on to say that by letting the dweller take charge instead of my Christ Self, I was therefore not able to prevent this particular situation from happening.

She told me she loved me and supported me, but that the Master said I had to undertake this initiation alone and she couldn't help me. Not only that, but she could have no contact with me and the next time she spoke with me, I would know I had passed through this initiation.

"Here is what you have to do, Andrew!" She said, "Visualize it as a plant with a root that is so deep, deep, deep in your consciousness and you have to use all the spiritual tools available to you to pull out that root! The root is representative of the entanglements of your dweller in your consciousness. If you're successful, you can win the battle over your dweller. You can overcome the dweller, and what will be there is a void filled with light that will give you the healing of the pain in your soul." At this point I was crying and Mother was crying. It hurt us both that she could not have any contact with me. But this was the Master's instruction—Morya's.

I thought to myself, I'm going to walk out of this room screwed up royally, and I have to do this by myself. It was so overwhelming to me. At the end of the meeting, Mother repeated that she couldn't have any further contact with me, as a result of my past sin of omission.

Leaving there was the toughest part. I wished her good night and left the room. It was a strange situation. My daughter was a couple of years old and I wanted to play with her. I was supposed to function normally, but it was all I could do not to panic.

This was a very intense cycle for me during the late fall of '88. I was consumed with the intense spiritual work and a very heavy work schedule at the same time.

Eight months later, I was up in the Heart and I heard someone calling me. I turned around and there was Mother. She was actually speaking to me! She said she had several questions and wanted me to answer them for her. I looked at her in a state of disbelief. "You just spoke to me!"

"That's right! The Master said, 'Job well done!' And that was El Morya!"

This experience shows that it's a "do-it-yourself path," based on a one-on-one relationship with the Guru. When push comes to shove, the chela has to undertake the Path himself. It's a do-it-yourself program and we sit under our own vine and fig tree.

Milarepa, Nicholas Roerich

A wedding conducted by Mother.

38
DOUBLE TROUBLE
The True Meaning of Sacrifice
by Carl Showalter

So what do you need to do if upon receiving the chastening fire you feel hurt or unfairly treated? First, if you can, remember the exact words spoken by the guru in delivering the rebuke. Think of them as a mantra or a koan to be solved. A koan is a riddle that can be solved only by intuition or by a flash of inspiration. That flash of inspiration doesn't just come from koans. It comes from the moment when you merge with your guru or let's say an Ascended Master or an angel. And out of that moment of oneness, even if it is very brief, there comes this flash of inspiration. And you understand suddenly the chastening. You understand why that happened to you and you don't get angry with God because God did something to you that you don't like.
— Elizabeth Clare Prophet, February 20, 1997

Of all the occupations upon the planet one of the hardest, I suppose, is to be a chela of the Ascended Masters. This is because we don't quite understand what it is to sacrifice ourselves. In fact, probably that is our worst problem, our greatest fear—to give ourselves up. I know many chelas who just can't quite get it into their system that something higher than themselves is at work. So many times I'll say to someone, "Did you check that out with your Master?" "Well, no, I hadn't really thought about that."

I remember when I was in that same position. During a spring conference in Los Angeles, Mother told me that Jesus had appeared to her in a vision. He asked that my staff and I be called to Los Angeles where we would be assigned to create many small groups.

So we resigned as ministers of a church and travelled to L.A. We were leaders of the Teaching Center and we worked with the people in Los Angeles establishing 18 study groups. Not really realizing the closeness of the Master, one day I made the comment to my wife, Nancy, "You know, I don't mind being here at the Teaching Center, but I don't think I ever want to get into the red-hot center of this organization working directly under Mother. I think that would be too hot. I think I would rather just be here."

Well, Morya heard that, I'm sure, because within a week we had our new assignment. We went on the staff of The Summit Lighthouse. Soon after, Nancy and I were walking outside one day and out of a building came Mother. She looked at us and said, "I would like to see you two in my office." We went along with her and sat down. Then Mother asked, "Have you ever read this book?" She pointed out a book about Milarepa[1] in her library and said, "You need to read this book because you have some of this kind of work ahead of you." Not knowing what that meant, I was soon to find out.

The Ultimate Price for the Ultimate Gift

This great saint of the Far East was born in 1052 A.D. His father was a trader in wool and very well off, probably the most abundantly blessed of anyone in the area — the

---

[1] **Milarepa** is one of the most widely known Tibetan saints. In a superhuman effort he rose above the miseries of his younger life. With the assistance of his guru, Marpa, he endured extreme hard tests and initiations to balance his karma and achieve enlightenment.

biggest house, the best clothes and the best food. But a problem arose when his father was on his deathbed and he told his brother and sister, "I want you to hold our property until Milarepa comes of age," which was 15. So when the father died his brother and sister took charge. However, instead of holding the property for Milarepa, they stole it and divided it between themselves. In fact, they put Milarepa, his mother and young sister in a small room and gave them only the bare necessities. So when Milarepa turned 15, his mother called the family together and reminded them of her husband's dying wish: "My husband said when Milarepa turns 15 the property reverts back to us, and we want it back!" As a result the mother with Milarepa was turned out of the house and they became beggars on the street.

One day Milarepa, who had a beautiful voice, was singing. He would sing to his friends, conveying tremendous feeling. His mother, being filled with resentment and hurt, cajoled him, "If you don't go out and learn magic so we can get revenge for what's happened I'm going to kill myself right in front of you!" So she sent her son to a sorcerer -lama who practiced the black arts and he learned how to take vengeance.

During a large wedding, all his family who had robbed him were in the big house. Milarepa caused the house to crumble and kill all of them—all but two, his father's brother and sister. When some of the neighbors heard that, they decided they should kill Milarepa because of his black arts. When the mother got wind of this she had Milarepa learn more black magic to destroy the neighbors' crops. However, by now Milarepa was profoundly repenting all his evil deeds. He worried deeply over the heavy karma he had incurred.

So Milarepa sought out a learned lama named Marpa. Marpa told Milarepa that if he really wanted the Truth, he would have to pay a high price in order to balance the karma he had created. So Marpa gave Milarepa the assignment to build a wall–and later a building– which he had to tear down and rebuild a number of times before he was finished. When Milarepa showed Marpa his bleeding and bruised body, Marpa told him not to boast.

Now this is a lesson each of us ought to take seriously. We think we're doing so well, working so hard and yet we haven't paid back the ultimate price.

And so I found myself in the same kind of situation. Nancy and I read the book well. And I think that's the only thing that saved the day for me. Many times I just wanted to get in my car and drive as far away as I could get because I felt I was being treated too harshly. But Milarepa's story always came back to me.

I remember one time I came back from a tour and found someone had complained to Mother that I hadn't treated them quite right. For this Mother pulled me aside and gave me a tongue-lashing. And when I tried to explain, Mother said, "Don't you dare argue with me." This is the kind of situation that Milarepa went through over and over again where you begin to actually work out your own protectionisms. As I look back on these incidents now I can chuckle. So what if the guy thought I wasn't treating him right. I love him. I bless him. Why do I have to come up with excuses, why do I have to protect myself?

I was working under a Guru, not so much Mother as Morya working through Mother. When I looked at how things came about, it was obvious it was Morya. So I began to contemplate: How do I work with the Guru? How do I become one with the Christ?

Jesus said, "It isn't I who do these things, it's the Father who doeth these things through me." We cannot become one with the Christ until we get rid of the human ego part of us. The question is, who operates in your life? Is it you or the Christ or an entity? As long as I see God out there, I am in duality. The moment I become aware that I AM the Christ and I am operating out of that consciousness, it is no longer I who live (as Paul said), it's the Father who lives through me.

This is the whole business of the guru-chela relationship, where the chela becomes the Guru. When the chela speaks, it's the Guru speaking. My thoughts are the Master's thoughts, my feelings are the Master's feelings. We need not bow down and worship the Guru, we need to take on the Master's consciousness. This way we become more of the manifestation of the Master.

So we have to look at Mother as the Guru. And we have the dictation that made her a Guru. Mother resisted being called "Guru" for a long time. Finally the Master said they had waited long enough. Padma Sambhava gave her the mantle of Guru.[2] From that time Mother was called "Guru Ma."

I went through a number of Milarepa-like experiences. Maybe not as bad, since I didn't have to carry any heavy rocks. I am so grateful I had the opportunity to be under the Guru Elizabeth Clare Prophet. I am what I am because of her.

---

[2] **Mantle of Guru**, "Guru Ma": Dictation by Padma Sambhava 7-2-77, Pearls of Wisdom ,Vol. 27, No. 33a.

39

BE THOU MADE WHOLE
Mother's Miraculous Healing Touch
by Lucille Yaney

Blessed hearts, it is an hour for healing. And I, Saint Germain, wish to tell you that I have come today, yes, with the Lord Maha Chohan. For we shall not wait till Pentecost and we shall not wait till the July conference to activate once again the mantle of healing that our Messenger has worn for many thousands of years. Blessed ones, you should fear not to seek and find healing from God and to be willing if necessary to balance the karma that you are required to balance before that healing is complete.

Blessed hearts, in this hour it is truly upon you to recognize the full power of God's healing that is available. In past ages some of you have been with Jesus, some with Gautama, some with Padma Sambhava and other adepts.

–Saint Germain, *Pearls of Wisdom*, Vol. 37, No. 20

I was studying Buddhism. My future husband, Ralph, and I were dating. I had been studying for about three years and had gone to San Francisco for retreats. I needed a teacher for the next step in my search for Truth. At that time, we were experimenting with energy, sometimes feeling energy on our bodies through people's auras—some spots would feel cold and others would be warm. We were also very sensitive to our environment and could feel vibrations in a room.

For instance, I would put my hands over books. With some books of various teachings, I could feel heat and others were cold, meaning they drain energy. This is how we decided we would be able to know the true teachings of God. If we perceived heat from certain teachings, we equated it to the fire of God being in those teachings and that they were authentic.

When I decided to search for a teacher, I put my name on a number of mailing lists of spiritual organizations and the responses came in. Before I opened any of them, I would put my hands over the material and if I felt that it would drain me, being cold, I would reject it and throw it away.

The Most Energy Ever

One day we received a brochure about a conference from an activity that I had not heard of before, called The Summit Lighthouse. On the cover was a picture, "Angels of White Fire" by Gustave Doré. Ralph recognized the picture. So we ran our hands over it, and it was the most energy we had ever felt. We attended the conference and heard our first dictation from an ascended being, and we both had the sense that we were coming home and burst out crying, it affected us so deeply.

But the miracle happened when we went to the Mailing Department to thank the person who had put us on their list, since I knew I had not signed up myself. But they assured me this announcement had only gone to those who had either attended a previous conference or had inquired about the Teachings. They said they did not buy names for their mailings. No one knew how our name got added. I wondered what miracle caused me to receive this material that changed the course of our lives.

We felt we were looking at the "Y" in the road. On the one hand we were involved in a pretty upscale ragtag lifestyle, and on the other we just knew this was our Teaching. So we signed up as Keepers of the Flame.

Ma came to L.A. another time and we both attended the event. Afterward we invited her and some conferees to come up to our place at Big Sur in northern California, which we called Maitreya Mountain. On the other side of our property was a monastery with Zen monks. She accepted and I was so grateful. So I took a bus from Santa Barbara up there to meet her.

She came up with a few of her staff and then blessed the land. But she told us that the energies were not right. (We were growing marijuana.) And she told staff that accompanied her that it was not for them to be critical of us.

Fog Lifts in Response to Her Call

When Mother was blessing Maitreya Mountain, it was all covered in fog. I watched as she made the call to be able to see the retreat. At that moment I saw that the fog lifted for 10 minutes—just long enough for her to see it— and then it rolled back in.

She went around our house and did a clearance to remove negative energy. I remember when she walked in, her mouth dropped open. We had a three-story octagonal tower, with decks at different levels. One of the decks even had a little altar on it. And she said, "You tuned into the architecture of my etheric retreat!" She then described it. She said there was even an octagonal tower there. When she was leaving, we thanked her for all that she had done for us.

Sometime later there was a horrible fire at Maitreya Mountain threatening our retreat. Eighty percent of the land burned. We called Mother and she immediately had decrees going at the Ranch by her staff. The fire burned right up to the front gate, which was charred. It then continued to spread on the outside of our walls, but never came on our property. After the fire had run its course, the only things that were left untouched on Maitreya Mountain were our place and the Tasahara Monastery.

The Higher Way

The Masters had told their students to work on healing their psychology. We are both therapists—in fact, Ralph is a psychoanalyst. At a conference, Mother did an exposé on Sigmund Freud. Now Freud himself was very open to a lot of attacks, in part because he was the first person who tried to unlock the unconscious. Because of my training, I took offense at this exposé and walked out. We then made the decision that maybe this was not the place for us. Just as we decided to leave, Mother invited us to teach at Summit University in Santa Barbara. Instead of quitting, we accepted and went over to the Motherhouse where Summit University was in session and started teaching.

We did the lecture and then had dinner with her. We had come out of a hippie commune and had one foot in Beverly Hills and the other in a hippie consciousness. In our presentations we had some sexual connotations. Mother did not scold us for doing this in a public setting at a spiritual gathering. Instead she gave us teachings on the effect it had on others. She said we had no disturbance in our auras, but that we created a disturbance in others, and that we needed to be sensitive about the effect we have on other people. She talked about the example we were setting. So we gave up a lot of things and our consciousness took a 180-degree shift over the next two years.

In the beginning I was critical. I didn't like the idea of control, hierarchy and other concepts I had taken a stand against previously. I told Mother about this. She said, "Oh, don't worry about that. In time you will be in a place where if you see something you don't like, your head just goes to a much holier place and you see a different perspective."

Abortion—A Perspective from the Soul

We took one thing at a time. I was still skeptical. Ralph wasn't. I had such respect for him that I overlooked things and stayed the course. I was one thing when we were with Ma and then another on my own. Much later, we came to accept her wisdom, except for one issue: abortion. I had a mindset that a person should have an abortion instead of having an unwanted child. But Mother turned us around completely with one sentence:

"You're not seeing it from the perspective of the child and their attempt to get into embodiment. Instead you're seeing it from the parents' perspective."

Her explanation began to make so much sense to me when she approached it from the level of the soul.

As a result of our increased awareness of the plight of the unborn and their struggle to be born, we wrote *10,001: A Handbook for Survival . . . of Man—You Know Not What Goes On behind Closed Doors.* I was pregnant at the time and Mother didn't want my name on the book. Mainly, it's my organization and Ralph's writing. It was published in 1979 but is currently out of print.

The Very Next Day I Got Pregnant

Some things just couldn't be explained. Like the time I decided to go ahead and have a child to balance karma. We were now aware of the karma that was on us for the number of souls that we were responsible for being aborted, directly or indirectly. Because we were very pro-abortion, we had counseled for it. At that time the law required that a woman who wanted an abortion had to have a psychiatric review before she could abort. Ralph would say things like "This is going to be too destructive to the mother," so they would allow the abortion. That didn't last very long, but it was right around the time of *Roe vs. Wade*.

We ourselves had abortions—both of us had. Then our heads got quite turned around. In that process we both agreed to bring those two souls in that we had aborted. I realized we had petitioned to bring in another soul, and Mother blessed us. I had gone through a whole cleansing and getting my body ready. This time we determined that we would do it right.

Up to that point, I had gotten pregnant the first time we tried to conceive. Now, months went by and I had still not conceived. It seemed like something was amiss. I said, "OK, God is trying to tell me something." I went to the altar and prayed that if there is a reason for our being unprepared, we would attend S.U. I got the message that I needed to go to S.U. and then He would give me a child. It was at that point that I vowed I would go and make that commitment, which I did.

I wrote my Karmic Board letter and said that if I get pregnant, I will go to Summit University. The day after I made the commitment I got pregnant. That was incredible! And I decided to go in my last trimester because those are the months that are not very productive anyway.

Ralph went to Archangel Michael's quarter. I went to Archangel Jophiel's quarter. We tried to continue with our patients while we went to Summit University, which I would never recommend. We graduated on a Sunday and Monday was my slosh day. The next day I had patients lined up for 14 hours.

On the Tuesday after graduation, Ralph and I were at the Ashram in West Los Angeles having lunch with Mother. We walked into the living room and I sat on one of her beautiful blue couches. And then my water broke! So, there I was. Mother blessed the baby and we jumped in the car and proceeded to go back to our little apartment in Pasadena. Along the way we ran out of gas. Ralph jumped the fence and ran to a gas station. The man took pity on him and brought the gas back and we made it to Pasadena. The home delivery was lovely, except there were some major complications because I was older. Mine was the last home delivery Mother ever authorized.

I felt that this was part of the balancing of my karma. Ralph said the only way he knew that I was in pain was that I was clenching my fists. With natural childbirth I had worked on dealing with intense pain. With God's help everything turned out OK. No doubt it was by the grace of God and Mother's intense calls at the altar.

The birth was successful and Max was born. That day there were *five planets in retrograde*. That's the end of the miracle. Ma had counseled us beforehand. She explained that because of the way I had handled my daughter, I had earned the right to have a very difficult child. So we knew this child was going to be a great challenge for us.

Jesus Restores Max through His Messenger

An incredible thing happened that I will *never* forget. When Max was 1½ years old we moved out to the beach in Malibu and took a house with a Keeper. One day without warning, Max fell over a ledge to the sand—30 feet below! We were frantic when we saw him lying there limp. We were pushing on him and calling to him, to no avail. He was comatose. So we called a doctor friend who was a neurosurgeon. He said there was nothing to do but wait it out at the hospital. He didn't even call the paramedics.

Then Ralph called Mother. Mother immediately got on the phone and said to put the phone up to Max's ear. At that point even his pupils were not dilating when we put a light in them. I was very concerned because I knew that when the pupils don't dilate this is the fifth stage of a coma. This means the damage was all the way down into the very interior of his brain. So it was the very deepest coma that somebody could be in.

So we put the telephone up to his ear and Max immediately came out of the coma. It was *instantaneous!* But when we took the phone away from his ear, he went back into the deep coma, and he couldn't respond. Then Mother went in to make calls at her altar. Jesus told Mother to get into the car right away and go down to Max. One half hour later she arrived.

She rushed over to Max where he was lying. She was given precise instructions by Jesus to put her right hand on his toe and her left hand on top of his head. So she touched those two points and then spoke to him, and Max came back into his body. He began calling for mommy and started struggling to come back into my arms. It was necessary for Mother to be there physically in person for this to happen. She held him for a while until she was sure that he would be all right. He was really struggling and fighting. And then it was OK.

We drove to the hospital. Ralph and I were in the back and Mother was in the front seat holding Max. She did this all the way to the hospital. By the time we got there, he was running all over the place, jumping up and down, even *laughing* and throwing things out of the crib. We were in the emergency room. They had gotten in touch with the neurologist at Cedar Sinai, so he was on the way into the hospital. Cedar Sinai is the top hospital in Los Angeles.

They were sure this was a battered child. We were questioned. Even our housekeeper was taken and questioned individually. Max had backed into a wall heater prior to this incident and had three big burns on the back of his bottom. That didn't help matters. As sane as we sounded, they kept bringing in one person after another to interview us.

When they pulled down his diapers, I said to one of the interviewers, "I really didn't abuse this child," because we knew what they were doing. He turned on me and said, "This isn't a laughing matter!" So I said, "I know you have to do your job, but we're not that kind of parents."

We had a friend who is a very good professional on the board of Cedar Sinai, a very well-respected doctor, and we knew he would find the best neurosurgeon. When we spoke to this neurosurgeon, we told him what the truth was. Because we came so well referred, he didn't just look at us as though we were crazy. He believed us because he didn't have any other explanation for it. But the people who were investigating us, the other people in the hospital, didn't. We kept telling them that he had been healed. But these people just assumed that we were lying.

The other doctors couldn't believe that Max had been healed. So the only other explanation they had was that we were lying, even though Ralph himself was a doctor. I remember that was their conclusion based on the facts. What they felt was that we probably had thrown him and he went unconscious and we had to invent this fall, and that he hadn't really been in a fifth-stage coma. What this real-life experience says is that no child could be in a fifth-stage coma and be running around an hour later.

Unbeknownst to us, after asking us who our family doctor was, they called Dr. Burns and he said, "Listen, I'll put my full medical license on the line that this family does not abuse this child." He said that he would give up his medical license if it ever turned out that we battered the child. Only when he did that, did they decide not to turn in a report.

So it was really good that Dr. Burns was there, even though we didn't know what he did until later. We only knew that they just called off the investigation. All the while our neurosurgeon was staying supportive on our side. Both of us stayed with Max at the hospital all night long. And we insisted that we wouldn't leave him alone during his stay. So we took turns staying up with him and had to pay for a private room. All that didn't sound like parents that would batter a child. Max was kept under observation for two days. After that he was OK'd to go home because there were no residuals.

At 1½ years Max didn't want to come back into his body because he knew about karma. But thanks to the intercession of Jesus' healing power through Mother as his Messenger, he pulled through.

We Stayed Vigilant

We knew that we had been given custody of this great soul of light and that he could go either way—on the left-handed path or on the right. Because we knew the whole story about his lifestream, we stayed vigilant to defend Max and to lead him away from the darkness pitted against him.

We knew the soul of this child and we knew that we were entrusted to turn him around. If he had gotten into drugs, we would have lost him. To discourage him I used to bring him into the waiting room when people came into the office with drug problems. He saw the consequences firsthand and it worked. He couldn't understand why we never gave up on him. It was because we had the vision that Ma gave us.

Today he's grown up, he is a principled, ethical person and he has his own company and website.

We Almost Lost the Inn

As owner of the Inn of the Seventh Ray in Topanga Canyon, California, I witnessed such miracles! We never, ever should have made it. We were right on the edge all the time, so close to going into foreclosure. One day I needed $100. If I didn't get it, the Inn would be gone. At that moment the angels sent Jean A., a staff member, into our bookstore with $100 cash she spent on books.

We did 15 years of wedding receptions at the Inn in the area outside where there was no roof. So we learned to work with the elementals. In all those years when it rained, it would stop at 12:00 noon sharp, just in time for the reception to begin. And the rain would start up again at 4:00 pm, like clockwork! That's when the bride got into her car. As soon as we started putting up see-through plastic tents for the reception, it would rain during the reception itself—almost as though it now happened because the bride and groom had a protective cover. We came to the conclusion that our lives were working out. Nothing was worth worrying about. We learned that everything would work out, as long as we made the highest decisions, and as long as we did not compromise the laws of God.

Only once in 27 years was the restaurant closed. So much caring has gone into it over the years. People keep asking if it's the same restaurant. They can't believe we're still going strong.

Storming Granada

My daughter was a paratrooper and went with her troops into Granada. Because she spoke Russian, she was among the first to be parachuted in. She was sent to do interrogation. As they were landing they were being fired at. It was very dangerous. Mother did a full weekend of decrees in support of our troops in Granada. My daughter, Cindy, had some exposure to decrees. Mother had told her, "You have to open up your mouth and make the calls!" And that's exactly what my daughter did. She made calls on the way down from the air transport all the way to her barracks. Others kept warning her to bend down. But she had no fear because she had such a strong feeling of protection.

Mother Responds When We Call to Lanello

Ralph and I were very seldom divided in our viewpoints. But there was one time I got caught between my loyalty to Ralph and one of my children. So I went to the altar and prayed to Lady Master Magda.[1] The Inn was

[1]**Magda:** Jesus dictated through his Messenger, Elizabeth Clare Prophet, that Magda was embodied as Mary Magdalene in the Bible. He also said that she is his twin flame and serves with him in Heaven. The property where the Inn is located is rumored to have been the property of the charismatic preacher Aimée Semple McPherson in the 1930s. She ascended at the close of that embodiment and is now Lady Master Magda.

always her home even though we weren't in the Teachings when we bought it.

One minute later Ma called and asked Ralph, "What's going on with Kurt?" She reminded Ralph about some advice he had once given her about a situation that she had been dealing with. This turned him around. With Mother, it was never "you have to do this and this." She never gave us orders or told us what to do. She just took in the consciousness of the other person and allowed that person to make his or her own decision.

I had one patient whose life was falling apart. This person was in the Teachings but was on the brink of suicide. In desperation, I called out to Lanello. Two minutes later Ma called and said to him, "Lanello wants you to come and join staff." As a result, he packed up everything, came out to Pasadena and worked part-time on staff for years.

That's the way it worked when Ma was in charge. I am grateful I was able to witness to some of these situations.

Ralph and Lucy Yaney sing with Mother and other devotees during a stump in South America in 1977

40

THE ACID TEST
Searching for Truth
by Burt A. Bialozynski

*Friends, neighbors, lightbearers, Keepers of the Flame, all
who gather—let it be known that this land is a haven, a place
for the coming together of souls who would pursue the mystical
quest of the Holy Grail, who would drink of the chalice cup of the
Teaching, the eternal mysteries that the Lord Christ shared with the
beloved disciples 40 days after the resurrection in the Upper Room.*
—Lanello

After being shocked to find out that the faith I had
been raised in was corrupt, I determined in my heart to find
the "real Jesus Christ," my Saviour, and not listen to what
everyone was feeding me. Well, after three years of much
violent, tumultuous grappling with myself and other worldly
forces, I made contact with my Mighty I AM Presence.

I was in extremely dire straits when I first met Mother.
I had pawned everything I owned to attend the 1983 winter
conference at Camelot in Malibu, California.

I was also very scared, not wanting to get involved
with some strange cult. I had not told any of my family
where I was. Fully prepared to be disowned by my parents, I
flew from Florida to Los Angles alone, ready to wash dishes
at a restaurant, if necessary, to survive.

Expecting to Find a Charlatan

Once at Camelot, I entered into the back of the large church packed with people making strange sounds with their voices. I saw Mother up at the altar in fine raiment with huge diamonds, rubies and other precious and expensive gems on every one of her fingers! (I later learned they belonged to the Church.)

I thought to myself, *Boy, what in the heck have you gotten yourself into? You know for a fact that this lady is cashing in. And she has this group of willing mesmerized subjects who undoubtedly throw money and other worldly goods at her feet — and in California no less, known hangout for cults and cult leaders!*

After the service I was bound and determined to see this so-called Messenger face to face. I worked my way through the crowds and waited for her at the back entrance by the altar. After changing into everyday garb, she emerged alone with a pleasant smile on her face.

It was almost as if she sensed my reason for being there. She calmly lifted up her eyes, looked dead center directly into my eyes, and simply yet graciously said, "Nice to see you again." Now, I had never met this woman before in my life! And the Catholic tradition I came from is very anti-reincarnation.

At that very moment, Mother, august being that she is and has become — because of her devotion to the living God I AM THAT I AM — in that very "cosmic interval," if you will, Mother unscrambled my thoughts, dispelled my fears and spoke the Truth to my very heart of hearts!

Unspeakable Joy

I haven't had much contact with Mother on a personal basis since then, except one time during the Summit University class of 1986 that I was attending. In the years since, I haven't been physically present in the same room as the Messenger, but it doesn't matter. For even now, these many years later, I feel once again that unspeakable joy rush through my being like the air of a fresh spring morning, when I attune my thoughts to her office and her mission. And I think of the very personal and very real sacrifices she has gladly accepted. These she has had to endure to make and keep reliable and trustworthy the communication between the human and Ascended Master octaves. For this I am grateful.

Mother with Judy Sue Christenson and conferees

Jesus Christ, Our Lord and Saviour

Saint Germain, Our Knight Commander

41

MOTHER KNOWS BEST
Morya's Love for My Soul
by Rosemary Galgano

The one who commiserates with the offender [the one who has been chastised] offers sympathy rather than compassion, which does not help anyone. Sympathy is like finding a person going down in the quicksand and you jump in to try to pull him out. You both go down. If you were to be compassionate, you would throw the person a rope or branch and pull him out of the quicksand instead of jumping in with him.
—Elizabeth Clare Prophet, February 20, 1997

Mother came to Philadelphia in 1979 to give her stump message on the twelfth planet. The night before her delivery I sensed I needed healing and I wanted an encounter with my Guru. So I made a call to El Morya for an alignment of my soul.

Next day the lecture was held in a large auditorium at the local university, and the hall was filled to near capacity. I was working as an usher and was told to hand out more decree sheets, but I had not heard Ma request that this take place. I didn't want to do it, yet I wanted to be obedient to the head usher. I was standing in front of the stage when I heard a stern voice say, "Will you please sit down!"

As I looked up, Ma was looking directly at me. Seeing I was the only one standing, I decided to go back to my seat, which was in the back of the hall. Along the way a number of people held out their hands, so I continued passing out decrees. In retrospect, I realized I should have sat in the first available seat.

Afterward, to my amazement, a number of Keepers came over to me in sympathy. From their perspective, the Messenger had yelled at me and they came to console me. They saw it from the reaction of their egos. Yet I knew that my call to Master Morya was being answered. It was my personal initiation with Ma. Now I began to understand the heart tie and the love of Maitreya and El Morya for my soul. During this entire time I was enveloped by the love of the Divine Mother. My soul was being aligned and I was in bliss.

No one could have known the great blessing that had been given to me. Later on I met Mother at the Teaching Center. She looked at me and gave me a big hug! I recognized that it was because she knew that I had internalized the discipline and allowed the light to flow through me, rather than resist it.

The Deck Was Stacked

Mother said this was the hardest lecture she ever had to give because of the fierce opposition. Her acknowledgment of the existence of the twelfth planet had met with hostility from Nephilim and fallen angels.

The energies were so heavy before the lecture that Mother did not do the scheduled radio broadcast but sent a staff member instead. As the interview ended, the moderator fielded questions from the listening audience on a call-in line.

As soon as the moderator announced he was taking questions for the speaker, I called in. But I still had to wait two hours before I could get my question across. By his attitude I quickly found that he wouldn't take any question, unless the caller was against Elizabeth Clare Prophet. I understood why the questions seemed so one-sided. So I said I was a Christian lady and didn't believe anything this person was saying—even though I knew these to be the true teachings of Jesus. I said this so I could get my question through and remembered the quote: Be ye therefore wise as serpents and harmless as doves. (Matt. 10:16)

Despite All Odds, Saint Germain Had His Victory!

I was the last caller taken that night. As soon as I was on the air I stated my question: "I know that Jesus healed by the power of the Word. What can you tell me to prove that what you are saying is true about the Teachings of the Ascended Masters?"

This gave Mother's stand-in the perfect opportunity to lead into the teachings of the violet flame. He jumped at the opportunity and began by saying that what you have to do is give the mantra, "I AM a being of violet fire, I AM the purity God desires!" He explained that the power of the violet flame could remove darkness and replace it with light in anyone who is willing to try. So the program ended on a positive note. Saint Germain got his message delivered and had his victory!

Saint Germain has told us that he gave us this mantra as our initiation into the Aquarian Age. He asked us to give it as often as possible.

I AM a being of violet fire,
I AM the purity God desires!

I AM Saint Germain, and I say to you: Give this life your all! Give it to me and I promise you that you shall have your ascension at the conclusion of this embodiment. Furthermore, you shall have rings upon rings of the seven rays added to your Causal Body, commensurate with your levels of service. And as angels escort your soul to the retreats of the heaven-world each night, you may visit golden-age civilizations that are in progress in the higher octaves. –March 2, 1996

Anandamayi Ma
by Margaret Reichardt

Mother spoke of an Eastern guru, Anandamayi Ma.
She was fascinated by this holy woman. Anandamayi
was so much in the higher realms, so disconnected
from her physical existence, she had to be taken care
of as if an infant. Mother explained that she saw the
future for herself as being completely helpless and at
the mercy of her chelas whom she loved so much.
Anandamayi Ma lived her life for the sake of her
devotees and the world. Mother would follow in
her footsteps.

42

JUST A STONE'S THROW AWAY
The Pull of Light and Darkness
by Dr. Anna Nordin

Always bear this in mind: Everything is in God's hands, and you are His tool to be used by Him as He pleases. Try to grasp the significance of "all is His" and you will immediately feel free from all burdens. What will be the result of your surrender to Him? None will seem alien, all will be your very own Self.
—Anandamayi Ma, Elizabeth Clare Prophet's heroine

I was first introduced to the Teachings in 1979 when I was an undergraduate student at McGill University in Montreal. I was going through a very difficult time, having given custody of my four-year-old son to his father, from whom I was separated, so I could pursue my dream of being a physician. I missed my son and was very depressed.

Two Keepers held an introduction on the campus. I don't recall much of the content of the lecture. However I did immediately recognize the Teachings and the teacher, embraced them and began attending the study group meetings in Montreal. I regret not having noted which Ascended Master dictated, because I later learned that one may have a special relationship with the Ascended Being who gives the first dictation one hears.

I kept going to the study group, learned how to decree and began to have quite a few mystical experiences. Since finding the Teachings, I have felt a comfort and strength that had previously been missing in my life.

Finding My Dharma

In 1982 I discovered that a brand new college of naturopathic medicine was opening in Canada in September. I didn't walk, I *ran* to apply and was accepted. I had found my dharma!

I aced all my courses at the University of Waterloo while living out in the country on a farm and felt a sense of calm and peace. I decreed in my room in the farmhouse, since there was no study group nearby.

This is about the time when Guru Ma began to appear to me in the etheric while I was sleeping and talked to me while I was awake via a small prompting inside my heart. She would appear to me in beautiful violet garments.

Then I went to Los Angeles for the summer of 1986 to become acquainted with Camelot and to experience life in Hollywood. I did this against the advice of my clinical director, who expected us to continue our internship through the summer in order to graduate.

I arrived at Camelot with just a pillow and blanket that I got from the airplane and a few belongings, but not much money. I wasn't able to sleep for three nights. Finally a couple in Sherman Oaks, with a son named Gabriel, took me in and helped me find a job as a nanny. I was given a car to use with this job, which allowed me to go out to Camelot.

Torn between Hollywood and Camelot

I was very attracted to the Hollywood scene and the glamour of the movie star life. I spent just as much time in Hollywood as I did at Camelot. I realized that I had internalized the energy of rock music and the fantasy of Hollywood as a very young child. I escaped into this world to avoid a very painful and abusive childhood. It really has its hooks in me, even today, and I must call specifically to have this base energy transmuted. In retrospect I can see how this tie has kept me torn and conflicted internally by being simultaneously attracted to both right and wrong.

At Camelot in the summer of 1986, I was present at several of Mother's lectures and dictations in the chapel. I was baptized by her and felt a great presence of the Holy Spirit. But this experience was both elating and confusing. I had gotten to know this guru so personally "on the inner." Why didn't she recognize me and say "Hi" when my turn came in the line to receive from her the rose petals with water? (Later I realized she had been in an exalted state in communion with the Masters.)

I was beginning to learn discernment, because I felt something deeper and more meaningful at Camelot than I did on the streets and in the parties of Hollywood. I was still in my infancy because I had taken on a rock musician as a boyfriend, albeit one who was also struggling with the same light-and-dark issue I was.

In September I returned to Canada to complete my last year of school and found I was under a great discipline for having taken the summer off instead of beginning my internship. My life was made very difficult around the college. If not for the decrees, I question if I would have survived emotionally.

I fought for my medical degree the entire last year of medical school, and then ran back to Southern California. The Church had already moved to Montana. I took up with my rock 'n' roll boyfriend and attended the L.A. Study Group services in Canoga Park. I would drive by Camelot to experience what remaining presence of the light was still there and got permission from the new owners to take a walk on the property.

The Day That Shattered My Idolatry

In 1987 I had a significant experience that shattered my idolatry of Mother. She was giving a presentation at a hotel on Wilshire Boulevard in L.A. There were several hundred people and I was sitting closer to the back. The Chart of the I AM Presence was up on the screen, but I was fixated on and obsessed with the beauty and light coming from Guru Ma and I was looking only at her.

Suddenly, she focused her eyes on me and motioned with her eyes for me to move my attention from her to the Chart of the Presence. In that one brief exchange, she taught me that it is the Teachings that are important, and one should not worship the Messenger who brings them. I later saw her again at the L.A. Study Group and for the first time I perceived she also had normal human traits and characteristics like everyone else.

I lasted one year in the rock 'n' roll and movie star scene in Los Angeles. I never felt quite comfortable in that environment and could never really let myself go. I was seeking something else. My father visited me and we decided to take a drive north of Los Angeles along the Pacific Coast Highway. He suggested a shortcut through Topanga Canyon. This was another life-changing experience for me. I knew I had to move to Topanga. There was that peace that was desperately missing in the L.A. celebrity scene.

I broke with my boyfriend in July 1989 and moved into a 15-foot trailer with no running water or electricity high up in the mountains, only to learn that the Inn of the Seventh Ray, run by Lucille Yaney, an elder of the Church, was just a couple of miles from me. It was here that my most profound healing took place.

I took a weekend job to care for boys who had been taken from their homes because of abuse. They were trying to heal themselves from their traumatic experiences. I was also beginning to recognize my own trauma and began a healing process. I mentioned my healing quest to a hostess at the Inn of the Seventh Ray one evening and she told me that the owner, Lucy Yaney, was a therapist.

I immediately set up an appointment to see her. She held therapy sessions in her home. Upon my first visit I realized we had been neighbors for two years, just a stone's throw across the canyon. I spent every week for five years in that therapy room in the back of her house. Often in Lucy's office I found a copy of "I AM the Witness"[1] turned up on her table and each time I read it, it was speaking to me regarding a particular issue I was going through at the time.

He Recognized Her Immediately

I had been decreeing "Lightbearers of the World Unite, in the name of Saint Germain" for some time when I met a group of lightbearers called the Sserulanda Foundation who had a community in Uganda, East Africa. They were visiting their focus in the city and advertised a lecture they were giving.

I attended and shared my path with the Sserulanda delegate named Jonnamikisa Sseruwamikisa. When I showed Mr. Sseruwamikisa Mother's picture, he nearly collapsed to his knees and said he needed to meet her immediately. I was willing to help him. However, I'd never had any success in meeting her myself, so I took the party of Sserulanda visitors to the Inn of the Seventh Ray, hoping Lucy might be able to help me. Lucy called the Ranch and Mother herself answered and expressed her desire to receive them. So I purchased their airline tickets to Montana. Lucy told me that Mother rarely answered the phone.

They bought an orchid to present to Mother when they reached Montana. She told them it was the most beautiful orchid she had ever seen. They expressed their profound interest in the Teachings of the Ascended Masters,

---

[1] "**I AM the Witness**" is printed as part of various *Pearls of Wisdom*.

and Mother had several boxes of books shipped to their headquarters in Africa. She invited their leader Bambi Baba to visit her at the Ranch when he returned to the United States.

When the Sserulanda visitors returned to Los Angeles, Mother sent back a daikon radish that she had eaten from. I was invited to partake of it, and I did. That night, Guru Ma was teaching in an etheric classroom. When I entered the room and she saw me, she beamed, hugged me, thanked me for making a connection between her and the Sserulanda Foundation possible and invited me to sit in the first row!

Learning Not to Judge

I recall there were three instances of "pummeling" by Mother. Two involved my being upset with fellow chelas whose behavior I judged not in keeping with that of a light-bearer. One person was dragging heavy boxes across the floor at the back of the sanctuary and making a lot of noise while I was trying to focus on the Masters' presence at the altar. Another person had even been "kicked out" from the Ranch by staff because of a particular behavior.

Even though I felt it was a reasonable reaction to be annoyed by these people's conduct, Mother was very stern with me. She told me if I became annoyed at the particular actions of another, I did not understand the deeper meaning of what was going on. She was very displeased with me for making judgments without understanding the whole picture.

In one case, the next day, she sent a presence over me while I was in a busy shopping mall in Santa Monica that caused me to experience being tied to the heart flame of the 100 or so people around me. I felt such a connection with all life around me that small blunders they might make would seem insignificant.

Breaking Down the Barriers

Up to this time I was never able to really meet Mother in person, or talk with her on the phone. There seemed to be an impenetrable wall of "guards" around her that made any contact difficult. When she was visiting Los Angeles in April 1997 to give a conference "The Practical Art of Living a Spiritual Life" at the Airport Hilton, a certain few people at our Study Group decided to host a dinner at Bravo Cuccino in Santa Monica in her honor.

I found out about it, but when I arrived, I was denied entrance because I had not been invited. I stood outside on the sidewalk while my Guru was indoors with this select group. I knew there was a reason I had to experience this pain of separation from my Guru and that someday it would be of benefit.

At one point during this conference Mother was speaking about reincarnation and asked if anyone would like to share anything about their experiences. I jumped up and spoke with little fear or nervousness to the large group of over a thousand people. This was not typical, as I normally wouldn't be able to do such a thing so calmly. As I spoke, I felt Mother, who was sitting on the stage behind me reading my records—scanning my soul on a very deep level, like she was looking at the very origin of my soul. I felt this was the first time she had ever consciously connected with me. After that, I would run into her in restrooms, hallways and elevators.

Quite opposite to my being shunned at the dinner, a man I did not recognize called to tell me that Mother would be at Nicholas Canyon Beach in Malibu at 4:00 pm that day. I went there and spoke my first words to her. I introduced myself and said I was the person who shared my experiences at the recent conference. She said, "I'm glad you did that." I was self-conscious, so I clammed up. In her graciousness she took hold of the conversation and said, "I heard the seaweed is alive up here" (north of the industrial area of Southern California).

I Couldn't Get the Words Out

I knew exactly what to say to confirm that her statement was indeed correct, but I could not get the words out. It was a combination of being awestruck to have her attention and being self-conscious because I was being observed. I left kind of dazed and disoriented.

Soon after, I attended the 1997 July conference "Practical Spirituality" at the Marina Sheraton in San Diego, where I ran into Mother in the hallway and on the elevator. There was a cruise in the San Diego harbor scheduled one night for Guru Ma and chelas. The cruise was sold out. There were no tickets left. However, I was prompted to remain in line anyway. This turned out to be the right thing to do because all who were in line were allowed to board. I was self-conscious because I had not brought a nice dress, but being there was much more important than my appearance.

No sooner had I boarded than I met Guru Ma on the top level of the cruise ship. I told her I had waited to meet her for 17 years and I loved her. She said, "I'm glad you're here." Unlike our meeting earlier that year on the beach, when I left with a sense of unfinished interaction, this time our meeting was complete and nothing further needed to be said.

At the end of the cruise, Mother was standing at the exit of the ship to greet everyone who was leaving. I told her I would like to speak with her sometime and could I call her. She said, "Yes, you can call me." Being accustomed to being blocked from access to her by her staff, I said with amazement, "You mean I can just call and ask to speak with you?" She looked surprised—as if to say "Of course, isn't that the obvious procedure?" Then she replied, "Yes, that's the idea."

Mother's Story about a Guru in India

I was not consciously aware yet of Mother's health problems that led to her retirement, though I had been feeling a sense of urgency for a couple of years that I had to connect with her as soon as possible. She had, however, prepared me for this inevitability. She had told me about a Guru in India who was being fed and clothed by her chelas. I later found out this was Anandamayi Ma, who left embodiment in 1996. It was some time later that I figured out that she showed me this in preparation for the eventuality that she too would be in a state like this.

Another intense moment was when Mother was beginning to get sick and came to Los Angeles in 1998 to visit a doctor. She was staying at my friend's just a short distance away. However, Lucy had strict orders that no one was to visit Mother. I looked across the canyon at the house where she was, felt her presence there and was in so much agony that I could not be with her. The sense of separation from her was virtually more pain than I could bear. I was just crying out all night.

Then a huge storm developed and a large tree between my house and my friend's house cracked in two. I blamed her for years and secretly shunned her for not allowing me to see Mother one last time. Only recently have I realized that the responsibility lay with me to be more assertive and go to my Guru when I needed her and not wimp out because of rules and limitations imposed by others. Big, painful lesson, that one!

Since her retirement, Mother continues to speak to my heart when I need advice or confirmation that I have passed an important test, or when I need to heed a particular person or situation, or at various other times. After all these painful experiences of being separated from her, I learned I have to detach emotionally and to become my own mentor.

There are no guarantees for the ascension. Today is June 23, 2003, and I am firmly entrenched on my spiritual path, having made momentous strides. I have made the transition from focusing on myself and my problems to focusing on others and the world and how I can be of benefit to mankind.

I know I could lose this attunement in a heartbeat but for the grace of God. I continue to diligently implore El Morya to never leave me nor allow me to slip off the Path, and I also ask this for others. I feel that is the greatest thing I can ask for, for everyone who reads these words.

Louis Difo (above) and Kenneth McNeel spin Mother around the dance floor.

43

AN ATTITUDE OF GRATITUDE

Mother Came to Live with Me When I Was Four
by Michael Villeneuve

*In every age the Lord has sent his emissaries to initiate
spirals of renewed Self-awareness. Our Messenger is the taper
which we hold in our hand to kindle anew the crystallization of
the God flame within you. Through the release of the spoken Word
at conferences, through the blessing of your chakras with special
jeweled focuses which we have secured especially for this purpose,
our messenger is appointed to be the instrument of a greater concentration of the light of hierarchy in the body of God upon earth.*
–Saint Germain, *Pearls of Wisdom,* Vol. 18, No. 31

I grew up with Ma. She came to live with me when
I was four years old. I knew her presence with me and she
was part of my life. We grew up together. Ma also came to
live with another staff member when he was a child and
they grew up together as well. Growing up with Ma prepared me for my mission to serve with her, protect her and
help her fulfill her mission. This went on until 1978 when
Mother gave her stump lecture in Virginia Beach. I had
studied Edgar Cayce for years and was in Virginia Beach
(headquarters for the Cayce foundation). I went up on the
stage and she sealed my third eye. When I saw her in the

physical as an adult, I never again had the experience of being with her as a child.

The following year Sanat Kumara released the Ruby Ray[1] in a dictation and he said America is essential for the platform of the Golden Age. This tied in with my awareness of my mission to help protect America. Saint Germain said if America is destroyed, he will raise us all up in a twinkling of an eye.

In the fall of 1979 I attended S.U. Level II at Camelot, sponsored by the Goddess of Liberty. The classes were held in El Morya's room. There were 11 students and Ma. There were two eight-foot tables. Ma sat on one side and the students sat on the other. One day she interrupted her lecture and started talking directly to me. I told Ma about my experiences of growing up with her, and that I had put these experiences on the altar because I thought possibly they were psychic. She looked at me intently and said, "Morya wants you to take it back." It was then that I realized that these experiences were true.

Mother's Mission

Mother has been sent to rally the people. She came to Earth to redeem the fallen ones and to find the lost sheep. Mark followed so she wouldn't be alone. Mother told me she left heaven and came down to the fallen ones to bring them love. The fallen ones were given the opportunity to experience her love so they could be inspired to turn around and work their way back to God.

We don't want Mother to have to experience the heartbreak of the loss of the people she loves and we don't know who that is. So we must do whatever we can to make sure that none of our brothers and sisters are lost. We

---

[1]The **Ruby Ray** is the fiery core of the love ray. The Ruby Ray is an intense light for a purging of darkness as no other ray can purge. It is the intensity of the essence of the very Blood of Christ. This fiery light manifests as the judgment of all darkness.

don't want to make our ascension and look back and ask where they are. When you go into your heart you're in the heart of the guru and you know the deep love of the guru for her chelas. We must pay the price for the guru to rescue these people. We must put on our Christhood and walk the stations of the Divine Mother and her children. This is the teaching of the Fifteenth Rosary[2] — to give away your Christhood to rescue your brothers and sisters and set life free.

Daughter of the Cosmic Virgin

Ma told the S.U. students she is the daughter of the Cosmic Virgin. We have no idea how high she is in hierarchy. Her job is to bring the Everlasting Gospel to the lightbearers, setting them free, and to bring judgment on the reprobate.

Part of Mother's mission was aborted in the early 1900s when she was embodied, along with Mark, in Russia as a member of the Czar's family. They were destined to bring in a Golden Age. Edgar Cayce said that Russia will be the next/future flame of freedom. What America is today, Russia will be tomorrow.

Murder of the Divine Mother on Mu

In 1998 Mother and I had the opportunity to talk at length. I told her I was seeing a counselor to clear up my psychology stuff, which Morya had said every chela needs to do. I told her I found out during these sessions that my issues go way back — to the lost continent of Mu.

There was a central temple and Mother was the representative of the Divine Mother. She had "Champions" — soldier guards, spiritual warriors who had spiritual powers they could use to defend her. I was one of these Champions. One day I entered a room and found Mother being assaulted by my boss, the head of the Champions. This murderer inserted a wedge in my heart and I froze momentarily,

[2]**Fifteenth Rosary:** See *Pearls of Wisdom,* Vol. 23, No. 27, from Mother Mary.

experiencing a temporary paralysis. Not only did this man murder Mother physically, but he used black magic to put curses on her, to try to mess her up psychologically, even to destroy her soul. Mother said this was a correct reading of the record and told me who it was that had murdered her—someone she knows in this embodiment.

Mother told me how I and others presently on staff who were part of the Champions could have saved her. These Champions had not done the spiritual work necessary to protect her. They were not on the cutting edge. They had let things slip. The head of the Champions (the instigator of the murder) knew their weaknesses and arranged to have women distract them from their duty. Thus the way was opened for the murder of the Divine Mother on Mu.

I have carried the burden of the record of this murder with me through all these centuries; I have relived all these experiences in color. Thus I have felt partly responsible for her problems. Mother, the representative of the Divine Mother in embodiment, was murdered by Luciferians, by betrayers, by someone she trusted most.

On May 12, 1983, Jesus described the judgment of the betrayers and their seed. He said the betrayers have always been there to try to murder the representative of the Divine Mother.

"No One Can Thwart Your Mission except You!"

In 1938 I was in the Farm Department at North Ranch. At that time there were two farm departments—one at North Ranch and one at South Ranch. There had been numerous complaints by staff in these departments about the abuse of power by some supervisors.

In response to these concerns, Mother visited each department separately. She listened to everything each one had to say—the facts of what happened and their reaction to how they were being treated. In each meeting there were those who stepped forward and said that the actions of these supervisors were interfering with the workers' manifesting their Christhood.

Mother's immediate reply was exactly this: "You are going to hell unless you get rid of that idea. Nobody can stand between you and your personal Christhood. What they are doing is irrelevant. Your reaction is going to deny you your victory. No one can thwart your mission except you."

Initiation Failed by Many

In the fall of 1989 El Morya warned staff about an initiation that was coming. This was during the shelter cycle. The men on staff were racing against time to get the shelters ready. There was much work to be done and a timeline to be met. Men from Big Spur and North Ranch (45 miles from the shelters) had been working at South Ranch and hadn't seen their families for many weeks.

On Christmas Eve there was a service with dictations given in King Arthur's Court. All staff were to attend. Some of the men from the north end decided to leave early and go back home to spend Christmas Eve with their families. I had the flu and was sick but went to the service at South Ranch anyway. While there I was told that the bus was leaving to go to North Ranch, even though the service was not over. I had to make a choice because this was my only transportation, my only opportunity to go home, and I needed to go because I was sick.

When Mother found out about this group leaving the service early, she said that all who had left early had to write a confession letter to Morya. The resulting discipline — the opportunity to balance the karma — was that these men all had to go to the Heart of the Inner Retreat and stay there. The weather was bitter cold, ranging from −20° to −4°. We had to stay in tents with inadequate heaters and eat canned food. It was a great challenge trying to stay warm during the day while working outside building the shelters. This was Morya's discipline.

The only thing that sustained me was my trust in God. I was concerned that Morya not kick me out of the Community because that would have ended it for me, since all I knew was the Teachings. We stayed in the Heart until the night the whole staff were buckled into the shelters. This was because India and Pakistan were planning a nuclear war and the Soviet Union had nuclear weapons targeting America.

Guru-Chela Relationship

The highest love is the love of the guru for the chela and the chela for the guru. This is a greater love than the love of twin flames. The fallen ones have never returned Mother's love, but we have the opportunity to give her that love. We can stand at our altar as she did, with the full fire and belief that one with God is a majority.

Ma's work is her chelas, publishing the Everlasting Gospel, leading the decrees needed for the labors.[3] We must not allow ourselves to have a sense of separation or fall into a feeling of isolation from the Mother, the Masters or God. We need to stand up and put on our Christhood. We are just in an interlude called the tribulation—ours and Mother's.

One of the last things I said to Mother when I left staff in 1998 to get more training was "When you need me, I'll be back."

"From the Beginning We Were Winning!"

The Masters have promised that when the fallen ones are judged and removed, the lightbearers will rise. We have been told that in the twinkling of an eye the fallen ones will be gone. When God is ready, He will act and move through His own and Mother will be free. The Teachings will then be spread as the waters over the sea.

The battle is already won in the etheric. Although we are going through the tribulation right now, we should

---

[3] **Labors:** An assignment given by the Brotherhood to the chelas of Guru Ma to do the necessary decree work at the altar to rid the planet of a certain body of dark ones.

not be depressed. We need to learn to go into our heart. Only those who can enter into their heart will go forward. Lanello told us in a dictation that there are nine evolutions simultaneously occupying nine planes of consciousness. Planet Earth is going to become Freedom's Star. The battle is already won in heaven.

Dance the Jig
by Theresa Yui

During a busy publishing cycle, Mother really wanted a project done in a few days. We thought it would take at least a week. Mother said that if we could meet her timeline, she might dance a jig.

Amazingly, as a result of a great team effort and some heavenly assistance, we were able to complete a major portion of the project by the time she had requested. I let Mother know and reminded her of what she had said. Her heartwarming reply:

44

OUT ON A LIMB
The Masters Intercede
by Mark Chapin

You know the great joy that you take in surprising someone with a gift, especially a loved one. God likes to surprise you with his gifts. Don't weary him and weary him and weary him with continual calls for this or that healing, this or that physical manifestation, this or that want, thereby revealing to him that you know more of your unwholeness than your wholeness. Let us take a new tack. Let us let the sails of our ship be full with the billows of the Holy Spirit. Let us call upon the Lord for wholeness by affirming wholeness, by being wholeness. Let our life be the dynamic decree. Let our very life be the expression, "I AM whole. Lo, I AM THAT I AM."
— Elizabeth Clare Prophet, August 14, 1981

One summer I was walking along the path at Camelot. Suddenly there was a loud crack followed by an instantaneous thud on my back. A huge branch from a towering California oak came crashing down around me! I was just passing under the branch when it split in two and the main body of the branch landed on me. It must have been at least two feet in diameter. At the time it fell, hundreds of staff and students were walking right along this same path. This mishap transpired during the John the Beloved Seminar in July 1982, following our Freedom class.

I started to lose consciousness, but fortunately I came back. I was taken to the hospital and had X-rays. Mother probably told me more about the causes for this accident when she visited me in the hospital, but I was so dazed and shaken by the event that I don't recall what she said. Miraculously, nothing was broken and I was released.

When I returned to Camelot, I had one chiropractic treatment and a sore back and neck for a few weeks—but that was it from a physical aspect. Considering where the branch hit me and how heavy it was, it was indeed a miracle that I was not seriously injured. There is no doubt in my mind that there was divine intervention.

Another interesting anecdote: A witness to the event told me later when he heard the crack, he looked over to the tree and saw a young lady who was walking ahead of me. He marveled that it looked like she was lifted off the ground and swept away from danger by unseen hands.

Afterward I learned that Mother had told others that I had volunteered and that the message of the branch falling on me symbolized a government that looks fine on the outside but is rotten at the core. Mother made other comments about the accident and its symbolism to the students attending the seminar.

Mother's Commentary to the Students

So clearly, accidents are witchcraft, and you can see how that witchcraft is practiced. I will tell you that there was a false guru who was very angry that many of his followers left him and came into this organization. And I was told by one of his followers that he always gave a fire mantra to the fire elementals, whereby he would control those elementals. They were very afraid of him and very afraid of his mantra. He had pronounced a tremendous judgment and curse upon those who had left him.

So I learned what this mantra was, and I did my own inner work to counteract it. One of the ways that I saw it out-pictured was that one of our oak trees suddenly fell across the path at a time when students were walking by. And by the miracle of Almighty God, no one was seriously hurt. One person was brazed slightly and was checked at the hospital. Even in a period of the maximum number of people passing by and this thing suddenly coming down, no one was seriously harmed.

But the virulence and the intensity of the black magic of this false guru of India were certainly clearly evident. And I even had people tell me that they were told by God to move out from under the tree just before it fell. And therefore they obeyed the voice and moved, and the tree fell where they had been standing. So this is an amazing demonstration of the protection of God.

Mother having a good time with chelas

45

MY BROTHER'S KEEPER
Key to Balancing Your Karma Quickly
by Louis Difo

Remember this, beloved: all Archangels and angels are here to serve the sons and daughters of God and their children who are of the Light, who seek the Light and who ultimately become the Light. And as they move through time and eternity they become manifestations of the piercing descent of Sacred Fire.

So, beloved, please make a commitment to me that each day you will give fifteen to thirty minutes of dynamic decrees to me for the protection of every lightbearer on Earth. Do it in idle moments when you move from place to place. And thereby empower us, through the science of the spoken Word, to work through you.

–Archangel Michael, *Pearls of Wisdom*, Vol. 40, No. 24

I found the Teachings of the Ascended Masters in New York City in 1982. These teachings became a major part of my life as I was quietly pursuing a banking career as Vice President at the Chase Manhattan Bank, now called JPMorgan Chase. I had a 20-year career in banking while I was in the Church.

On my way back from Asia on business in May of 1983, I decided to stop at Camelot in California. I was there for two days. On my last day I was supposed to have a meeting with Mother at 8 in the morning. I planned to meet with her for one hour. That would give me ample time to catch my plane at 11:30. My job responsibilities required me to get back to New York as soon as possible.

My bags were packed and I drove out to Camelot, up the long drive, and parked outside the white stucco Spanish-style mansion. I got there at 8 am sharp and let Mother's secretary know that I was waiting downstairs to see her. Every 15 minutes I was looking at my watch, knowing I would have to leave by 10 at the latest to make my connections. With no response by 9, I again rang upstairs asking if Mother knew I was there.

"Yes, she knows," the secretary assured me. At 9:15 I called again. "I'm still here." By 9:45, I thought I had better check once more and wondered if I should call the whole thing off. I reminded the secretary that I had to be at the airport by 10:30. Then a message came down from Mother that piqued my interest. She told me that there were some tapes she wanted me to listen to. They were of her lectures given in Africa. She explained these were important teachings I needed to know. I decided to put my chelaship before my work responsibilities and made plans to leave two days later.

At 11 am Mother's assistant came downstairs to see if I was still there and returned with a message for me. Mother was inviting me to dinner at 7 that evening. As it turned out I had a wonderful day at Camelot absorbing all these marvelous teachings. They were truly life transforming for me!

At 7 pm Mother came downstairs, smiling, and gave me a big hug. She was with one of her daughters. She said, "Well, let's go to dinner." Mother asked that I sit next to her in the car. The first thing she asked was "How is your father?" That surprised me because my father had passed away a year before. She perceived that I was still in mourning and feeling his absence.

She next said she was going to give me an important key to help balance my karma. She told me I needed to bring the Teachings of the Ascended Masters to Africa. Sharing the Teachings is the quickest way to balance your karma. This was one of the main reasons why she and Mark traveled throughout Europe, thereby balancing old karma on the Continent. That was why getting the tapes and Teachings published was given a number one priority. When people read the books and watch the tapes, they get freed and it helps you get free.

Play the Tapes for the Judgment of the Dark Ones

During dinner Mother told us that she could not anchor enough light in her aura to counteract the tremendous darkness on the planet. She said the Archangels had dictated the year before, during the New Year's Class 1980-1981 "The Class of the Archangels" at Camelot. They came for the judgment. Mother asked us to play these dictations repeatedly so that this action can be recreated and the judgment can be anchored upon the fallen ones. This way we can help Mother counteract the darkness so evident in this day and age.

Mother's Great Love for Africa

Mother said Africa has a very important role to play in the Age of Aquarius. When she traveled there on her stump tours, she was well received everywhere, almost like a head of state, because the people recognized the Mother. When they saw her they knew exactly who she was. Mother taught that race is irrelevant. White or black, it doesn't matter. Every race, every country has its own divine plan.

From the late 1980s to the early 1990s I was a group coordinator for Africa with Rev. Annice B. And I did many things at my own expense, sharing teachings and working with the groups. There are many students there. When I approached Mother about the cost of the publications and said, "The people of Africa cannot afford the books and the *Pearls of Wisdom,*" she reduced the cost so that it was almost nothing, barely covering the postage. She spoke of the great devotion of the African people and how they would pray for hours. She was so concerned about their souls, but she didn't want them to become attached to her personally.

One time I was on a business trip in Dakar, Senegal, on the west coast of Africa. I received a message that Mother wanted me to call her. She knew I was in contact with some heads of state and asked me, "Do you know the president of Zaire?" Ebola was raging in the country, killing many people. Mother had read about it and called me. She said, "Louis, my heart is aching, for the mother in me sees all this suffering from Ebola."

She had met with someone who claimed to have a natural cure for Ebola. She was hoping I could make contact with the president of Zaire to let him know there might be someone who could help. She said she didn't know if this cure could really end the epidemic but thought it was worth a try. She said we have to try anything and everything to alleviate suffering, not only spiritually but physically. This was one example of Mother's constant concern and love for all people.

Mother continued to advise and support me and my family throughout the years. She has always been there for us. She never imposed her ideas. She always allowed me to make my own decisions and respected my free will. But she did give me great counsel and consolation.

On August 15, 1995, I phoned Mother and expressed my concerns about the harmful worldly influences on my teenagers. I remember her profound humility and her trust in the Presence of God in everybody. She said, "Louis, don't be too attached. Children will go through their stuff. But most important is that you introduce them to the Presence of God in them and pray for them. If we do our part, they will never forget. At the right time for them, between them and God, they will return to the Path."

Her devotion to the one God, to her Guru El Morya, are memories that will never leave me.

46

BEHIND THE EIGHT BALL
A Case of Mistaken Identity
by Andrew Kramer

Remember that you are the tree that must be pruned, that the chastening of the law is the action of God's love. You ought to look with utter compassion upon those parts of life who have no one to chasten them, who are allowed to roam the world free and in rebellion and to perform all manner of atrocities against the divine image.

These, indeed, need to be pitied. For did not anyone love them enough to chasten them? I say to you, if you are chastened, know that you are loved. If you would be free of the chastening, then, I say, be free of the chastening as well as of the love, for the two go hand in hand. —Serapis Bey, September 29, 1974

Here's a chelaship story that happened in Holland at a weekend retreat. This was part of the European Stump in the fall of 1985. Many people throughout Europe came. I was one of the two security team members.

None of us ever got much sleep on this trip. Mother did a 30-plus-night lecture tour we called a "stump." I averaged about 1½ hours of sleep each night, decreeing all night long because of the need for decrees for Mother. We truly learned the power of God's grace, which is what sustained us because of our unswerving commitment to the mission of the Messenger's message getting to those who were seeking the Path.

The Teaching from Mother

The night before the weekend retreat, the staff had the opportunity to get a real night's sleep (the only break in the whole trip). Mother was happy to have two of her daughters there with a friend. And she was looking forward to a good night's sleep to recharge for the weekend conference.

Now Ma had a certain fur coat, a big white coat, and her hair was curly at that time. As I was walking to my cabin I saw in the distance two girls walking with a woman in a fur coat and curly hair. So in my mind it equated that Mother's two daughters were walking with her. What I didn't know was that that person was actually another lady who had a coat just like Ma's.

Right after that I saw her daughter, who asked, "Where is my mother?" So I told her that I had just seen her walking. I then went to my own cabin to get some much-needed sleep. Unbeknownst to me, at that moment Mother had just gone to bed.

I was staying in a cabin with six other guys and was just falling asleep when there was a knock on my door. It was Mother's daughter, who told me she had a message for me from Mother. She said she went into Mother's cabin, believing that she was out walking as I had said, and didn't close the door properly. The wind kept the door clanging and woke Mother up out of a very deep sleep.

She continued, "Here's Mother's instruction to you on what happened: The force played all of us like a xylophone and we were all tools of the force. This was a setup. All of us have weak notes (points), just like the letters from a senior devil instructing a junior devil in the art of temptation, as described by C. S. Lewis in his *Screwtape Letters*. Here's what Ma wants you to do. Go to the farthest place the group has on the property from where Mother is sleeping, and do violet flame decrees so she can get some sleep. And keep decreeing until she tells you to stop."

At this point it was about 10 pm. So I stayed up the entire night decreeing until early in the morning and watched the sun come up. Then I received a message from Ma via her daughter about 7 am. "She said she so appreciated all the violet flame that you did!" She then told me that Mother was going over to the lecture hall and wanted to know if I could get her car to take her there.

Even though I was extremely fatigued, having been up all night decreeing, I went to the cabin and met Mother. She said, "Good morning, how are you? Why aren't you getting in the car with me?" So I told her I hadn't slept, shaved, or taken a shower. She said, "Get in the car!" — twice. So I went to the main lecture hall with Mother to look around.

Then we drove back to her cabin so she could get ready to go to the conference. I said I was going to catch some sleep, being in no shape to guard her at the lecture. But Ma said, "There is no way that I can go into this lecture hall without you in the front seat!" And I thought, *Yeah, sleeping in the front seat!*

The whole day I was fighting sleep and people in the audience, knowing I was security, kept nudging me to stay awake. It was embarrassing. But I knew that Mother needed me there to help hold the balance for new people in the audience and to help deflect some of the energy. I also knew that it was a spiritual office and not just a physical one. After the end of the day's events, Mother spoke to me with so much love and thanked me for my devotion and dedication. I told her no matter how much I did for her it would never repay her for what she had done for me and my family.

The end of the stump was bittersweet. When I finally got to sleep I slept 14 hours straight because my body was so fatigued. But I was unhappy that the stump was over because I had been in another plane the whole time — the etheric plane. It was a whole different state of consciousness and I didn't want it to end. We truly felt the presence and sponsorship of the Brotherhood.

Mother's Selfless Commitment to Her Chelas

I was with Mother while she was giving a lecture in Los Angeles. Afterward she was giving personal time to people who wanted to talk with her until way into the wee hours of the morning. So I turned to her and said, "Ma, you need to get your rest!" She answered, "How can I do that when they waited hours to see me?" So I told her, "The reason they can do that is that you are the living example." The point of the story is that many people do not realize how much of her life and energy she gave to everyone, and how much of herself she gave to this movement on behalf of the Masters and the Brotherhood.

I traveled all over the country and the world with her and Ma got very, very little sleep. She spent hours and hours counseling people and stayed up all hours of the night at great personal sacrifice, making calls for people and counseling them.

I was blessed to witness time after time her love and dedication to her mission and watch her day by day, increment by increment, truly lay down her life for her chelas.

47

BALM OF GILEAD
The Teaching Touches My Heart
by Alexandra Tolmatskaya

I am as near as the breath that you breathe. And there is nowhere that you can go that I am not, for I have projected an Electronic Presence of myself to each one of you who will receive me. . . . My reward is the ascension! My reward is Light! And if you will receive me as a Prophet of your ascension, then you can have my Electronic Presence walking next to you.

–Lanello, *Pearls of Wisdom*, Vol. 16, No. 32

I live in the Ukraine and began to study English when I was 15. It was in 1986. I had a wonderful English teacher (she immigrated to the United States in 1989). Our manuals were poor. They consisted only of texts about Marxism-Leninism, communism, the October Revolution, the nuclear threat coming from America and other stuff in bad English (now it is really funny but it was not so then).

Longfellow Taught Me English

If you were a Soviet pupil you could hate English because of English lessons. However, our teacher recited to us the poems of Longfellow. We didn't even know Longfellow's name and couldn't find his poems in any books.

The most amazing thing was that I began to recite those poems aloud many, many times. I "decreed" them at home and even at school breaks. My fellow students were also infected with this idea. Almost all of our class stood on breaks repeating one verse several times loudly and then another verse and then another. Pupils of other classes said that we were all crazy. But we didn't care because this repetition was great fun for us. Soon we became the best English class at school. So, even without decrees I decreed. And even after my school years I didn't quit my habit of reciting the verses of Longfellow. My favorite one was "I shot an arrow into the air."

> I shot an arrow into the air,
> It fell to earth, I knew not where;
> For, so swiftly it flew, the sight
> Could not follow it in its flight.
> I breathed a song into the air,
> It fell to earth, I knew not where;
> For who has sight so keen and strong,
> That it can follow the flight of song?
> Long, long afterward, in an oak
> I found the arrow, still unbroke;
> And the song, from beginning to end,
> I found again in the heart of a friend.

Exactly 12 years later (in September 1998), my sister Olga gave me *The Science of the Spoken Word*. And I found the "wonderful verses," which reminded me of Longfellow. I began to read them aloud—all the decrees from the beginning to the ending of the book. My daughter Nika (she was six at this time) began to repeat the "verses" with me! I didn't even care about the mystical sense of decrees. I liked it because it was English. But my daughter realized it was God.

Angels Flew into Our Room

The next evening we began to read decrees. And suddenly one huge angel and a multitude of small angels flew into our room! We heard them and we saw them both physically and tangibly. I was greatly surprised because I didn't believe in angels. At this time I knew only Jesus, Mary and God Almighty, and those angels didn't look like traditional angels in classical pictures. They were mighty beings spreading their presence all over the room and the space around the room. We heard the rustling of their wings and saw how swiftly they flew!

The next day we began to read decrees again. And for a moment we saw a handsome young fellow with blond hair. After a time I recognized it was Sanat Kumara. Sanat Kumara often came to me, even before I began reading this book. I knew him and wasn't frightened, although angels frightened me a little.

The Messengers Taught Me

I realized this teaching was meant especially for me, because this "young boy" always came to me when I was sick. When I slept I saw Mother and Mark and they explained many things to me. So the next week I called Montana asking to speak with Elizabeth. And then more great miracles occurred in my life. Since that time I began to live.

48

CLEAR AS A BELL
The Biggest Cinnamon Rolls in Town
by Janice Feuer Haugen

Those whom the Keeper of the Scrolls has singled out as selfless servants of God will receive a mitigation of their karma in these twenty-four hours. This dispensation is unto those who have received Saint Germain into their hearts and who religiously apply his violet flame for the transmutation of personal and planetary karma. And thereby, through the Holy Spirit, they are balancing their karma and moving on in the ascending cycles of being.
—Jesus Christ, *Pearls of Wisdom*, Vol. 39, No. 40

In 1986 I volunteered part-time on staff in the kitchen at Camelot while simultaneously catering part-time and teaching cooking part-time in the Los Angeles area. When the Ranch Kitchen restaurant at the Royal Teton Ranch in Montana was first announced by Mother, I immediately wrote that I would love to be a part of it.

One day most unexpectedly, Marcia, my supervisor, told me to get into the kitchen golf cart and she whisked me to the sacristy for my first-ever personal meeting with Mother. We spoke of the restaurant and she told me about the "Famous Cinnamon Rolls" that would be served there. When I returned to the kitchen, Marcia showed me the proposed menu, which included Famous Cinnamon Rolls. So I asked to see the recipe. "We don't have one," she said. "You'll need to create it."

In short order I moved to Montana and was living in a trailer behind the restaurant and gift store. Once I got there I began working on cinnamon rolls, among other new menu items. I would bring each batch of cinnamon rolls to the restaurant manager. First thing she did was go straight to the center, the heart of a cinnamon roll, to judge the quality of each batch. They continued to improve in size, frosting, filling and texture. If these were to be famous, every aspect needed to be perfect. Finally one afternoon we had the recipe that was declared worthy of being called "famous." When Mother called from Malibu and was told about the cinnamon rolls she exclaimed, "I *can* see them and they're huge!" She was very right; they were each a quarter pound, four inches square and around two inches high.

Well, very quickly they did become famous. We had 12 pans that could each hold 12 cinnamon rolls, so each day we made 144. It was in the making of these cinnamon rolls that the bakers began an important ritual—the blessing of our baked goods. As the just-formed, huge roll lay on the table, it was blessed with enough light and love to neutralize any negative effects of the sugar.

During the winter months when the restaurant was much quieter, there was only one baker. This wonderful baker continued blessing the cinnamon rolls and muffins each morning. One of her customers, Timothy, was a regular, enjoying a muffin each morning.

One morning this baker questioned the blessing of the baked goods—so she didn't bless them. That afternoon when Timothy and the baker happened to see one another, Timothy told her that the morning's muffin looked the same, but something was different, something was missing. Smiling inwardly, the baker knew immediately what was different, and learned her lesson well.

We touched so many lives in the Kitchen--especially during conferences. I remember one Thanksgiving when I was still working part-time in the Kitchen. I needed to be there early to bake the many pies. After a very late night I decided to sleep in my little Honda Civic instead of driving home, so that I could complete the baking early enough to clear the ovens for the stuffing and potatoes and turkeys. There was much to be done to serve 1,500 or more people. The wonderful kitchen staff worked many, many hours in joy, in harmony, in love to prepare the Thanksgiving feast.

When the kitchen staff finally had the opportunity to eat Thanksgiving dinner, I placed my hands over my plate of food to bless it, and instead, the food was so charged with that love, harmony and joy that it was blessing me! I could feel it blessing me through my hands all the way to my heart. Such a gift it was to serve on the staff.

My Karma Was Greatly Mitigated

Early on Pentecost morning 1992, moments after the Ranch Kitchen opened, I slipped outside and fell and broke my right wrist. It was extremely painful. But most fortunately a table of nurses was having breakfast and one of the nurses, dear Marjo, came out to help me. She called one of the staff doctors and received permission to give me a shot of a strong painkiller and then drove me to the emergency room at the hospital in Bozeman. After a cast was put on and an X-ray taken, it was determined that the break was severe enough that surgery was required to be performed in a couple of days.

When we arrived back at the Ranch I was given a room for the night with a phone. Soon after I was settled in, Mother came to visit me. With so much love she spoke with me and gave me a message from El Morya. He said I was not to have even a moment of self-pity. The accident had been *greatly mitigated* by my service and decrees over the years. Although the pain at times was very intense, I could only wonder what horrendous act I must have committed to bring about the need for such pain to balance the karma. Balance it I did, and was then fortunate to meet and marry the most wonderful man the following year.

Little did I know what exactly "greatly mitigated" meant until many years later. A new friend with an opened third eye happened to see my right hand as I was gesturing in conversation. She looked at my palm more closely and said, "You were supposed to have died earlier. Did you have an accident?" I mentioned the broken wrist. The next year, in a meditation with El Morya, it was explained to me just what "greatly mitigated" meant. Our beloved Mother, through her great love, actually gave a portion of her attainment so that I could live and be here today to share this story and my gratitude for our Guru Ma.

Janice Haugen
and Mother

Susan Harrow
with Mother

49

A CUP OF TEA
I Will Always Love You, Mother
by Susan Harrow

You can remember the smile of your teacher and you can remember that a person, the Guru, loved you personally. The love of Guru is the love of God. We are totally, completely loved.
—Mother

I do not remember the day or the hour. But I will never forget the words she spoke to me. Those words will follow me into other galaxies. Those words are etched upon my soul and recorded in my heart.

It was a day in California. There were many days there that all seem to have slipped together into a pocket folder of memory. I assisted Mother in her household, mostly providing meals. And always wondering why I had been requested to take the task—being unskilled altogether in the art of cooking.

And things needed to be just so. There were Mother's preferences, of course, but then also the refinement of my soul in the process. If you ignore the details, you don't always produce food that is filled with love and perfection. When there are many details at the same time, the mind must give up and the heart must take over. A fine theory in retrospect, but it's not always easy to find the joy in the midst of the discipline.

All kinds of situations came my way. Cooking here, cooking there, cooking on the spur of the moment. Doing this and doing that while the vegetables burned, mastering the art of being everywhere at once and having everything under control, but often not being the master.

It was a testing and a trying but I knew it was for the betterment of my being. I knew I had found the dharma (the duty) and the sangha (the community). I knew I had found the Buddha (the Guru, the enlightenment) who would lead me forward on my path. But sometimes I wanted to do well just to get approval. Sometimes I disliked myself a lot when I didn't get it. But the lesson seemed to be to keep on trying. No matter what.

Sometimes the food wasn't hot enough, there was too much or too little. Sometimes the vegetables were over-cooked and I had to start over. Sometimes there was no time to start over and the opportunity was lost. Would that I had found more joy, but often I found the serious nature of the testing was the serious nature by which I viewed my life and my path. Serious because I have always sensed that this lifetime around there is a lot at stake.

So it was a day like many others, cooking and serving. The meal had concluded and in some way had been a disaster. The details are gone. But I recall the feeling of utter hopelessness that beset me. Once again I had failed. I had made a mess of things. Oh, woe! Would I ever make the grade? Be good enough? Be the master of this humble task? And the last duty before I left was to serve tea to Mother in her office. I dreaded it. Having made quite a fool of myself during the serving of the meal, I just wanted to go away quietly. Not to be.

The office was large and deep in wood and flagstone floor. Long were the windows and rich the seats of leather. Old England come again. Mother sat in serious contemplation at her deep dark desk. All within me hesitated. Yet I entered to take the drink, hoping that the exploits of my day would not be commented upon. Hoping that silence would release me, no matter how uncomfortable the silence. But more often God holds surprises, gifts in golden packages on days when they are least expected. As I deposited the tea before her, Mother looked up from her work. I braced myself to receive comment on the sorry state of my being.

"You know," she said, "that I will always love you...." Her heart, as often, opened like a flower, and love flowed to me in that moment that is still stored within me for all its grace and power. I am sure my tears fell. I am sure I could not speak. I do not remember being able to do so. I just remember that for all that I had done or not done, for all eternity's weaving of my path with the path of the Ascended Masters and the Messenger, to have come to a moment such as this was worth more than all the rewards the world could ever offer.

There are many memories, but this is one of the fondest. Fond not just because I felt loved and appreciated in that moment. Fond because those words fly with me throughout my life. Fond because those words are true. Fond because this kind of love is the love of eternity. Where souls have met and been flung afar. When souls have met again and remembered who they are.

And so to our beloved Mother with all my heart I say, "You know that I will always love you, too."

50
GUIDING LIGHT
Mother's Consolation
by Diana Difo

*Walking by that Light, we find the blessed souls. We take
them to our heart. We wrap them in our arms of love. We succor
them. And, precious hearts, there is truly a oneness that can be felt
through this ultimate sacrifice of the Son of God that can be felt in
no other way.*

*Once you have experienced the pain within your heart
of the crucifixion, you experience world pain in every part of the
body of God. You are there—witnessing, releasing the Word,
releasing the Light! And in its very release, that Light swallows
up that pain by the sacred fire breath—tending the altar of God
at the bed of the sick, at the heart of those who hunger and thirst
after Him, for whom there is no consolation in this world save His
coming, save the morning of the resurrection when He appears
once again.*

—Archangel Uriel, *Pearls of Wisdom*, Vol. 24, No. 18

Mother came to Vancouver, Canada, to give a seminar
at the University of British Columbia. I decided to go and
invited my mom along with her friend Heather, who was
very ill. Heather had an advanced stage of cancer and I
wanted her to see Mother before it was too late.

We were sitting in the audience when Mother came out on the platform. Looking out at the spectators, she unexpectedly zeroed in on us and gave us a long gaze. She then started speaking about reasons people get cancer. It was amazing. It felt like a personal message for Heather, as her talk began addressing difficult issues Heather was facing. This was a very timely moment. Through her gracious talk, Mother gave Heather and us an opportunity to understand the causes for her illness and how to best cope with it.

Afterward Mother gave a dictation by our Lord and Saviour Jesus Christ. I still remember his fiery dissertation: "I AM real; I AM here!" He admonished people to leave their old thinking and ways behind. He was practically physical! I was a little embarrassed because my mother was there and I felt like I wanted to hide under a chair, it was so very powerful.

Although my mom could not be moved, to me this experience of both the talk on cancer and the dictation were life-transforming and a witness to the authenticity of the Messenger! And Mother's sermon gave us so much comfort and a greater understanding of what we were dealing with.

51

KEEP ON WALKING
Affirm Your Victories
by Judy Sue Christenson

*Charge! charge! charge! I say. Move swiftly through maya
and illusion and self-attachment—and such pride. Let it all go,
beloved. For I promise you, you are ready. Your Christ Self is
ready. And as though there were a great silence all heaven is poised
and ready for your declaration of Victory! Victory! Victory! in the
cups of time and space day by day. I promise you it will not be
arduous forever.*
—Lord Maitreya, *Pearls of Wisdom*, Vol. 31, No. 85

When the Church moved from Camelot to Montana
in 1987, I wrote to Mother and asked for additional guidance and any discipline that might help me. In response I
received the most beautiful short message. Her recommen-
dation transformed my life. It was "to study and really know
the book *Corona Class Lessons* by Jesus and Kuthumi, and
to accept, internalize and become what you read, page by
page." She advised me to give Mother Mary's rosary without fail daily and ask for Mother Mary to come into my
heart and help to re-form me in the image of Christ.

Initially I thought that this might be a very large
assignment, but as I began reading from *Corona Class Lessons*,
I found it gentle and healing. I later learned that this was

one of the books the Masters recommend for the healing of our psychology. Years later Mother was in Minneapolis and gave the lecture "It Is Possible to Fail." She mentioned that two key books for success on the Path were *Corona Class Lessons* and *Understanding Yourself* by Kuthumi, Lanto, and Meru.

Another assistance and comfort on my path to wholeness was Mother Mary's landmark dictation delivered August 14, 1989.[1] She stated that we could not decree above our psychology, that we had to "take apart (and put back together again) elements of the soul and the soul's personality development in this life and sometimes in previous lifetimes."

Over the years I received several letters from Mother supporting my work on healing my psychology and advising me to seek therapy when needed. I received a letter in 1991 from the secretary to the Messenger, as I was resolving a burden.

Beloved Mother wanted you to know that she is holding you in her heart's love. She has said that the foundations of spiritual problems are within our psychology and that we will only resolve our spiritual problems if we resolve our psychology first.

Mother suggests you do the Tube of Light often when you think of it and call to Archangel Michael to cut you free from any forces seen or unseen that would be moving against you for the vulnerabilities in your psychology.

The development of your heart chakra, the development of love in your heart as you extend personal love to all people you meet, is a certain means to overcoming all problems. You can use "Saint Germain's Heart Meditation I and II" for this purpose.

One Million Escaped Hell!

There came a time when a decision was made to decrease the number of decrees to Astrea (10.14 in our decree

---

[1] *Pearls of Wisdom*, Vol. 32 No. 44 "The Re-Creation of Self – A New Realm of the Possible."

book)[2] given during the services. I was distressed about this because I recalled how Mother had taught us that we needed to carve people out of the astral plane with our Astrea decrees. As a result I wrote a long letter to Mother and others requesting that more decrees to Astrea be given. I later learned that Mother received letters from other students asking for the same thing.

The following Friday was Saint Patrick's Day. To my great surprise, when I joined the broadcast from the Church, Mother was leading 144 Astreas. I was so excited! The following Friday Mother led another service with 144 Astreas. At the end of the service she told us that Enoch was on the platform. She stated that by giving 144 Astreas we earned a dispensation for the cutting free of those souls tied to us. That was the year that my husband, Matthew, and I were cut free to be together at last.

Saint Germain, Jesus and Cuzco dictated, commending the work that had been done by the giving of these Astreas. In Jesus' dictation on October 8, 1995, he stated: "Approximately one million souls on Earth have totally escaped hell solely by the work of the Astreas that you, the staff and the Keepers of the Flame have given since you began giving 144 Astreas three times a week."

When some staff visited Minneapolis for outreach, one person approached me with a personal message from Mother: "Are we doing enough Astreas for you?" This was such a wonderful validation.

Letters of Comfort from Mother

In the summer of 1992, I was working day-night rotation at the hospital in a float pool. One night I had a patient who had an obstructive pulmonary disease. This was a serious matter. The doctors wanted to talk this patient into being a "no-code," meaning that if she went into a

---

[2] **Decree to the Elohim Astrea:** Number 10.14 in *Prayers, Meditations, Dynamic Decrees* published by The Summit Lighthouse.

cardiac arrest, we would do nothing to save her life. To make matters worse, I had trouble getting some other doctors to assist with this patient.

I became quite disturbed and went into the bathroom and got on my knees, praying to God, asking what to do. I was prompted to go into this patient's room and show her the I AM Presence Chart (which I give out freely at the hospital). I showed her who she was and how valuable her life was—even now. I also told her that I had taken care of patients in intensive care, even on respirators, to help them with their healing. I encouraged her to pray about her decision, and said we would be there to support her. I remember rallying some other nurses. In the morning the nursing supervisor exclaimed how pleased she was with the nurses in our communications with the doctors and *particularly* the care of this patient.

After getting off work that morning, I went to breakfast and wrote Mother to share my experience with her. Following is her response via her secretary:

Beloved Mother sends her love to you and said that God has placed her on earth to help you make it back home all the way to his heart. She was grateful for your stand for life and for your victories. Keep on affirming them! As Mark Prophet said to Mother just before he left this world, "Elizabeth, may you win all the way." So she says to you, "Judy, may you win all the way." That means that you are determined to win in everything you do each day, to serve with excellence, no matter how low or insignificant, to be thorough, to give your very best, to be kind, to be loving, to be forgiving.

Judy, Mother sends you the joy of her heart, which is the joy she holds for your victory. Just make as your motto: "Keep on keeping on, and never a backward step."

What was amazing is that in this letter Mother also answered a question I had without my asking! There were some who tended to feel that if you were not on staff and were serving in the field, it was not significant enough. Mother addressed this concern of mine:

The first thing you must know is that it does not matter where you are in physical location. You can attain union with God. Union with God is not conditioned by circumstance or karma. Union with God is based upon the soul's recognition of the wrong she has done and her willingness to pay the price, which you are doing by your dharma, decrees and love.

Miracles of God can happen, but you must put your attention on being the manifestation of God where you are. You must affirm:

"Behold, I am everywhere in the consciousness of God. I am a prisoner of my Lord, yet a soul freeborn. I can go forth from my body at night and journey to the retreats of the Ascended Masters and the Great White Brotherhood. I can study and do penance and serve with the legions of Archangel Michael out of the body and return to keep my vigil on behalf of all those who are suffering."

There is no more important work that you can do for yourself and the world than to decree.

What profound messages these were to my soul at that time, and not even what I was outwardly requesting!

Trust your Holy Christ Self

In the early 1990s I wrote to Mother and told her that I would wait forever for the right man to come into my life. I did not want a karmic relationship unless it was necessary, as I had the violet flame. Not long after Mother received my letter, El Morya had a message for Matthew (my future husband) that it was time for him to leave staff. Since he was born near Minneapolis and had lived here, he came to our Teaching Center.

El Morya had told us never to focus on someone coming into our life. When it was God's Will El Morya would put our "partner" face to face with us. So there I was, on fire for leading the services at the Teaching Center, and there he was, on A.V.! God is wonderful and most especially our Messenger, who later interceded to help bring Matthew and me together.

In 1996 Matthew and I were married at the Ranch. Once again I wrote to Mother and part of her response literally jumped off the page and has guided me for several years. It was indispensable to my path and I believe also the path of others.

She again encouraged professional counseling as needed and to "trust your Holy Christ Self—your inner man of the heart—to guide you rather than relying on advice from others." The reason this was so profound was my common tendency to look outside myself, when in the final testing we must all rely on our attunement from within, which of course is so very empowering! This is the bonding with our own beloved Holy Christ Self.

In that same letter Mother included the words of God Meru given in his dictation on September 1, 1973:

Thrust your sins into the fire as the ancient sacrifice of the children of Israel, symbolical of putting into the flame the menagerie of the subconscious—the animal forms, the darkness, the density. How do you do this? You simply say,

"In the name of Jesus the Christ, I cast all that is less than the Christ into the flame. O God, consume it! I ask it. Hear my plea and answer. I accept it done this hour in full power, in fulfillment of the promise of the Creator."

If you will but make that call, all of heaven will move this very hour to lift the burden of the sense of sin from you.

We can also burn letters to Mother and the Masters to receive answers on the instant.

52

ON THE SPOT
Stop This Car!
by Carl Showalter

Countless miracles of Christ have been duplicated by men and women of various times and climes since his wondrous advent, and yet because of human skepticism and forgetfulness, the wonder of it all has been relegated to the realm of myth or the imaginings of gullible minds. Let me plead for a renewal of faith in the power of God, for this is a requirement of everyone who would be a wonderman of spiritual accomplishment on behalf of the holy purposes of the universal law itself.
—Saint Germain, *Pearls of Wisdom*, Vol. 5, No. 29

I had the privilege of being Mother's bodyguard on her first five stump tours. I learned that when accompanying an adept or guru in her travels, one experiences many interesting phenomena. Working close to one who is connected intimately with the Source made a real believer out of me.

I remember one night in mid-America. It was winter and it was raining. The temperature was at freezing. Being on the security team always meant being aware of all the dangers, and this evening was certainly one of great challenge. In spite of the weather we had a good turnout of people. The hotel that hosted the meeting was on top of a hill, and the bus that Mother rode in was parked a block away down a very steep hill. Across the street from the hotel was a parking lot that went all the way down to where the bus was parked. The street that we had to cross was already rather steep.

After the lecture and anointings that night, we found everything covered with a thick coat of ice. Now the question became how to get Mother down to her bus. We finally decided to drive across the street to the parking lot and work our way down their stair-step parking configuration. This way we could go down a little at a time. So we proceeded very slowly and cautiously.

I was the driver, with Mother to my right and other staff filling the car. I didn't get halfway across the street when the front of the vehicle slid sideways and we began sliding downhill. So I steered over against the curb—to no avail!

Feeling powerless to do anything about it, I exclaimed, "I am sorry, but I can do nothing to stop this car."

With no feeling of fear, Mother said with a very powerful voice, "In the name of my Mighty I AM Presence, stop this car!"

The vehicle stopped immediately and the staff assisted Mother out of the car. They carefully proceeded to the bus. There was no physical way for that vehicle to be stopped. It truly taught many of us the power of the spoken Word and the adeptship of our Messenger.

53

THE INSIDE SCOOP
Mother's Attunement
by Tonya Gamman

The Messenger knows full well that she is not perfect. But she also knows that God is perfect and that God perfects her and you in divine love. Seek not the human condition of anyone. What shall you find? You shall find the same old human condition. Those who can rise above it and resolve it come to new heights of glory and visions of angels beyond.
—John the Beloved, *Pearls of Wisdom*, Vol. 46, No. 25

Mother was given some misinformation about Paul and me. As a result she gave us a discipline. I was very confused about this, since I was not expecting her to make a mistake like this. So I decided to write to her. I started the letter, "Dear Mother, I don't know you personally, so I will write you as if you were my own mother." I then told her the truth of the situation.

Later that afternoon, a trusted staff member agreed to take the letter for me to the post office when she came to see Paul for an appointment—but she was late! So I rushed over and personally put it in the post office in Bozeman. But I knew it was too late to go out that day. I prayed to the angels and the Mighty Blue Eagle from Sirius for God-speed.

The next morning the phone rang and it was Mother. She explained that she had received my letter at her office at the Ranch. I was dumbfounded. It was not physically possible to even get the letter from Bozeman to Corwin Springs, then to the Ranch that fast, let alone get it through her secretaries to her desk.

She apologized that she had been misinformed and was sorry for this misunderstanding. She said she would like to meet with us at North Ranch the following Sunday. As a result of meeting her in person, I found that Mother was very loving, just like my mother.

People have complained to me that it was difficult to get letters to her. I myself have had letters that never got through. In hindsight I realized these were situations I needed to handle myself. Then there were times when I didn't even need to write. She would just begin talking about what I had on my mind, even though I had never mentioned it. That happened frequently. It all depended on the situation and what was best for the development of my soul. All in all, it was a very Holy Spirit thing.

One time I was concerned about a certain happening in my marriage. I knew my husband would be seeing Mother that day, and I thought I would call her and ask her to talk to him about it. I picked up the phone and called her secretary, but chickened out. I just said, "Never mind!" and got off the phone. I knew Mother would be glad to help me, but she was so busy and I just didn't want to bother her.

After I got off the phone, I prayed to Mother Mary and asked her to help me. Later that day my husband said he had had a "strange" conversation with Mother. When he explained, I was flabbergasted. It was the very subject I was going to call her about! Not only that, but it was the first thing she brought up when she came into the room to meet with him. I guess Mother Mary delivered my message firsthand!

Mother Is 99 Percent Accurate When Taking Dictations

One time I asked Mother to clear up my confusion regarding her attunement. I told her that sometimes she made mistakes and I was used to K.H. (the Ascended Master Kuthumi) who knew everything and could read my thoughts, so he never made mistakes. It was hard to know how to take things that she told me at times, because she was human and not always perfect.

She responded, "Well, when I'm giving a dictation and I am one with the Master, I'm 99 percent accurate. There is a little of my human self involved, but very little. Then sometimes when the Masters impress something on me and leave it up to me to carry it out how I feel is best, the accuracy goes down somewhat." Then she said in humility with a chuckle, "Other times, I am a human being just like you and I make mistakes too." It helped me a lot to understand that she was still on Earth, subject to its influence and therefore not perfect. I understood, but I was often bothered by not knowing which way she was when.

Do Not Use Subliminal Tapes
by Dr. Paul Gamman

Tonya's relative got a set of subliminal tapes with positive affirmations on them. I talked to Mother about this. She was adamantly opposed to using them and said that these techniques and methods were not correct.

Mother explained that the conscious mind acts as a filter to the subconscious, but with subliminal tapes it was not allowed to filter out the dweller of the person on the tape giving the affirmation. If the conscious mind is not there to filter this out, you can have their subconscious mind influence your mind without any discretion.

She said, "Who is going to bind the dweller of the person talking on the tape? You take on their dweller when you listen to these tapes!"

54

BETWEEN A ROCK AND A HARD PLACE
You Cannot Pick and Choose at the Lord's Table
by Christopher Allen

*I am in the hope that you will prepare yourself to succeed
in your endeavors. Above all, stand ready to make the necessary
changes in your thoughts and preconceived ideas that will make
it possible for you to be victorious. If man expects to succeed in
alchemy, which is in truth dependent on the higher laws of spiritual science, he must nurture the faith on which the strength of his
invocation and concentration will rest.*
— Saint Germain, *Pearls of Wisdom*, Vol. 5, No. 29

As wonderful as it is remembering the moments of
sweet interaction with Mother, there were also those
moments of pointed teaching, of chastisement, and of life-
changing disciplines. It is the latter of these that is the
foundation of this story.

There are always many facets to the giving and
receiving of disciplines in the guru-chela relationship. Many
teachings have been given regarding this relationship, and
it is the luminous essence for all of the disciple's experiences
upon the Path. It is my belief that the Master will never
give us a discipline or initiation that cannot be passed, even
though drastic change may be required to pass through
victoriously.

This change may be excruciating to the psyche as it currently exists, but liberating to the soul who embraces the path. You must fully believe that the Guru is the greatest gift you have been given in life, and have faith and utmost trust that the Guru will not lead you astray. This is especially important when you feel that you have been misunderstood or betrayed somehow, or that the guru's personal idiosyncrasies are at play instead of God's pure love for you. You cannot pick and choose at the Lord's Table; you partake of the body and blood of Christ, or you only get bread!

I had been on staff for quite a few years when change became the order of the day in my life. My main duty on staff was in the print shop, with service in various other ways in the Camelot community. Staff life and service to Mother's mission was my total passion, and I fully believed that I would be a staff member for life.

The Order of Saint Francis

I was also an "eligible" young man in my twenties, and the inevitable laws of attraction to the eligible young and equally devoted ladies serving on staff did sometimes afflict us all. Don't get me wrong—all were expected to live joyously in the principles of a monastic lifestyle and I think we did a pretty good job of doing so. Attraction letters would be written to Mother from either side unbeknownst to the other, asking permission to pursue a relationship, but permission was not an easy thing to come by.

After several years of the merry-go-round attractions and letters (some more serious than others), Mother had me walk with her one day. After we had discussed the nature of one such relationship that was not going to work out, she asked me if I would like to renew my vows to the order of Saint Francis. I had always had a soul tie to Saint Francis and wholeheartedly agreed. I also accepted her request to draw up bylaws for the founding of the Order of Saint Francis within the Church.

It is funny how things work. When I presented Mother with the bylaws, she told me that I couldn't take the vows outwardly this time around because I would be getting married. She did not want to cause misunderstanding in the community at large by allowing me to take the outer vows and then having me change at a future time. My inner vows were intact, but you can imagine how this turn of events stirred the pot! It was around this time that I began to have retreat visits with a beautiful little child who was waiting to be born into my future family. Obviously this child was more aware of what was progressing than I was.

Then I Saw Her

A number of months later, I looked across the lawn and I saw her. With all my being I said to myself, "That's the girl I'm going to marry!" I had never seen her and could hardly see her now, she was so far away, but I knew it was her.

Sometimes on Sunday afternoons, there would be an old movie (from the golden age of Hollywood) showing in the S.U. classroom. On one occasion, I went up to catch the latest film but I was a little late getting there. There was only one seat left. As I scooted in, I realized it was right next to my future wife! So we finally met. Thank goodness she was beautiful, too. Over the next year we talked and smiled at each other, and we both realized that we were falling deeply in love.

Our letters had been written, and Mother was working with us in preparing the inner foundations of our life together and in service to the community. I was the permanent staff member who knew the necessity of the rules of staff life, the importance of patience in this process. It was also my lack of patience and discipline that upended the applecart.

We were on a six-month "no interaction" time allowing Mother to do her work for us, when I sent her *another* letter stating my desire to get married. I wanted to still work in the print shop and work a little part-time in town to earn some extra money that we would need. The response I received wasn't quite what I was hoping for. In fact, it hit me like a ton of bricks! Mother sent word that El Morya wanted me off staff and to leave immediately that night.

There were other things told to me, one regarding what I would now do. This even included a suggestion by Mother that I could look into joining the Marines. I was still allowed to come to all services, so at least I had that to hold onto. Some dear friends offered to let me stay with them and I arrived at their home that night. Their kindness to me exemplified their spirit. The man provided me with work as I needed to earn money, and his wife was so gracious.

"This Is Not a Suggestion!"

I had many things to sort out in my life. I considered Mother's suggestion about joining the Marines, but I had absolutely no desire to do this. So I figured that I would get a job at a local print shop and work there. That information made its way back to Mother and she immediately sent a message to me regarding joining the Marines. "This is NOT a suggestion; it is a COMMAND from El Morya!"

Now the equation was even worse. If I don't join, what will that mean to my life? I would always wonder if I made the right decision. If I join, it is a minimum of a four-year commitment. At this time I had no idea what was happening with my dreams of marriage. Four years in the Marines . . . they might be the worst years of my life. This was my thought process. I went and joined the U.S. Marine Corps pronto, after they approved a waiver for me since I was 28 and past the cut-off age.

My sweetheart was also in turmoil through all of this, but supported my decision to join the Marines. I am awed at her support and her love for me during this unfolding drama. It would have been easy to understand if she had decided on a different course for her own life. Before I shipped off to boot camp, Mother invited us to the Saint Patrick's Day shindig at Camelot, where she announced our engagement. Not long afterward, we were married at Camelot in the company of incredible lifelong friends and family.

El Morya Makes His Presence Known

My years in the Marine Corps seem like another lifetime now. There were some rough memories, but also some really great ones. El Morya made his presence known to me while I served, always letting me know of his guiding hand in my life. With his guidance also came his great love.

A special child from the inner retreats was born to us during this time and she looked just like in my dreams. I never regretted for an instant the decision to follow the discipline we were given. The direction of my life was altered completely, yet perfectly. I am still working on living up to my part in it all—that of being a worthy chela.

Mother's Eternal Promise

Through this discipline, a great blessing occurred for my life personally, and that of my wife, my children, and any who meet us along the way, because it is integrated within us. It is the blessing of the eternal guru-chela promise that Mother wrote to us in a letter:

"Because you have been obedient to the command of El Morya, I will be your Guru for as long as you desire."

Chelaship Was Paramount
by Margaret Reichardt

To earn the right to get the Teachings in print, a price had to be paid. The more important the release, the more sacrifice was required on the part of Mother and everyone who worked with her. Unless we put every last ounce of energy into getting the job done, it didn't happen. Many projects demanded all night sessions, pushing, pushing, pushing with all we had. The more fire of the heart invested in the publication, the more quickly it manifested.

The process started with Mother and her editorial staff. Then the final phase went to the Graphic Arts department and the print shop. A razor's edge mentality had to be maintained by all to ensure the accuracy of the releases as we were most always working on the fly. Once I asked Mother why we had to function under crisis management. She said that "Often Saint Germain doesn't tell me until the last minute what is to be published." This repeatedly happened for the quarterly conference announcements, posters, flyers. We seemed to be always overdue getting the information out so people could make their plans to attend.

I remember one conference, the "Golden Harvest Conference" October 1985 at Camelot. We were late and getting later on producing the poster. The front had 18 pictures of Ascended Masters, in addition to the Chart of Your Divine Self, Mother's picture and two other full-color pictures. The back was filled with small type explaining everything about the conference and the Healing Seminar with 15 workshops which was held just prior to the conference. We were late, very late. Another eleventh-hour, barely in time, assignment.

We had just gone through a marathon getting "The Lost Years of Jesus" into print. And once again we had to gather our resources and create. When the poster was finally in the hands of the posterers, Mother explained that we had to put a certain quotient of our light into the making of this piece in order to earn the right to have it available for those who might be interested.

It was incredible to witness how much the Masters and Messengers did for even just one soul! I remember one very large mailing in Montana that kept all our publishing and distribution staff up and working day and night for five days. Mother really had us push and push to get it out by a certain date. Later Mother said there was a soul, someone out there, who needed this material right at that time and it was crucial to get it to them immediately.

Getting out the Masters' words was Mother's fundamental concern. We had barely enough printers to keep the presses going round the clock which is what it took to meet the Masters' timelines. To thoroughly train a printer to run our large presses required years. Christopher was an experienced printer and vital to our operation. It was a great loss to the press shop when Mother gave him this initiation. We were all pained at the thought of doing without his services for four years, including Mother. Another lesson on how Mother and the Masters put a priority on the growth of the soul.

It was always a God-victory to publish a book of the Ascended Masters' teachings. This is what the Messengers lived for.

55

A KING'S RANSOM
My Blazing Vision
by Joni Wallace

The precious violet flame, an aspect of the Comforter's consciousness, is the friend of every alchemist. It is both the cup and the elixir of Life that cannot fail to produce perfection everywhere when it is called into action. After the violet flame has performed its perfect work, then let all rest in their labors that God may move upon the waters (waves of light) of the creation to produce and sustain the righteousness of his eternal law.
—Saint Germain, *Pearls of Wisdom*, Vol. 5, No. 34

My first encounter with Elizabeth Clare Prophet was when I read her books *The Lost Teachings of Jesus*, at the time of the Gulf War. I had just given birth to my second child and my firstborn was a toddler. Nevertheless, I found time to read through the books quickly. My husband had brought them home. He told me one had literally fallen off the shelf at the store and it caught his attention.

I knew there was truth in those pages, yet at the same time I was terrified. There were all those unfamiliar names. I set the books aside and didn't pick them up again for a long, long time. Years went by, and I became pregnant with my fifth child. I was very sick for a long time with pneumonia/bronchitis symptoms. I remember being very sad and struggling greatly on many levels.

My husband arranged for a massage therapist to come work on me. As she was giving me her treatment she had me wear earphones and listen to a guided imagery tape for healing. To this day I don't know what was on the tape. Instead my heartfelt prayers for divine intervention were answered in the form of a blazing vision of Elizabeth Clare Prophet and a very large Archangel Michael! A shaft of bright light went through the top of my head and along my spine.

Elizabeth Prophet began to talk to me and I found myself sobbing at her words. I became aware of some of the outer as well as the inner reasons for my illness. The massage therapist ("message" therapist in this case), my husband and two other people in the room witnessed only my intense sobbing as I released years of hurts through cleansing tears. Needless to say, after that my recovery was quick and complete. I was profoundly changed. My first physical contact with Mother occurred several years later.

I had received my first decree tape when I signed up for Keepers of the Flame Lessons. I didn't realize that that gift was part of my membership, so it was a pleasant surprise. I could hardly wait to hear a decree. I'd been doing the decrees from *The Science of the Spoken Word*, but this was my first experience doing them with a group of voices—most importantly, Mother's voice.

Wonderful Things Happened with the Violet Flame

So, after everyone was asleep, I would grab a tape recorder and take it into what I thought would be the room where I was least likely to wake my sleeping children—the bathroom. As quietly as I could, I did the decrees so as not to wake the baby. What joy!

Up until this time I had often hid in the closet so the little ones wouldn't find me and disrupt my concentration.

I decreed alone and counted on makeshift beaded strings. It didn't take long for the sound of decrees to echo through our home, despite "kid noise" and interruptions! Many wonderful things happened because of these decrees, as the violet flame did its perfect work.

Eventually we found out that Elizabeth Clare Prophet was going to be in Chicago for the Easter conference. Easter has always been "my" holiday, and I've always loved everything about it, especially the Easter lilies—"my" flowers. I'll skip all the wonderful experiences at the conference—the visions, the contacts—and I'll move ahead to the birthday celebration for Mother at the new Chicago church.

I went to the restroom to breastfeed the baby. There were several other ladies in the room. Then Mother came in. I said something to her to express my tremendous gratitude for all that she has done for our family in changing our lives, something insignificant to describe something so magnificent. To this day when I get near her all I can mutter is "Thank you, thank you, thank you!" Or else tears of gratitude and joy well up within me and I cannot verbalize anything at all.

I find it humorous that my first encounter would be in the bathroom! Remember, the first time I heard Mother's voice on tape I was in the bathroom, hiding out. I suspect that I had spent a lot of time reading *Lost Teachings* there as well. In our smaller house it was the place of greatest privacy. It is wonderful to realize that the Ascended Masters have such a great sense of humor.

So Mother has touched me and healed me in the secret and hidden places of my being, while in the hidden rooms of my home. So what was hidden could no longer remain hidden and what was just a flicker could shine ever more brightly. I am forever changed. I love her greatly! To Mother I give my heartfelt thanks!

56

NO TIME LIKE THE PRESENT
It Wasn't My Time
by Esta Buckland

I come to give you the awareness which has been spoken of in dictations in this past year of the tremendous necessity for concentration on the balance of the threefold flame, both by the devotional songs and decrees to the Christ Self, the threefold flame, and the I AM Presence and by the awareness within one-self of those things of karma and personality and underdeveloped chakras that are an actual block, whether to the will of God and its power, whether to the wisdom of God and its practical application or to the love of God and its compassionate, self-sacrificing offering upon the altar.
— Lord Maitreya, *Pearls of Wisdom,* Vol. 29, No. 22

In 1992 I had a pacemaker put in and I often wondered (and made calls) that it would not affect my heart flame or my Threefold Flame in any way. So I wrote Mother and here's what she said:

"No, Esta, it will not affect your Threefold Flame or your heart chakra. Is it not a wondrous gift from Saint Germain to have the prolonging of life through this technology? You are in your rightful place both physically and in the purity of your heart."

Last May 1998 was my 90th birthday. We were still living at North Ranch. Grace and Celeste invited many people to come for that celebration. There were over 125 people. Mother came and really enjoyed herself. She told me it was the best party ever! Mother visited with everyone, taking pictures. The children flocked around her to love her and talk to her—just to touch her dress.

Late afternoon we all followed Mother out to Deer Park Chapel and she sat me down in Lanello's chair. She sealed the light in the chapel. It had been wonderful to live that close to the chapel and be able to go out there at any time day or night to decree, to play music, to pray or meditate. The following day everything was removed except the chair, and the chapel was closed down. It was rather sad—but we hadn't had services there for about a year

I Wasn't Expected to Live

In July I had a blood clot in my left thigh and was rushed to Billings Hospital in a big plane for immediate surgery. I had no time to think of any danger, but I wasn't afraid. I had talked to Mother that morning and she assured me I would be OK. She told me that she was looking at Lanello's picture and he said, "It's not time for Esta yet. She has work to do."

So I went into surgery knowing Lanello was right by my side. I woke up at 11 to see Grace, Carl and Lanello holding my hands. Grace and Carl had come to stay with me all night, because I wasn't expected to live. I was very much alive and after a while they decided they could leave. I got along very well and every day since then my prayer of gratitude is: "I am grateful for another chance and I am grateful to be alive. Thank you, God."

57

SEVERAL DIPS IN THE JORDAN RIVER
Mother and I Both Got Life Extensions
by Tonya Gamman

Do you think you do service to God and country? I tell you, all service is unto the Divine Flame within. And, beloved, some of you who have rendered such services in this life have truly had years added to your lifestreams in this incarnation, and you know not of it. But El Morya has seen to it, as he does take charge of his own chelas with such tender caring.
—Godfre, *Pearls of Wisdom*, Vol. 30, No. 45

Ever since I can remember, I had a feeling that when I was 36, my life would go through some major change. My Teacher, K.H. (Kuthumi), had shown me things in my future only up to that time, and nothing beyond. My predominant feeling was that my life would end at that time or something traumatic would happen. Thirty-six came and went. Nothing significant happened and I assumed that all was well.

My Life Changes Forever
My feeling of security was premature. The year I turned 37 brought with it an experience that would change my life forever.

I was on a vacation trip with my husband and his parents in the Caribbean. We were having a great time seeing the sights, but it was stressful for me. Our baby, Clare, was with us since she was still nursing at the time. The hard part was that she was also teething and fussy. My father-in-law had very little tolerance for her baby noises.

The result of all this was that I had to hold the baby practically the entire time to "keep her quiet," not to mention keeping the peace with my father-in-law. The problem was that I had recently been in an auto accident that, unknown to me, damaged my spine, and I shouldn't have been holding her at all.

To top things off, I was supposed to go to visit an old friend on a neighboring island. That situation was causing me terrible conflict. On the one hand I really wanted to see my friend, and on the other hand I had a very strong feeling not to go.

I realize now if I had gone and not listened to my inner guidance, I might have died. My intuition won and I didn't go. It was a good thing because the airlines went on strike the next morning and I would not have been able to get back to the island or home to the United States for quite a while.

The stress of this decision was heavy on me as I went to sleep that evening. I awoke in the night from a tremendous pain in my heart, radiating down my left arm and out my little finger. I was also having difficulty breathing. Immediately I recognized the symptoms of a heart attack. Quickly my mind flashed to the fact that I carried a bottle of capsicum in my purse for just such a situation.

I had previously witnessed a person who was having a heart attack return to normal within 15 minutes of taking capsicum, so I foolishly thought I should just go take it and I would be fine in a few minutes. I didn't want to disturb my husband and daughter, who were sleeping soundly in the same room.

I found my purse, took the capsule and waited for the symptoms to improve, but they only worsened. By that time I began to get scared. I started to call to my husband but couldn't get enough breath to get any sound out. I felt like I was about to pass out when I reached out and grabbed the sheet on our bed and pulled it.

My Life Changes Forever

The angels must have been working overtime, because Paul bolted out of bed and was at my side in seconds. That was very unusual for him, as he was a deep sleeper and difficult to awaken. He was able to find out enough information to know what was happening and began working on me. For about an hour he did everything he knew how to do from adjusting my spine to pressing acupuncture points with his fingers.

Slowly I began to improve and I finally was able to get a complete breath. The pain subsided. It began to look like I was going to be OK. Still it felt like my heart was three times as large and heavy as a rock. The feeling of heaviness didn't go away for over three days.

That night after the pain was subsiding, I walked into the bathroom to get something. As I stepped into the room I "felt" and "saw" a white cloud of light, brilliant and beautiful, descend upon me. It completely surrounded me. A voice "spoke" gently from this cloud as a thought/feeling transfer.

The voice said very lovingly, "Your time is up!" I replied, "But I am only 37 and I'm not finished yet!" It simply repeated, "Your time is up!" A few things about my life flashed before me. First and foremost was my children without their mother, and then there was a pie-shaped graph that showed how much karma I had balanced so far in this lifetime.

The pie graph was showing 49 percent of my karma balanced. It was not enough to make a passing grade. I knew I had to be at 51 percent to graduate if I was to make my ascension in this life. I thought to myself disappointedly, I have not graduated to the next level again. I was very disappointed when that information had sunk in.

Well, the voice spoke again. "Your life is extended because of your children." The children referred to were my two last children, the ones I had not planned to have. One had even made it into my life despite birth control measures. I now call these two children my life-extension specialists.

After the last communication, the cloud pulled away and ascended back from where it had come. I was never scared during all of this. But I was concerned for my children having to live without me, and disappointed that I had almost missed the mark — again. Now I had another chance, and it would take me over four years to complete balancing that last 2 percent of my karma and finally reach the 51 percent required!

My Inner Sight Expanded

Just after the attack was brought under control, I laid back down on my bed. I could see through the roof of our building right into the etheric plane. Archangel Zadkiel's retreat was right above me. As I was looking at it and at the room at the same time, it was sort of like looking through gossamer. The place was filled with angels, violet and golden light. The lights formed geometric patterns and a sort of stairway, a moving stairway the angels were traveling on.

My husband was well aware of all this. When we returned from the trip, Paul spoke to Mother about my heart attack. She told him it was my time to go but I had been given a life extension.

For months following I was in an altered state, like living half on Earth and half in heaven. Often I could read people's minds and hear their thoughts like they were actually talking to me. I could "see" things just before they happened. It was like viewing a movie in my mind. It kind of spooked me. I could also see into heaven and saw the angels and the heavenly retreats during that period. Occasionally I would see things that were happening far away, but I felt they were as real as if they were taking place right beside me.

One time was especially traumatic. I saw a man get onto a subway train and open fire on an innocent group of people. I had seen it when it happened, but I did not know what it was until the next day. One of our patients (Mother) told the story to my husband because she had just heard it on the news. It had actually happened in New York, and somehow I had seen it on the inner here in Montana.

Having these events going on was somewhat disturbing if not intriguing, yet interesting. However, I was very relieved when they lessened until they finally disappeared from my life. Once again I felt like I was cemented into my second life cycle and fully integrated into the world as we know it.

A New Life Lay before Us

The time period after I almost died was an intense time for my husband, Paul, and me, especially emotionally. When you almost lose someone you love, it really makes you come to terms with the fact that things are not forever on this plane. We took turns waking up in the night and looking at each other, thanking God deeply that we were still together. Every moment became precious. Relationships with other people, especially family members, became more meaningful. It was a great time of unity.

As time passed we seemed to be opening a whole new life together. It felt as if the burden we had been carrying from that last life had been lifted. That era had finished and a new lighter life lay before us. I felt unsure about the length of the life extension, though, since I was not told the details at the time of my near-death experience.

I prayed fervently and finally received an answer to how long the life extension was. Four years, I was told. Well, it wasn't a long time, but it was *some* time. Perhaps there would be a way to earn more time before that period was up. It was definitely a new cycle, sort of like a rebirth. It felt so refreshing, like being reborn!

Jeremiah's Vision and Warning

One day I was enjoying a quiet moment, which is rare at my house. Jeremiah, who was about seven years old, came into the room crying. At first I thought that he had hurt himself and I just comforted him. When I asked him if he had been hurt, he said no. He would not speak about what was wrong, but only sobbed. He kept saying that it was so bad, that no one had ever had such a terrible thing as this happen. It was obvious that this was very painful for him. I tried my best to convince him to tell me what was wrong. He would not do it and we went on like this for about half an hour. I continued to comfort him.

I assured him that whatever it was we could resolve this, if he would just tell me what it was. I even explained I could not help if he didn't tell me what was wrong. He just continued to sob.

Finally I closed my eyes for a minute, and immediately I had an impression of what it was. Then other things began to make sense too. Recently he had acted strange when we parted. He would cling to me and say he felt sad, his heart hurt and he felt an empty feeling. I had wondered what was wrong and questioned him, but he didn't explain. That had been going on for about a week. He must have been intuiting the situation.

Then I asked him, "Has it anything to do with me?" He answered, "Yes!" and cried louder. I knew in my soul that what I suspected was true. Then I asked him if it had anything to do with *my life*. He said, "Yes, but how did you know?" "I just had a feeling" was my reply. At that point he finally opened up and told me what had happened.

Visitation by an Angel

He said he had been playing his violin in his bedroom, when for no apparent reason he fell to the floor with his violin beside him and began crying. He moved to the bed, and then saw a very large light blue angel in the corner by the closet doors. The angel had on a light blue robe with long sleeves that hung down his arms. His eyes were pure bright blue. The angel told him that he needed to concentrate with all his might on his violin. The angel said Jeremiah should try hard to do things right in his life and as perfect as he could. He told my son not to lie or do any other wrong things, so he could play better. He expressed that he was pleased that Jeremiah was playing the violin, but that he must concentrate on playing it more.

He said the angel also showed him a vision of himself falling out of a window and hurting his legs. The angel had said he would come to warn him later in life when he was in danger.

Then he told him something about me that made him sad. He told him that his mother's time on earth was almost up, and that she was calculating her remaining time wrong. Then the angel went back into a blue ball until there was only a bright ball of light left, and then disappeared. Jeremiah then ran to tell me, and all he could do was cry.

Hearing this, I explained to Jeremiah what had happened to me earlier in the Caribbean and about my life extension. I thought about what the angel had said regarding the time. I realized I had been calculating my time from the date when I asked how long my extension was. I understood now that I should have been calculating the time from the actual event in the Caribbean when the extension was first given to me. That was nine months difference. This event explained why the angel that appeared to Jeremiah and told him my time was almost up. Jeremiah and I cried together, and then we shared heart to heart. This also helped Jeremiah understand what the angel had explained to him about the importance of his violin playing.

I told him I would always be with him in his heart. For some reason during that time period, I had been teaching him how to contact me with his heart when we were apart. This was practice so he could learn to do this when I was gone away traveling, and eventually for use when one of us returns to the etheric.

My Secret Revealed

At this point I felt that I should share a secret with Jeremiah that I had known about him since before his birth. It was given to me in a vision while he was in the womb. One day in 1988 I felt the presence of God as I was praying. He spoke to me about the child Jeremiah that I was carrying. He told me that Jeremiah would have to learn to concentrate with his full attention on something for him to succeed in his life's mission. He said if Jeremiah were able to do this, things would go well with him. However, if life was not able to teach him that lesson, then he would be crippled and have to learn to walk again. He would have to learn the lesson of extreme concentration in that manner.

I was told that it would not be my fault if this happened and he would suffer no permanent damage. He would totally overcome all handicaps. I was not to blame myself if it happened, but just help him either way to learn this lesson. Later I was told to have him play the violin to learn that concentration was necessary for him to succeed.

Jeremiah and I bonded in a way difficult to describe. We both had a hard test coming up, and we both were looking to pass it with the least stress to our family and ourselves. The angel had shown Jeremiah a fall from a high place and an injury. When I told him what I knew from before his birth, it all made sense to him. All he needed to do was to place his attention on playing his violin. We decided he should practice an hour in the morning and at night.

Trying to Earn More Time

My situation was not so easy. I had felt a prompting by one of the master teachers, Saint Germain, to get up at 5 am and do a three-hour violet flame prayer vigil. My son Jeremiah had a vision that confirmed that I needed to do this. I tried for several months to do it. I had studied other people who had received life extensions like mine, and I was trying to figure out what if anything I could do to earn more time.

I was pregnant with Michael-Sean at the time when the angels appeared to us. It was a difficult pregnancy. I had been very sick this time, had very little energy and often had to lie down. I became very discouraged because of my inability to do the prayer vigil, and finally one day I just gave up. I decided if it was my time, I would just go, since I was unable to fulfill what God had asked of me. I would quit trying and "go home."

Three years passed and it was getting close to the end of the four-year extension. One day Paul was speaking to Mother. He then handed me the phone and encouraged me to tell her what was happening. "Tell her everything," he pleaded. I had shared my near-death experience with her previously, so she already knew I was on a life extension. So I told her about the recent events and how I was feeling like giving up and was very discouraged.

"I know what you are saying is the truth and I understand. We must do something here—your children need their mother and so you need to stay. We have to find the way to get an extension for you. Don't worry," she said. "We can do it. I am on my third extension. It can be done."

I cannot tell you how wonderful it is to be validated and understood when you are going through something like this. There are few who understand it, and very few who can really identify with it. It is a very lonely experience.

Then Mother asked me if I had been decreeing when I was in the Caribbean.

"Well, of course I was," I replied. "Every day!"

"Well," she said, "you certainly challenged some dark forces down there, and it most likely contributed to or caused your heart attack. There have probably been no calls made down there for a hundred years!

"Next time don't forget to call me for help before you try tackling something like this yourself. Make your calls in the name of the Messengers Mark and Elizabeth Prophet and the entire Spirit of the Great White Brotherhood. The dark forces would not want to take us on."

My mind immediately flashed back to the first time I ever saw Mother. She had come to teach a class for the retreat I was attending. I remember that my first impression was that she was not going to be here on earth much longer, and I could almost see through her. There was so little of her left in the physical octave.

She married shortly after that and I did not see her again until after the marriage. The change was dramatic! And I was surprised but pleased, because she looked very much anchored in the physical. I realized now what I had not understood then, that she had been given a life extension just as I had. That was why I had observed such a change in her. I could really identify with her experience since I had just lived through it myself. This realization took place in a millisecond, a flash of insight.

Mother asked me to hold the phone while she went to her altar to pray for me. I could hear her as she prayed. One thing in particular stood out as I listened. She called to the Angel of Record to look through the record of my lives, and find the place for a dispensation for me to continue this life. Her calls were so soothing to me. I felt a floodtide of hope wash over me.

When she returned to the phone, I thanked her. She asked if I would please keep her posted. She encouraged me to follow my intuitive feeling, to do my prayers, but Saint Germain said I could do them any time of day. She said she would pray for me every day. She added that I needed to say prayers regarding my children's lives because since this is in my karma, it would be in theirs also, as we share group karma. She said, "It's in your chart, so it's in theirs too. Do violet flame on them all."

She then also told me that I needed to do something big, something that would affect many other people's lives in a positive way. "Well," I said, "God has been prompting me to write a book about Paul's and my last life together." She said, "If God is prompting you, what are you waiting for? Write that book now!"

My Pledge to God

I said, "I'm not a writer!" "Just write it," she replied. She went on to explain about how I should write it. But I still did not feel confident to write this book. So I thought about it more and decided to publish a children's book that I had written years before. I felt I could gain experience with the process, and that book was so near ready to be published it could be done quickly. I began with that idea and discussed it at length with my husband. Then the idea came to me one night that I should make the book a fundraiser for our church building project and it could affect even more people. That night I decided to go ahead with that project, and I pledged to God that I would do it.

One intensely sunny day, I was leaving my office, absorbed in a conversation with our secretary, and I stepped out into the street without looking. As I did so I heard my husband yell, "Tonya, step back!"

Instinctively I stepped back without any hesitation as a speeding car whizzed by, missing me by a hair's breadth. Electrifying chills swept over my entire body. When I heard the roar of its accelerating engine, time stood still for what seemed an eternity. It was like life was on hold. I felt like I was floating in time and space.

It seemed as if a page in time turned. I had a feeling of knowing that the time of my death had just passed me by. On some level I knew it was OK now, that I had passed the time of danger. I had gone beyond when I would have left. Michael-Sean was safe in my womb and we were going to meet each other soon here on Earth instead of in heaven.

I felt relieved after that. I wasn't waiting for the other shoe to drop or feeling like I was standing under the sword of Damocles. Still, when I actually reached the exact month and date of the four-year extension, I was apprehensive. But nothing happened, except that it was a difficult and confusing month with many changes for our lives.

Later that month I received a puzzling call from my astrologer. She asked me if anything had happened during this month that was out of the ordinary or strange. I said, "No, not that I am aware of." She continued along this line for a while until I finally said to her, "What are you getting at? Would you get to the point!"

"Well," she said, "you had an aspect in your chart that indicated that you could have died, but obviously you are still here."

"What!" I said. "Why didn't you warn me?" She said, "It is generally agreed that we don't do that as astrologers, lest we plant something in the mind of the client that could trigger them to cause such as event because they expect it to happen."

That made sense to me. I told her about the last month's events and how I had once again received the grace of God to stay here and be with my family. She said she was glad I was still here. I said I was too!

I thought it was amazing that this would be in my chart. And Mother had mentioned the charts when she spoke to me, although it had not occurred to me to get our actual charts and decree over them. It would have been a good idea.

The astrologer said my chart showed if I made it through that time, I would be on Earth for a long time so not to worry. That made me very happy.

Jeremiah's Message from Heaven

The next morning, about one month from the first visitation, the angel returned to Jeremiah, who knew nothing about my decision or pledge made the night before. The angel told him that I had been granted 10 more years, but five years were contingent on my prayer work and 5 on my book being published. The angel was very pleased and praised Jeremiah's diligent work on the violin. He was very excited to come and tell me what the angel had said to him this time, and we were both very relieved to hear that message from heaven.

Whenever something seems to be going "wrong," I affirm out loud or to myself, "God is in charge!" Then I look for how He is in charge and what I have to gain or learn from the experience in which I find myself. It has turned situations around for me many times.

58

I AND MY MOTHER ARE ONE
Rekindling an Ancient Memory
by Larry Stanley

The Mother of the Flame knows the deep registering upon her being of world pain. So too, you must know this pain; for you cannot be sensitive to God and have ultimate communion with the Ascended Masters without being sensitive to the pain in the hearts and minds of the billions of people upon earth. Know this, beloved.

We the Ascended Masters do not walk in the fullness of joy ourselves, for while we work with earth's evolutions we also carry the burden of world pain. The sorrow of the Blessed Mary's heart is the sorrow of many souls in pain for want of shepherds, for want of teachers, for want of ministering servants who will give their lives for the consolation of many.
–Gautama Buddha, *Pearls of Wisdom*, Vol. 38, No. 21

I joined staff in July of 1973 when the Church was at La Tourelle in Colorado Springs. Like many of my new young friends who had been drawn to the teachings of Mark and Elizabeth Prophet, I had recognized the ancient lineage of the Masters and felt a calling to pursue the spiritual path.

I became keenly interested in these Teachings and had begun practicing decrees when I received the notice of

Mark Prophet's ascension. It was an incredible idea to me that someone had actually reached liberation from rebirth and had ascended just like Jesus Christ. I had to meet these people for myself, so I made quick arrangements to visit Colorado Springs for the Easter ascension class.

It was a remarkable experience. When I left to go back home at the end of that week, I felt like I was leaving home rather than returning. I knew I would be back. In July of that same year, my brother and I were accepted on the staff of The Summit Lighthouse. Knowing that I was renouncing a more worldly life, I packed up and moved to La Tourelle.

My first job was in the Graphics Department under the direction of Tom and Florence Miller, who soon became lifelong friends. One of my new acquaintances and fellow staff members was Donald. He taught me the ropes on how to do my job creating half-tone negatives that would print on the printing press.

The Power of Fiats

Donald loved to give fiats[1] while he worked and taught me some of them. After a while we would give them together. Donald and I became very creative and made up lists of positive affirmations that released great light. These fiats can raise the frequency of your environment when used correctly. They move energy and so we used them to help move the projects along quicker without hitches. They also are capable of raising your awareness and causing a spiritual high, to the point of making you giddy and quite happy. Pure spiritual energy was much more effective in raising my consciousness than the drugs of the day that I had given up and left behind.

This was the beginning of 25 years of service to the Ascended Masters, which were rich with personal spiritual experiences, personal instruction from my teacher, Elizabeth

---

[1] **Fiats** are verbal statements, affirmations of being that are given aloud.

Prophet, and the companionship of many fine devotees. During these years I became a staff photographer. This gave me the opportunity to work closely with Elizabeth, and over time we became very close friends. My position took me around the world with Mother to places like Australia and the Philippines, documenting her life and teachings.

Since Mother's illness I have continued to visit her from time to time. As the illness has progressed, her ability to speak has diminished but I can tell that she recognizes me. The twinkle in her eye and joy in her heart tells the story. I always fill her in on the current events of my life and occasionally she will surprise me with a short profound comment.

Only Female Disciple of Padma Sambhava

Tibetan history says that Yeshe Tsogya[2] was the only female disciple of Padma Sambhava.[3] She had perfect recall. She could listen to hours of teaching given by him and write it down verbatim. Mother told one of her assistants that this devotee was one of her embodiments. One of the great books that I have found is titled *Advice from the Lotus-Born*. This is a compilation of direct teaching by Padma Sambhava given to his 25 disciples, written by Yeshe Tsogyal. It's a marvelous book for serious devotees.

In 1999 I made a trip to Lhasa, Tibet, with my good friend Christopher and several other wonderful friends. There we met Bangri Rinpoche, a Tibetan lama who is also thought to be an embodiment of one of the 25 original disciples of Padma Sambhava. One evening in our hotel, Christopher, Debra and I were discussing how we might

[2] Though a consort of Padma Sambhava, Yeshe Tsogyal became a master in her own right. Both the Nyingma and Karma Kagyu schools of Tibetan Buddhism recognize Yeshe Tsogyal as a female Buddha.

[3] Padma Sambhava was the Indian yogi who laid the foundation for Lamaism, the Tibetan form of Buddhism. He is one of the most eminent figures in Tibetan Buddhism and lived in the eighth century A.D. The great Padma Sambhav teaches that one need only to look within oneself to find Truth.

broach the subject of his tie with Mother if it came up in conversation. We wanted to be careful not to offend the lama. Being in a foreign land we were unsure of what was appropriate and what might be seen as disrespectful. Our discussion was without a conclusion and we dropped the subject.

The next day when we went to tea with Bangri, he asked, "So, what do you have to tell me?" He explained that the night before "Your big Western God came to me and told me that you have something important to tell me." We looked at each other in disbelief and sensing the ever-watchful eye of El Morya, we proceeded to tell Rinpoche about our teacher.

We showed him a picture of Mother and told him that she was ill and that she was a student of Padma Sambhava. We then told him that she was our teacher as well. Tears then came to his eyes and he swooned. I believe he recognized Mother on the spot. Bangri then revealed to us that in Tibetan text it was stated that a woman would be reembodied in the West who would bring the teachings of Padma Sambhava to the Western world, confirming Mother was this woman. He selected an ancient Tibetan text that was in his prayer room and carefully unwrapped the aged paper, then proceeded to read to us this amazing revelation by Padma Sambhava. With firm conviction, Rinpoche then told us that he must come to America and see our teacher. He wanted to help.

Earlier in the day, we had attended the giving of mantras by Bangri and some of his monks. He then asked us to give him a demonstration of our prayers, so we demonstrated decrees for him. He was keenly interested in our teachings and commented that he had been studying the same teachings for 600 years and was excited to learn new practices.

The Defining Moment

Later that year it would come to pass that a trip for him to visit Mother was accomplished. Bangri came to

America to see Mother and traveled to the Inner Retreat in Montana. He was invited to teach from the altar in the chapel. That afternoon, Mother was in attendance and at the conclusion of the event they stood together on the altar in mutual respect and devotion to their common teacher, the Great Guru Padma Sambhava. It was the first time that I had ever witnessed Mother attempt to kneel before anyone other than the Ascended Masters. I believe she was kneeling in the presence of Padma Sambhava that she recognized in the person of Bangri Rinpoche. It was a moving moment for me and many others.

Upon his return to Tibet, Bangri was jailed by the Chinese government and given a 15-year prison sentence for actions against the state. He was accused of teaching his students Tibetan Buddhism and other subjects outside of the government's approved curriculum. After nearly 10 years, he is still in jail. We are all hoping that he will be released in the near future.[4] Please pray for my friend Bangri Rinpoche and his other monks. This is a holy man who dearly loves our Guru Ma. Personally, I would like to see him teaching and continuing the great lineage of Padma Sambhava in the United States in years to come. His wife, Nyima Choedren, was also imprisoned with her husband. She was released in 2006.

Homage to the Great Guru Padma Sambhava. Homage and gratitude to my Teacher Guru Ma.

[4] At this writing his fate is not known.

59

LOOK BEFORE YOU LEAP
"How I Love My Chelas!"
by Andrea Selestow

I have loved each of you profoundly, from the depths of my being, the most profound reaches of my soul. And if I have not been a perfect guru, I believe that I had perfect love for my students.   —Elizabeth Clare Prophet

My first week on Mother's personal staff I was hoping to make a good impression. Why then was I so dense! There was only a small space to walk between the dining room and kitchen. This particular morning as I came through the kitchen doorway, I saw Mother approaching. I thought surely there was enough room for both of us to cross pathways, but to my dismay I miscalculated and boom I hit her—smack on—like, pow! I was quite startled because we both got a jolt, plus I got some fire for allowing this to happen. What a great learning experience to be a part of the mysteries of being initiated by the guru.

Now as I look back at all the density I came to Mother with, I can see how I came away receiving so much enlightenment. I attribute this to the violet flame decrees and my daily personal contact with Mother. How blessed I am because Mother is all love and as her student, I know I did not have the gift of discernment, vision, knowledge or clarity of one who is the Messenger for the Great White Brotherhood.

I can witness that when I was in the presence of Mother, I almost always felt like I was actually in heaven on Earth. That conviction is from experiencing live dictations as well as my very personal conversations and soul tutoring with Mother. It was her aura and her energy field that made a difference and lifted me to a place that is indescribable. This spoke volumes about who she really is. The divine energy she created around her was so different from anything I have ever experienced. This is one of the many reasons in my mind that *there is no doubt Elizabeth Clare Prophet is truly a prophet and Messenger.*

I will try to explain to those who may not understand. She brought me up to a level and frequency that is totally different from the density of the physical plane. I experienced it tangibly. I lived it for the 20 years I served and was so blessed to have an opportunity that cannot be explained because it is just part of a dimension that is unexplainable.

Mother cared for me so very much. She showed me kindness and love and fun. We had many good laughs together.

A Very Special Christmas Treat

Christmas 1998 was quite special and unforgettable for me. I am sharing this particular story because I want everyone to know the teacher's love for all her students and just how very much she loves them.

At 7 am Mother knocked at the door and gave me a big surprise! She announced she wanted me to join her and share Christmas as part of her family. Obviously this was a rare treat and most unexpected. I explained to Mother I was supposed to be replaced at 7:30. But Mother insisted that this would be fine. This is what she would like. I accepted graciously and humbly. I was more excited than a child on Christmas morn, I think. We were served a great breakfast.

What a special thing it was for my little soul to be able to share Christmas with Mother! This was the greatest gift God gave me that day—to be with my guru.

With every present she opened (not necessarily from chelas), Mother affirmed, "Oh, how I love my chelas and how my chelas love me!" The great love of Mother for her chelas radiated from her as a great joy! Her love for me was no different from her love for all the other chelas. It was just my opportunity and a special Christmas treat Santa gave me on this Christmas at the Royal Teton Ranch.

When I left the Ranch, it was as though my body was going down. It was difficult to adjust to the different plane—because when I worked for Mother, I know she graced me by keeping me in the spiritual realm.

Tuck this in your hearts and remember Mother's words: *Oh, how I love my chelas and how my chelas love me!*

Mother and Andrea Selestow had a wonderful Christmas day 1998 at the Ranch in Montana

60

OUR BRIGADOON
An Unparalleled Opportunity
by a Community Member

You have seen our Mother now decree for a while with you. You have seen my decrees. You have heard her prayers and invocations for many years. All these are by way of teaching you, not by words alone but by the quality of heart, what it takes to so increase the fire of the heart that a space is cleared and a Buddha will ensconce himself right where you are.

And then you have peace, and you'll go about your service — and the Buddha will keep the flame and you will keep the action. You then become, as a soul, the Shakti of the Buddha who has come to be where you are.

—Lanello, *Pearls of Wisdom*, Vol. 26, No. 30

My first contact with Mother was a poster for a stump lecture that someone thrust into my hands. It was in Chicago in 1978 or 1979, and the poster had her picture on it—a beautiful, other-worldly photo, very etheric. I knew her at once. I taped the poster to the wall as soon as I got home. But I couldn't find anyone to go with me, so I didn't go. First initiation failed. I never did get to one of Mother's stumps.

It was three years later in another city that I finally found a local study group. I went to the next conference, then S.U., and right after S.U. I joined staff. I was on staff for about seven years at Camelot and the Inner Retreat, but I never became a permanent staff member. Nor did my job assignments require contact with Mother.

But to be a community member was an unparalleled opportunity. The daily rituals (morning, noon, and evening decrees), the weekly round of services (Sunday service, sometimes with a dictation; Tuesday evening decrees to El Morya; the Wednesday Jesus Watch; Friday the Ascension Service; Saturday's Saint Germain Service), the simple life with beautiful meals prepared for us so we could concentrate on our work assignments, and the work itself—all of it thrilled my soul.

And it was all Mother. What God did through her was phenomenal. In retrospect, I can see how carefully the community was constructed, not just to get the work done, but to put each of us shoulder to shoulder with those we had karma to work out with, to give us the opportunity to balance our karma in world service, to teach us the science of the spoken Word, and to show us—up close or at some distance—Mother.

When Mother was coming to a Sunday service, for instance, decrees would start at 9 am. The foundation would be set with decrees to Archangel Michael, violet flame, dweller calls and judgment calls, and other decrees to address the need of the hour. Hour by hour the decrees would become more and more fiery, and the light in the chapel would grow. When Mother was about to come, decrees to Astrea would begin, to clear the forcefield.

Sometimes it was difficult to stay the course and clear the opposition to the release of the Word to come, but when Mother came out on the platform, the sense of struggle ceased and there was only joy. Mother would have AV start a piece of very high classical music that she had selected, and then she would begin her invocation, such as could be heard nowhere else on the planet. She would call to the hosts of the Lord, asking for specific blessings for the planet and for the people. Even today, far from that time and place, my heart leaps when I hear those recorded invocations.

On Sunday Mother would often read from the Bible and sometimes give a sermon. I loved those sermons. She gave them without notes, just commenting on the Bible passages. Or sometimes she would read to us, long passages from Buddhist devotional texts or perhaps *Hiawatha* or Homer's *Odyssey*. Being read to by the Mother was like the Balm of Gilead. When she was done with her reading or her sermon, she would take her seat beside the altar and the meditation music would begin. After the dictation, there would be more meditation music and probably Holy Communion.

The stillness in the chapel at those times was profound. To say you could hear a pin drop would be an understatement. We were totally in our hearts. I have only recently realized that those heights of devotion, when my heart was filled to bursting with the love of God, came by her grace. We laid the groundwork through our decrees, but it was Mother who lifted us and carried us to the heights we so desired.

It was all by the Holy Spirit and not a formula. Anything could change at any time. We could never second-guess Mother. We could never say, "This is what Mother would do." What Mother would do was to follow the Holy Spirit and do as she was directed. "For my thoughts are not your thoughts, neither are your ways my ways, saith the LORD." If a staff member needed to be disciplined mid-service, the discipline was given. It was all of a piece—there was no saying that prayer was holy but fiery discipline of the human consciousness was not. The purpose of it all was alignment with the Mind of God and the development of higher consciousness in us.

Attending a conference was like five or ten Sunday services in a row. We entered a realm where time and space ceased to exist, a realm inhabited by thousands instead of

our usual hundreds.. The multiplication factor of our decrees was immense. It was at the conferences that Mother
gave many of her lectures. For weeks or months before
the class, she would work with her staff to construct lecture notes, and she delivered them well. But what–almost
literally–took our breath away were the moments when she
would look up from her notes and speak extemporaneously,
giving teaching by the Holy Spirit as it was delivered to her
for us in that moment.

Mother's lectures brought alive for us the teachings
of many religious traditions and showed us how there is only
one Teaching behind them all. From the outside, it might
appear that she was eclectic, drawing on many exoteric traditions. In fact, she was showing us that the source of all these
traditions was the esoteric teachings of the Brotherhood,
the Reality of God. She was showing us how the Teachings
have been expressed in many traditions–like the story of the
blind men describing the elephant–and training us in how
to talk to people with other backgrounds.

We have been told that Mother and Mark are very
high souls, that they had no obligation to this planet but
out of love they came to help us. We have also been told
that Mother was given the choice of being a yogi in the
Himalayas with a few advanced disciples, or embodying in
the West and contacting many souls. Through her worldwide stump lectures and her conferences, Mother touched
thousands and thousands of people. Thousands and thousands received the sealing of the Emerald Matrix in their
foreheads. Thousands and thousands saw her and, in that
sense, knew her. She is truly a worldwide spiritual leader,
as well as being a Guru in the Eastern tradition.

In 1997, toward the end of her active ministry,
Mother held a series of Darshans in King Arthur's Court at
the Royal Teton Ranch. These were a community initiation
and an initiation for each of us individually. Morya offered
to give each staff member a reading of the percentage of

karma already balanced, plus a comment on our path, on condition that we receive that information publicly, as required in the tradition of the Gurus. Mother took our names to the altar one by one and received a message for each of us, which she then delivered to us in open meetings.

Some had balanced more than 51 percent of their karma and in that respect could be considered candidates for the ascension. But Mother cautioned us that many of us had gone back and forth over the 51 percent mark for centuries (if not longer). She said she would like to offer a special class for those who had balanced 51 percent of their karma, because at that point one enters the emotional quadrant of the Cosmic Clock and the initiations become more complex and difficult to pass. That class, however, was not to be.

There have been many tests of idolatry in this organization, first and foremost the test of idolatry of Mother. It is difficult to attain exactly the right perception of the Messenger—to recognize her high office in hierarchy while at the same time to see her as the example of what we are and shall become, the one *like us* who has shown us how to live as the Christ, to walk by the promptings of the Holy Spirit, to become one with God. The cure for idolatry is the Teaching itself. Like Mother, we have the flame of God within, and like Mother, we can become that flame. As Mother once told S.U., "Strawberries don't worship strawberries."

It's easy for us to acknowledge that without the Holy Spirit, we cannot comprehend the Mind of God. It's perhaps harder for us to acknowledge—though it is every bit as true—that *with* the Holy Spirit, we *can* comprehend the Mind of God, and like Mother, we can live in it and through it.

In a staff meeting in 1997, El Morya announced that he was withdrawing his thread of protection through the Messenger, and that henceforth his ability to intercede for us would be on an individual basis based on our decree momentum, our devotion to God and our service to man. Many times we were warned in dictations not to take the

Messenger and the Masters for granted. We were told that there would come a time when the dictations would cease. And they did, gradually. In 1999 Mother retired. Like the Gurus of the East, she had taught us, and then she was withdrawn. It was time for us to sit under our own vine and fig tree, to prove the Law that we had internalized.

I will always be grateful that I had that opportunity of a lifetime and many lifetimes, to participate in a mystery school that comes only once in perhaps 10,000 years, which was intended to lay the foundation for the survival of this Path for the evolutions of this Earth, like Tibet before the Communist invasion. The mission of the Two Witnesses is ongoing. The planet is in jeopardy, and on a personal level, in order to qualify to present ourselves to God for his consideration as candidates for the ascension, we each must balance 51 percent of our karma, balance and expand our Threefold Flame, fulfill our divine plan through our sacred labor, become the Christ and offer that Christhood on the altar.

Indeed, in our personal attainment lies the key to the survival of the planet, for it has no reason to exist except as a platform of evolution for souls of light who are karmically tied to it. Ages ago, Sanat Kumara came to rescue this planet at a time when Cosmic Councils had decreed it be destroyed because its people had left off the inner walk with God and no longer worshiped the Trinity in the Threefold Flame of the heart. The planet becomes more secular and humanistic day by day. One ascension a year is required for its continued existence. If spirituality can no longer be taught nor religion even mentioned on this planet in coming years, how will the Lightbearers find their God and the path of the ascension?

May we each earn our victory, and swiftly, to give to our Mother and those who sponsor us the fruit they deserve for their millennia of most gracious intercession on our behalf.

Mother offers
encouragement
to Esta Buckland

Mother loved being
with her chelas

Mother admires the gift of
a 7-1/2 caret diamond ring
Sir Winston (Kenneth McNeel)
gave the Church

"Uncle Kenneth"
expresses his deep
appreciation and
love for Mother and
pledges his support
to her. Land of
Lanello 1973

In parting we leave you with the words of Mary Ellen Maunz (shown above):

Mother and Mark are two of the greatest souls one could ever hope to know. I know and remember that we have served with them for centuries. Each and every one of us has a portion to fulfill of the great mission of the Two Witnesses, whoever we are, wherever we serve. As we recall the precious teaching of Catherine of Siena: "Of myself I can do nothing. God doeth all," I offer my entire service to Mark and Mother, to whom I owe my very soul's survival.

Mother seals the Light in Deer Park Chapel at the North Ranch while Esta Buckland, seated in Lanello's chair, looks on. This would be the last service in this chapel, 1998.

Epilogue

Your recourse is to the Causal Body of the Mother of the Flame...who is in embodiment.

When you have recourse to one such as this Messenger, then you must take advantage of it! Just call to the Messenger to reinforce you, to protect you....Call to the Causal Body of the Messenger....Take advantage of the use of the Messenger's Causal Body while she is in embodiment. For it is a powerful, living, pulsating presence.

It is also very important that you make a call to the I AM Presence of the Messenger when you are in distress and bowed down. She will make that call at inner or outer levels, but the call will be made. For this is the vow that the Mother of the Flame has made to you, beloved, that she will always make calls for those of you who call to her, whether silently in the night or directly in person.

It is not necessary for you to write a letter to the Messenger. It is not necessary for you even to communicate with her, for she does all of this in her Higher Self.

–K-17 and Lanello, June 29, 1996

The Eternal Lamb

Most beloved sons and daughters of my heart, I AM come. And my presence is unprecedented, for the Lord God Almighty has decreed the fullness of myself within this temple as the only recourse to the downward acceleration of the deceleration of death in the Earth. Therefore we will hold a flame in the center of our own.

I occupy the temple of the Messenger, for there is none other that is prepared. I occupy until the coming of Christ the Lord within your temple. As no other manifestation that has been brought to you in this dispensation, so is my coming. And we are determined that the outcome of my coming shall be this: there shall be salvation in the Earth and the salvation shall be unto those who believe on the One Sent. . . .

Let the chelas not be tempted. Let them remain with the wife of their youth. For that wife is the living mother, and I, Sanat Kumara, am the Mother dwelling in the mother, being the source of the mother, being the beginning and the ending of the Universal Presence of the Woman clothed with the Sun. . . .

Let the Earth listen well. Let the chelas break the spell of darkness, for every initiated chela will know that I AM in the heart of the chela as I dwell fully and bodily in the temple of the Messenger and the embodied Guru. This is as it shall be. This is as it will be. And there will be no turning back of the terrible crystal and the intense white fire.

And to all who are of it, it is the warmth of the womb of Mother. It is the love of the fire of her heart. It is the crown of the Father. It is the release of all that you have prayed for. God will no longer deny it to the body of the faithful. I AM here. I will not be removed into a corner, and I AM here to stay until the plan of God is fulfilled.

Keep the faith. Endure unto the end of the age.

–Lord Sanat Kumara, June 29, 1979

Afterword

It would be so wonderful if this part of the book were unnecessary. But the Powers that Be, the Universe, the God of Very Gods have chosen to remove our dear Guru, Mother, Messenger, Mentor, and Teacher from our company. Oh, yes, we know there are very valid reasons for this move, not the least of which is that we are now forced to rise up higher to follow in her footsteps.

Mother said it best when she announced her retirement in 1999:

My Beloved Friends Whom I See in the Retreats Every Night,

I would speak to you about empowerment—El Morya's empowerment, the Messenger's empowerment and your own empowerment.

Beloved El Morya has placed his mantle upon me and he has risen higher in consciousness and service to life. By his grace and love, I have received this mantle. All of us have been empowered by El Morya since he gives us the power to direct our own affairs. So I, too, am empowering you to come up higher. I am determined to see you all the way home to your ascension by your own efforts.

Because of the honor and responsibility of El Morya's mantle and my larger assignment of holding the balance of both positive and negative planetary karma, I am compelled to give you some guidelines about what I can and cannot do for you.

Because of my health and my upcoming retirement, my role has changed in some respects. However, I still retain my spiritual mantles and the sponsorship of the Great White Brotherhood.

K-17 and Lanello explained in their dictation of June 29, 1996, how your prayers can be answered and how I can maintain the Guru-chela relationship with you:

As the Messenger has mentioned, we ask you to write letters to us, Lanello and K-17. You may address us jointly in a letter. Keep a copy of your letter and burn another copy so that you can see

how we have answered your calls almost imme-
diately and what progress you are making by
writing to us. This is fruitful. And therefore, make
it the last thing you do as you retire. Write that let-
ter to us and burn it. This is our gift to you, beloved.

I have received countless confirmations of the above dispensation and I trust that you will take advantage of it. Many of you have written me saying that when you have called on the mantle of the Messengers or burned your letter to me or an Ascended Master, your problem was immediately resolved or alleviated in some way. It tickles me when I hear about these miracles and El Morya winks in agreement.

My answer to my staff and all who have written to me about becoming my chela is: I accept each and every one of you as my chela. Your chelaship is hereby approved and sustained as long as you do not compromise your responsibilities and continue to honor the Guru-chela relationship. Again, this is an inner relationship and does not have to be confirmed by me on the outer. I will help you at inner levels.

The moment you write to me, I receive your letter on inner levels. . . . My Holy Christ Self goes before the altar of God and petitions for intercession on your behalf. So you see that you do not even need to mail your letter. You may burn it as Lanello and K-17 have instructed or simply make the call to my Holy Christ Self.

My beloved one, as we transform ourselves into the likeness of God, we are moving with the winds of the Holy Spirit. This is not separation but bonding. The Guru-chela relationship comes down to a matter of oneness—the oneness that I feel with you and the oneness that, in reality, we are. We are as close as heartbeat, beloved.

I profoundly thank each and every one of you who have prayed for me and for the healing of my body temple.

May we continue to inwardly commune as friends, peers and living Christs in service to our Mighty I AM Presence, the Ascended Masters and our beloved Bapu, El Morya.

–Mother, March 22, 1999 (excerpts)

Mother did everything possible to prepare us to pass our tests and go up the mountain after her. She gave us the roadmap for our victory in a lecture given on May 20, 1989 entitled:

"The Temptation of the Chela: To Attain or Not to Attain God-Self Mastery"

The person of the Evil One will come to tempt you when you decide to displace the unreal self with the Real Self. Hasn't he come already? Maybe you didn't recognize him. Maybe you thought you heard yourself saying to yourself, "Why should I struggle? God did not intend me to struggle." Well, that's not you talking to yourself, that's the devil talking to you. Those are the words the fallen angels whisper in your ear. They say, "Take the broad way, the easy street. No need to struggle. Life should be a bowl of cherries—and if it isn't, then there's something wrong with your religion or your Guru."

But the mighty work of the ages is to attain self-mastery, and God-Self mastery, day by day, right while one is bearing and balancing one's karma. To be successful at it you have to become a career son or daughter of God. To stand, face, and conquer self and karma takes all of your strength and will and mind. It takes complete concentration. It takes self-discipline. It takes an unselfed love for God that grows and grows with each trial and testing of our souls.

For only Love can win the prize. Because to be your Real Self in this world means you are going to have to go against the tide of your past karma and the entire momentum of your human consciousness and creation. What's more, you'll be challenged by the whole world and its momentum of the human consciousness and creation. Because you're no longer going downstream with the people trends, you're going upstream with the God trends!

Just as Mother said she will never give up on us, we should never give up on her. Just as Mother said she would be our Guru as long as we would have her, we should remember to invoke the assistance of her mantles. Just as she would never stop praying for anyone in need, so we should never stop praying for her. Just as she would hold the immaculate concept for us, so let us do the same for her.

Bend the knee before your Holy Christ Self and say:

My beloved Holy Christ Self, I will listen to your voice and I will obey you, no matter what. I will not argue with you. I will not deny your voice. I will not drown it out with my human reason or my human desires or my human preferences.

Yes, I will seek you, my Holy Christ Self. I will seek the Rock of my Christhood. And I ask that my human consciousness be broken upon that Rock, once and for all, so that I might have my victory.

And in having that victory, may I remain in the earth in good health and in soundness of mind that God in me might deliver those souls who must also have their victory over their disobedience to the promptings of their Holy Christ Self.

I pray especially for those souls who are weak in body and weak in mind and weak in spirit that they might have their victory over the flesh as well as over all disobedience to their Holy Christ Self.

–The Maha Chohan, *Pearls of Wisdom*, Vol. 38, No.

GLOSSARY

Akasha: A subtle, etheric substance that fills all of space, on which is recorded everything that has ever happened in a particular location. The akashic records can be read by those with developed soul faculties.

Angel deva: A guardian spirit that dwells in nature and assists people to put on the higher consciousness specific to that particular locality.

Animal magnetism: A lower human substance that clouds the mind and causes people to be tools of darkness. This substance must be cast out and transmuted by the use of the violet flame. There are four types of animal magnetism: malicious, ignorant, sympathetic and delicious.

Ascended Masters: Beings like you and me who were quickened by the Holy Spirit, followed the Path to union with the Higher Self, completed their mission on Earth, balanced at least 51 percent of their karma, and returned to the heart of God in the ritual called the ascension. Every year at least one person must ascend from this planet in order to keep the Earth spinning. That person may be a pope, a yogi in the Himalayas or, as Mark said, your Aunt Millie.

Ascension: The permanent reunion of the soul with God—freedom from the cycle of death and rebirth.

Attunement: Becoming one with the presence of God and then acting from that level. Mother Mary said: Attunement is somewhat of a subconscious quality. It is begun with the outer mind; it is begun by its supplication, by the prayer to the Holy Christ Self to take command and continue the prayers and decrees of your heart throughout the twenty-four hours. This is an important request, and it should be made by you each morning before you even rise from your bed.

Calls: Powerful prayers, fervent commands given by the authority of the God within. It's a known fact that in life-and-death matters, people spontaneously cry out to God with an intense fire of the heart.

Causal Body: The bands of color around the I AM Presence. These are the reservoir of all the good that the soul has done since it first came into being.

Chela: A Hindi term used to designate the disciple of a teacher or guru; also, an exceptionally self-disciplined and devoted student of the Ascended Masters' teachings. In its highest manifestation, a chela is a devotee accepted by a specific Ascended Master for initiation. Derived from the Sanskrit word for "servant" or "slave."

Chelaship: The process in which a student or disciple of a Guru is tried, tested and initiated to strengthen his resolve and to prove his love for God and Guru. It is the path of initiation, the way to realize Christhood, and the means of transition from the plane of the mass consciousness to the heights of God consciousness. The byword of the chela is "Obey immediately!"

Christhood: Union with the Higher Self, also called the Christ Self or Holy Christ Self. One who achieves this union becomes the Christ, as did Jesus the Christ, who came to set the example of the path for us to follow.

Cosmic Clock: A science of understanding personal psychology and karma by plotting the qualities of God and their perversions by man on the twelve lines of the clock, and using this chart to anticipate the tests to come in the cycles of time. This science was a gift of Mother Mary to mankind through Mark and Elizabeth Prophet for our use in passing our tests on the Path.

Darjeeling Council: Led by El Morya and headquartered at his etheric retreat in Darjeeling, India, including the Ascended Masters and their chelas in embodiment. The Darjeeling Council tutors and guides those who serve in the governments and economies of the nations, as their free will permits.

Darshan: The Hindi word darshan comes from the Sanskrit darshana, meaning "seeing" or "looking at." According to the Encyclopedia of Eastern Philosophy and Religion, every encounter with a guru or holy person can be regarded as darshan. The Ascended Masters teach that darshan is the holy sight of the guru, through whom the light of God flows. It is communion with the Ascended Masters through the Messenger's "mantle," which brings blessings of holiness, purification and the transfer of light and the initiation of spirals of God consciousness within the chakras. A dictation from an Ascended Master is the highest form of darshan.

Decree: More powerful than other forms of prayer, a specifically worded petition to the Godhead for constructive personal and planetary change, given aloud by a son or daughter of God in His name and in accordance with His will. "Thou shalt also decree a thing, and it shall be established unto thee: and the light shall shine upon thy ways." (Job 22:28)

Discarnate: Generally a person who has died and has not merited entrance into the etheric plane, but is lingering for various reasons in the lower, astral plane. Also referred to as a discarnate entity.

Electronic belt: The residue of negative karma that requires redemption. It can be visualized in a kettledrum shape extending from the waist to beneath the feet. It contains the cause, effect, record, and memory of our personal karma in its negative aspect.

Elementals: Nature spirits who offer their selfless service to construct and maintain the physical plane so that we can evolve here. They do not have a Threefold Flame nor do they have the opportunity for personal immortality. There are four types of elementals corresponding to the four elements: salamanders (fire), sylphs (air), undines (water) and gnomes (earth).

Entity: A disembodied spirit; a discarnate.

Fohat: The constructive, creative power by which planetary systems are formed, Earth changes occur.

Four lower bodies: The physical, emotional, mental and etheric (or memory) bodies, which we use while we walk the Earth. We also have three higher bodies: the Holy Christ Self, the I AM Presence, and the Causal Body.

Great Karmic Board: A board of eight members (known as the Lords of Karma) that administers divine justice and determines the destiny of souls, countries and planets. In effect, they are the Supreme Court of this solar system. Before each incarnation, the Karmic Board gives us our assignment for this lifetime and tells us what karma we will be required to balance. After the transition called death, we go before the Karmic Board again to receive a life review. Some people remember receiving their assignment before birth, and some people who have had near-death experiences remember the life review.

Great White Brotherhood: The group of ascended and some unascended masters; so called because their light is great enough to give them a white aura, although they may have any color of skin.

Hierarchy: The universal chain of individualized God-free beings fulfilling the attributes and aspects of God's infinite Selfhood. Included in the cosmic hierarchical scheme are Solar Logoi, Elohim, Sons and Daughters of God, ascended and unascended masters with their circles of chelas, Cosmic Beings, the Twelve hierarchies of the Sun, archangels and angels of the sacred fire, children of the light, nature spirits (called elementals) and twin flames of the Alpha/Omega polarity sponsoring planetary and galactic systems.

Holy Christ Self: The guardian angel, the Higher Self, the voice of conscience, the Mediator between your soul and God individualized in you, the I AM Presence.

I AM Presence: God personified for each individual; your God Source and your real identity. See Elizabeth Clare Prophet, Access the Power of Your Higher Self (Pocket Guide available from The Summit Lighthouse), for a full explanation. Also referred to as the Divine Presence.

Karma: The law of cause and effect, or the law of the circle, operating from lifetime to lifetime: "Whatsoever a man soweth, that shall he also reap." (Gal. 6:7)

Keepers of the Flame Fraternity: A nondenominational spiritual order founded by Saint Germain. Its members (both men and women) pledge to keep the flame for the incoming golden age of freedom, peace and enlightenment.

Keynote: A specific piece of music that brings forth the energy pattern of a particular soul of light, an angel, an Archangel or an Ascended Master. It is the key to their Causal Body and captures the frequency of their I AM Presence.

Lightbearers: A group of 144,000 souls originally from Venus, who incarnated on Earth eons ago. Their mission is to save the planet and liberate its people from the forces of darkness and ignorance of their true nature in God.

Mandala: A Sanskrit word, loosely translated to mean "circle."

Mantle, Spiritual: Best described as a spiritual office or a position in hierarchy. Another definition is a canopy, a sustaining presence. There are many mantles, even the mantle of chela. These mantles are earned by passing spiritual tests and gaining mastery, by maintaining God-control in the face of challenges. They are bestowed by the Ascended Masters and are not passed along from person to person like an inheritance.

Maya: A Hindu term meaning "illusion," generally applied to what we consider the reality of our normal daily life on Earth.

Messenger: One anointed by God to bear witness to the Truth and trained to bring forth the teachings of the Ascended Masters for a people and an age.

Mudra: A specific, powerful positioning of the hands to achieve a desired spiritual effect, most commonly used in India. Buddhas and Hindu deities are generally depicted in art and statuary using the mudra traditionally associated with them.

Path of the Ruby Ray: A path of intense initiation through the highest form of love, for those who are working toward their ascension.

Pearls of Wisdom: Messages from the Ascended Masters in the form of weekly letters to their students delivered through their Messengers Mark and Elizabeth Clare Prophet, beginning in 1958. Many of these weekly Pearls have been collected and bound in annual volumes.

Psychic: In its highest form, someone who has developed senses of the soul, an extraordinary spiritual awareness of the higher (etheric) octave and a protected awareness of lower planes. However, most commonly this term refers to a person who is sensitive to entities inhabiting the lower astral plane. Channels are connected to the astral plane, not to the etheric plane.

Rays: The seven color rays (blue, yellow, pink, white, green, purple and gold, and violet) are aspects of God's energy that emanate from Him. There are also five secret rays, whose colors have not all been revealed to us.

Ruby Ray: is the fiery core of the love ray. The Ruby Ray is an intense light for a purging of darkness as no other ray can purge. It is the intensity of the essence of the very Blood of Christ. This fiery light judges and rebukes every evil form.

Reincarnation: The means devised by God so that a soul whose work on Earth is not complete at the time of the change called death is granted another opportunity to be reborn in a new body. Also referred to as re-embodiment.

Tag: A specified time slot to decree directly for the Messenger, so called because each shift of taggers couldn't leave until replacements arrived.

Threefold Flame: The spark of God inside the secret chamber of the heart chakra. This spiritual focus consists of three plumes, representing the divine attributes of blue for power, yellow for wisdom and pink for love. It is the work of a lifetime to balance and expand this flame.

Twin flames: Masculine and feminine counterparts created by God in the beginning, out of the same I AM Presence. Each of us has a twin flame, whom we may or may not know in this life, depending on our karma. Some people are inspired to follow a spiritual path by their twin flame who is already ascended.

Violet flame: An aspect of the sacred fire, the "cosmic eraser" that can transform the past, the present, and the future when we invoke it in accordance with God's Will and with love for all mankind. Forgiveness, mercy and freedom are qualities of the violet flame. All who have ever ascended have used the violet flame for transmutation, either as an outward practice in the mystery schools of the Brotherhood or in their etheric retreats. In the early part of the twentieth century, Saint Germain at great personal risk was granted the dispensation by the Godhead to release this key teaching to the planet at large.

Watchers: Fallen angels.

SUGGESTED RESOURCES AND TOOLS

All for the Love of God: Life with Mark Prophet, a Modern-Day Mystic
by Alex Reichardt with Margaret Reichardt and Other Disciples
Read about Elizabeth Clare Prophet's life with her husband, Mark Prophet. Softbound 314 pages. Over 40 pages of photos. Available through www.Amazon.com or www.BarnesandNoble.com.

The following items are Summit Lighthouse publications (800-245 -5445, www.tsl.org.

In My Own Words: Memoirs of a Twentieth-Century Mystic
by Elizabeth Clare Prophet
Now for the first time, the real story—in her own words. From her birth in Long Branch, New Jersey until, at age 22, she goes to Washington D.C. to start her new life with her twin flame and future husband, Mark Prophet. Also available as an e-book on Amazon. com. Summit Lighthouse item #7002, Softbound 242 pages.

Wallet Cards (2-1/4 x 3-1/2 laminated full-color picture)
Mark L. Prophet: Summit Lighthouse item #2942
Elizabeth Clare Prophet: Summit Lighthouse item #3087
These are the two pictures of the Messengers recommended for altar use. The photo of Mother is signed, "All my love, Mother." This photo of Mark was taken as he was sending love to his chelas and holding the vision of our ascension, our victory in the light. Lanello expounded on this in his dictation given on March 1, 1992, printed as Pearl of Wisdom Vol. 35, No. 10.

Inner Perspectives: A Guidebook for the Spiritual Journey
Mark L. Prophet and Elizabeth Clare Prophet
A series of radio interviews with Elizabeth Clare Prophet in the spring of 1977 on the basic precepts of the Teachings of the Ascended Masters. Remarkable fifteen-minute programs covering a vast array of material with thoroughness and clarity, most of which had never been discussed publicly before, shedding light on some of life's deepest mysteries. Summit Lighthouse item #7011, softbound, 365 pages. Subscribe to free audio podcasts of these interviews at iTunes.

"I'm Stumping for the Coming Revolution in Higher Consciousness!"
On February 3, 1978, Elizabeth Clare Prophet left Los Angeles with a team of twenty-four men and women, two buses, one four-axle truck—and an urgent message to deliver to over five million people in fifty-four cities throughout the United States and Canada. When local newsmen asked what prompted the surprise visit, "I'm stumping for the Coming Revolution!" was her immediate, enthusiastic reply. Available from www.TSL.org / bookstore / CD on Demand.

Angels: A Seminar on How to Contact Angels–Your Guides, Guardians and Friends
Includes lectures, meditations, songs, decrees (introductory pace), invocations, and dictations. The Messenger Elizabeth Clare Prophet traveled throughout the United States and Canada to deliver this teaching on the reality of the angels, the great assistance they can render mankind, and how we can appeal to them and invoke their presence in our lives. Summit Lighthouse item #ME07002, Complete Seminar. 24 hours, 15 minutes (2 MP3 CDs).

Soul Mates and Twin Flames: The Spiritual Dimension of Love and Relationships
by Elizabeth Clare Prophet
Elizabeth Clare Prophet reveals some of the great mysteries regarding relationships. She explains the difference between:
• soul mates (drawn together to fulfill a specific mission)
• twin flames (created as one in the beginning)
• karmic partners
She also provides techniques that can help you develop deep and lasting relationships. Summit Lighthouse item #4465, softbound, 188 pages.

Community: A Journey to the Heart of Spiritual Community
by Elizabeth Clare Prophet
In every age the great spiritual teachers have established their communities—Gautama Buddha and his sangha, Jesus and his disciples, Saint Francis and his brothers. In this book Elizabeth Clare Prophet draws on the teachings of the Ascended Masters to explain the universal principles of true community. She also draws on her many years of experience as leader of a spiritual

community to present examples of the challenges and joys of applying these principles in the real world. The book also includes commentary on the spiritual classic New Era Community by Nicholas and Helena Roerich. Summit Lighthouse item #7005, softbound, 284 pages.

THE SCIENCE OF THE SPOKEN WORD

The Science of the Spoken Word
by Mark L. Prophet and Elizabeth Clare Prophet
Help from "heaven's 911 team"–the angels and Ascended Masters–is just a call away. This handbook will teach you how to invoke God's intercession to solve specific personal and planetary problems. The authors present the most powerful and profound message on techniques of spoken prayer in print today. Explains how to use prayers, mantras, affirmations, decrees and meditations. Softbound, 218 pages.

Rise and Shine! Morning Decrees with Mother
Summit Lighthouse item #D99019, 1 CD 74 min., Pace: Intermediate+, Booklet with words included,

Save the World with Violet Flame! #1 - Elizabeth Clare Prophet
Summit Lighthouse item #D88019, 2 CD Set (Introductory pace)

Save the World with Violet Flame! #2
Summit Lighthouse item #D88034, 2 CD Set (Intermediate pace)

Save the World with Violet Flame! #3
Summit Lighthouse item #D88083, 2 CD Set (Intermediate+ pace)

Save the World with Violet Flame! #4
Summit Lighthouse item #D88117, 2 CD Set (Intermediate+ pace)

Lightbearers of the World, Unite! Decree book–Ascended Master Decrees, Mantras and Songs
Excellent beginning decree book for all ages. Includes visualizations, basic instruction on leading decrees, complete chart of the seven rays with color, day, chakra, archangel and qualities for each. Full-color illustrations, spiral bound. Summit Lighthouse item #5205,181 pages. Companion CD available at The Summit Lighthouse.

Watch With Me Jesus' Vigil of the Hours
In 1964 the Ascended Master Jesus Christ inaugurated the "Watch With Me" Jesus' Vigil of the Hours--a worldwide service of prayers, affirmations and hymns for the protection of the Christ consciousness in every son and daughter of God. This service commemorates the vigil the Master kept alone in the Garden of Gethsemane when he said: "Could ye not watch with me one hour?" The Lord Jesus has called students of the Ascended Masters to give the Watch individually or in group action once a week, at the same time each week, so that at every hour of the day and night someone somewhere is keeping the vigil. On this recording Elizabeth Clare Prophet with disciples of Jesus join you in full voice as you give your Watch each week. The choir and musical accompaniment will enable you to participate in the singing of the hymns of praise that form a part of the service. This audio CD is the companion product for the Watch With Me booklet. Note: This CD does not include a Child's Rosary as does the booklet. Summit Lighthouse item #D87096, 1 Audio CD, total time 78 min. Summit Lighthouse item #115, booklet 44 pages

CLIMB THE HIGHEST MOUNTAIN SERIES
by Mark L. Prophet and Elizabeth Clare Prophet
This series includes teachings given to the Messengers that were to serve as the Everlasting Gospel for the Aquarian Age

The Path of the Higher Self, Volume 1
This cornerstone of metaphysical literature explores a cornucopia of topics important to every spiritual seeker: the destiny of the soul, the difference between soul and Spirit, the role of the Christ, positive and negative karma, and how to contact the Higher Self and the spark of God within the heart. Summit Lighthouse item #4399, softbound 700 pages

The Path of Self-Transformation, Volume 2
Continuation of teachings on the inner mysteries of God, lifting the veil to reveal the true understanding of biblical allegory, including the mystical meaning of the "fall" of Adam and Eve. Answers profound spiritual questions supremely relevant for today. Summit Lighthouse item #4482, softbound, 339 pages

The Masters and the Spiritual Path, Volume 3
There are Masters who have come out of all the world's great

spiritual traditions. These great lights of East and West have graduated from Earth's schoolroom and reunited with Spirit in the process known as the ascension. The Masters tell us that they are examples and not exceptions to the rule. We, too, are destined to fulfill our life's purpose and reunite with Spirit. This intriguing work offers an innovative perspective on the universe and your role in it. Summit Lighthouse item #4491, softbound, 334 pages

The Path of Brotherhood, Volume 4

Prior to the "Fall" on the ancient continent of Lemuria, men and women lived blissfully in a golden-age paradise. Their souls evolved in love, peace and harmony. Everyone embodied the principle of being their brother's keeper. In the dark ages that occurred after the fall, souls lost their moorings, their sense of unity and oneness with God and became increasingly aware of their sense of separation and outer differences. Today, many pay lip service to the principles of brotherly love while their minds are often full of condemnation, and they are seething with emotion against one another. Even some churches have become more engaged in the struggle with one another than in training men and women for the vicissitudes of life. In The Path of Brotherhood, Mark and Elizabeth Prophet demonstrate how brotherhood is possible, and crucial, today. They take a mystical look at the Twelve Tribes, the Twelve Apostles, the Golden-Age Family and spiritual keys to reaching world brotherhood, which includes the realization of a spirit of unity and cooperation in spiritual organizations. Summit Lighthouse item #4502, softbound, 242 pages

The Path of the Universal Christ, Volume 5

In this volume, the authors recapture the heart of the Master's message: You, like Jesus, are meant to realize your own innate Divinity. You are destined to become one with your own Higher Self, your "Christ Self." Church fathers suppressed Jesus' original teaching on the Christ within. This book reveals our true inner identity and the true goal of our life on Earth. Rediscover Jesus' lost keys to finding God within and learn how to contact your own inner source and access your unlimited potential. Summit Lighthouse item #4501, softbound, 288 pages

Paths of Light and Darkness, Volume 6

The battle of light and darkness is not new. But there is a prophesied end to this battle, and how the prophecy unfolds in the interplay of light and darkness is determined by free will. Learn the key strategies in this battle that affect your heart and mind and how to navigate them successfully. This may be the most important book in the entire Climb the Highest Mountain series. If you thought Star Wars was fun, wait until you read about our story that began in other galaxies and other systems of worlds! Summit Lighthouse item #4516, softbound 316 pages

The Path to Immortality, Volume 7
What is immortality? Here's a powerfully liberating perspective from the Ascended Masters: Immortality is our divine right and the destiny of our souls. Read about the mysteries of the Book of Life, tests of the Sacred Fire at Luxor, Entities: the psychic world, and much more. Summit Lighthouse item #4503, Softbound, 528 pages

The Path of Christ or Antichrist, Volume 8
If you had to choose right now between the light of Christ and darkness of Antichrist, which would you choose? Most would say the Light, of course! But if the strategies and practices of the forces of Antichrist were carefully calculated to deceive and confuse you, would you know the difference? Here's a true guide to help you divide the real from the unreal. Summit Lighthouse item #4504, softbound, 352 pages

The Path to Attainment, Volume 9
How to find your way Home. Your blueprint for graduating from Earth's schoolroom. The completion of the outline of the thirty-three steps of initiation on the ladder of attainment. Apply these keys from the Masters to propel your soul towards the ultimate reunion. Profound yet practical, what it takes to finally master life on Earth. Summit Lighthouse item #4509, softbound, 448 pages, 15 B&W Illustrations, 1 Color Illustration

THE MYSTICAL PATHS OF THE WORLD'S RELIGIONS
Beginning in 1992, Elizabeth Clare Prophet delivered a series of lectures in which she explored the mystical tradition and teaching in many of the world's major religions.

The Buddhic Essence
Bodhisattva is a Sanskrit term meaning literally a being of bodhi (or enlightenment), a being destined for enlightenment, or one

whose energy and power is directed toward enlightenment. A Bodhisattva is one who is destined to become a Buddha but has foregone the bliss of nirvana with a vow to save all children of God on Earth. Disc 1 Become the Buddha. Disc 2 The Ten Stages of the Bodhisattva Path. Summit Lighthouse item #DVSETL93010, 2 DVDs, 1 h. 55 m.

Roots of Christian Mysticism: The Indwelling Presence of God
Elizabeth Clare Prophet introduces you to a remarkable group of mystics who for hundreds of years have practiced their own brand of Christianity—from Origen of Alexandria and Meister Eckhart to Catherine of Siena and Mother Teresa. The Christian mystics talk about spiritual union and the love initiations that accompany it. Summit Lighthouse item #DVSETP09001, 3 DVD Set, 4 hr. 27 min.

The Kabbalah and the Temple of Man
DVD Titles:
• The Big Bang and Jewish Mysticism
• Creation of the Tree of Life
• Emanations of God
• The Origin of Evil
Summit Lighthouse item #DVSET92056, 4 60-minute DVDs

TSL Videos on YouTube (Volume 1)
Short excerpts of Elizabeth Clare Prophet explaining the Teachings of the Ascended Masters.
The first fourteen video clips of Elizabeth Clare Prophet uploaded to The Summit Lighthouse YouTube Channel.
Includes: Your Real Inner Self - Your Divine Self - Your Causal Body Treasures - Fulfilling Your Reason for Being - Kabbalah: Tiferet as the Universal Christ - Kabbalah: Secret Merkabah Mysticism; Ezekiel's Ascension Chariot - Kabbalah: Early Rabbinic Mysticism of the Prophets - Violet Flame and the Seven Chakras - Become the Buddha - Mantra for Healing Personal and National Economies - Creative Abundance: Keys to Spiritual Prosperity - On the Ascension - Learning to Care for the Soul - Strengthening the Soul - Gautama Buddha Meditation
1 DVD, 85 minutes. Summit Lighthouse item #DVP09007

Kabbalah: Key to Your Inner Power
by Elizabeth Clare Prophet, Patricia Spadaro, and Murray Steinman

Explore the once-secret Jewish mystical tradition known as Kabbalah. Elizabeth Clare Prophet says in the introduction, "My goal is to bring to life the path of the Jewish mystics—to share with you their joys and ecstasies, their sacred visions and their practical techniques for experiencing the sacred in everyday life." 36 Illustrations, 19 charts and diagrams, pronunciation guide included. Summit Lighthouse item #269183, softbound 284 pages

THE LOST TEACHINGS OF THE BIBLE AND JESUS

Fallen Angels and the Origins of Evil
by Elizabeth Clare Prophet
Did rebel angels take on human bodies to fulfill their lust for the "daughters of men"? Did these fallen angels teach men to build weapons of war? That is the premise of the Book of Enoch, a text cherished by the Essenes, early Jews and Christians but later condemned by both rabbis and Church Fathers. The book was denounced, banned and "lost" for over a thousand years—until in 1773 a Scottish explorer discovered three copies in Ethiopia.

Elizabeth Clare Prophet examines the controversy surrounding this book and sheds new light on Enoch's forbidden mysteries. She demonstrates that Jesus and the apostles studied the Book of Enoch and tells why Church Fathers suppressed its teaching that angels could incarnate in human bodies. Fallen Angels and the Origins of Evil takes you back to the primordial drama of Good and Evil, when the first hint of corruption entered a pristine world--Earth. Contains Richard Laurence's translation of the Book of Enoch, all the other Enoch texts (including the Book of the Secrets of Enoch), biblical parallels. Also available as an e-book on www.Amazon.com. Summit Lighthouse item #4483, softbound, 514 pages

The Lost Years and the Lost Teachings of Jesus
At age thirteen Jesus departs Jerusalem with merchants and sets out towards the Sind (present-day southeast Pakistan). His purpose: "perfecting himself in the Divine Word and studying the laws of the great Buddhas." Includes: Chronology of Jesus' travels to the East. Discussion of the extant writings and oral traditions proving that Jesus taught after his resurrection. *The Secret Gospel of Mark* discovered by scholar Morton Smith in 1958. Summit Lighthouse item DVD, #DVL08001

Mary Magdalene and the Divine Feminine: Jesus' Lost Teachings on Woman
by Elizabeth Clare Prophet with Annice Booth
Answers today's controversial questions: Is God only Male? Who is the Divine Mother? What was Jesus' relationship with Mary Magdalene? Were they married? What is "original sin" and why did early church fathers create it? Does celibacy for priests actually work? What was Jesus' teaching on women's roles in church and society? Does gender have a bearing on spiritual attainment? Summit Lighthouse item #6352, Softbound, 320 pages, Special Features: Question & Answer section, 2 maps, 1 color and 25 B&W illustrations

Reincarnation: The Missing Link in Christianity
by Elizabeth Clare Prophet with Erin L. Prophet
A long time ago Christians believed in reincarnation. This groundbreaking work makes the case that Jesus taught reincarnation. Elizabeth Clare Prophet traces the history of reincarnation in Christianity—from Jesus and the early Christians through Church councils and the persecution of so-called heretics. Using the latest scholarship and evidence from the Dead Sea scrolls and Gnostic texts, she also argues persuasively that Jesus was a mystic who taught that our destiny is to unite with the God within. Your view of Jesus—and of Christianity—will never be the same. Summit Lighthouse item #4380, softbound book, 393 pages

ASCENDED MASTERS

Lords of the Seven Rays: Mirror of Consciousness
by Mark L. Prophet and Elizabeth Clare Prophet
An introduction to seven Ascended Masters who are ready to tutor and revitalize your soul. Reviews their teachings, their past lives and their universities of the spirit. By exploring their unique paths to spiritual mastery, you will find comfort, inspiration and invaluable keys for your own walk with God.
Summit Lighthouse item #2079, pocketbook 608 page, 72 B&W illustrations

The Chela and the Path: Keys to Soul Mastery in the Aquarian Age
by El Morya through his Messenger Elizabeth Clare Prophet
Little traditional biographical information is available about El Morya Khan. He is perhaps the most revered of the Tibetan

Mahatmas, reputedly born as a Rajput Prince in the Indian class of warriors and rulers. His date of birth is uncertain. Here, however, the precious teachings of El Morya clearly point the way for all who aspire. With the incomparable skill of a Zen master, he teaches us to become who we are, to see beneath the surface of daily life. He teaches of the divine light above and the divine light below, and the many layers of awareness that surround the soul. Summit Lighthouse item #420, softbound, 168 pages

Dossier on the Ascension
by Serapis Bey through the Messenger Elizabeth Clare Prophet
A profound look into the life and destiny of the soul. Serapis Bey shows that the ascension--the soul's reunion with God--is the goal of life for all. He gives practical keys for spiritual growth that can help you earn your ascension and he answers the ultimate questions about life after death. Summit Lighthouse item #1038, softbound 212 pages

Saint Germain on Alchemy: Formulas for Self-Transformation
by Saint Germain through the Messenger Elizabeth Clare Prophet
Alchemy is a powerful method of transformation. In this greatest of all self-help books, Saint Germain reveals techniques to help you transform your life, your town, your planet. Learn to harness spiritual energy, control your emotions and get rid of anxiety. Summit Lighthouse item #1835, pocketbook 544 pages

Saint Germain's Prophecy for the New Millennium
by Elizabeth Clare Prophet
Includes dramatic prophecies from Nostradamus, Edgar Cayce and Mother Mary. What can we expect through 2025? We are entering a period that is unique—both in its opportunity for spiritual and technological progress and in its potential for war, turmoil and even cataclysm. Learn how to make your future a brighter day. First, explore the most compelling prophecies for our time, including new interpretations of the celebrated quatrains of Nostradamus. Discover what the handwriting in the skies--astrology--can tell us about our future challenges and opportunities. It also introduces us to decrees. Summit Lighthouse item #4468, pocketbook

Quietly Comes The Buddha-Awakening Your Inner Buddha-Nature
by Elizabeth Clare Prophet
This revised version of the original poetic text contains prose,

poetry and prayers, in addition to meditations to heal and purify your heart and chakras. Discover peace, transformation and divine solutions to your everyday challenges by following the path of Gautama Buddha. This work can help you develop your inner Buddhic nature to bring wholeness into your life and the lives of others. Summit Lighthouse item #4446, Illustrations and photographs, softbound, 208 pages

Maitreya on Initiation: The Coming Buddha Who Has Come
by Elizabeth Clare Prophet with Annice Booth
A compilation of Elizabeth Clare Prophet's lectures and writings on Maitreya throughout the years, plus five messages on initiation from the Great Initiator himself. Summit Lighthouse item #7116, softbound, 256 pages

The Opening of the Seventh Seal: Sanat Kumara on the Path of the Ruby Ray
by Elizabeth Clare Prophet
This volume includes teachings from Sanat Kumara on the Path of the Ruby Ray, These teachings are foundational for the Ascended Masters' devotees who would serve on Earth as initiates of Divine Love. Summit Lighthouse item #7000, softbound, 412 pages

The Masters and their Retreats
Mark L. Prophet and Elizabeth Clare Prophet
The great lights who have come out of all the world's spiritual traditions and graduated from Earth's schoolroom have become widely known as Masters. They demonstrate to us that in the world of Spirit, there is no division of race, religion or philosophy—there is simply oneness, ineffable sweetness and love. These great Masters have retreats—temples and cities of light in the heaven world—where we can go in spiritual meditation and while our bodies sleep at night. Summit Lighthouse item #7100, softbound 546 pages

THE DIVINE MOTHER EAST AND WEST

The Age of the Divine Mother
by Elizabeth Clare Prophet
Elizabeth Clare Prophet shares her personal experiences with Mary and offers to readers a deeper understanding of the mystic Mary and the Universal Mother that Mary represents for us all.

Mary never was a Catholic herself, of course. She belongs to all people, not any one faith. She is a master scientist of the fifth ray and teaches us about the mysteries of the spiritual path. Learn to recognize the Mother in her many guises and to make wise choices on your own personal road of life as you enter the Age of the Divine Mother. Dictations by Mother Mary are included, along with a full explanation of her new age rosary. Summit Lighthouse item #7028, Softbound trade paperback, 376 pages

Mary's Message for A New Day:
(Formerly My Soul Doth Magnify the Lord)
by Elizabeth Clare Prophet
First book in The Golden Word of Mary series. Includes "The Soul of Mary on Earth," the story of Mary's embodiments on Earth, from the Temple of Truth on Atlantis to the Holy Land, the full text of the scriptural rosaries for the seven rays and the eighth ray, 14 letters from Mother Mary, 14 dictations, and a history of the rosary. Summit Lighthouse item #7003, softbound, 368 pages

Mary's Message of Divine Love
by Mark L. Prophet and Elizabeth Clare Prophet
The second book in the Golden Word of Mary Series. Read the fascinating account of Mary's life after Jesus' ascension, including her travels throughout Europe and where she established spiritual focuses. Also chronicled are the appearances of Mary over the last 2,000 years. Contains 14 letters from Mother Mary, 14 dictations, and the text of the five secret-ray rosaries. Summit Lighthouse item #7025, softbound, 368 pages

A Child's Rosary to Mother Mary, Disc 16
Experience the quickening of the Divine Mother's light within you for illumination, healing and comfort with these inspiring 15-minute scriptural rosaries. Printed words to the responsive prayers are included.
Summit Lighthouse item #D99002, 1 Audio CD, 73 min.

Kuan Yin's Crystal Rosary: Devotions to the Divine Mother East and West
Kuan Yin, the Goddess of Mercy, is as near as prayer. Her assistance is tangible as you lovingly invoke her presence to help you overcome the conditions and circumstances of your karma. A magnificent ritual of hymns, prayers, and Chinese mantras. Exquisitely

recorded with temple bells, gongs, harmonium, kartals, balaram, guitar and hundreds of voices, a majestic synthesis of Eastern temple worship with Aquarian Age accents. Summit Lighthouse item #D88084, 4 audio CDs, 4 hrs. 41 min.

Kuan Yin's Crystal Rosary Booklet
Summit Lighthouse item #2501

OTHER TOPICS

Secrets of Prosperity: Abundance in the 21st Century
by Annice Booth
A devoted student of Mark and Elizabeth Prophet discusses, "what is prosperity?" Prosperity is not only money--in your pocket, in the bank, in your stock portfolio and CDs. True prosperity is the sense of abundance--the sense that you have the right to live an abundant life. That you are a child of a wealthy Father and Mother who love you and want to give you all their riches. Prosperity is your true inheritance. It is health, wealth, happiness, joy, peace, faith, hope, wisdom, being in tune with the flow of the universe and able to accept the abundance of God. And now, as the golden age of Aquarius dawns, it is time to claim your own prosperity. Includes meditations, workbook and glossary. Summit Lighthouse item #4479, softbound, 229 pages

NON-SUMMIT LIGHTHOUSE PUBLICATIONS

Journey to Reality
by Jean Inglis Allison
The story of how one seeker sacrificed everything to serve Elizabeth Clare Prophet and how she was rewarded many times over. Softbound, 211 pages, www.Amazon.com

Resume of a Disciple: Stepping Up Spiritually
by Alberta Velma Fredricksen
A manual to unlock your spiritual potential. Wouldn't it be great to have a step-by-step roadmap for our spiritual life! Gain an essential understanding of yourself. Become more aware of who you are and truly know how important you are to God's plan. Grow by maximizing Spirit in your life and transform the world, one soul at a time–beginning with you. Contains many of the teachings of Elizabeth Clare Prophet. Softbound, 248 pages, www.Amazon.com or www.resumeofadisciple.com

Miracles, Masters & Mirth: Adventures in Spirituality and Self-Awareness
by Therese Emmanuel Grey
A student of Elizabeth Clare Prophet shares the real, down-to-earth miracles that happened to her and brought her closer to the ever-expanding, all-encompassing mystery of love that is God. The author shares her discovery that beyond all preconceived ideas and expectations, the purpose of life emerges and sheds light on questions such as: Do we live once or many times? How can I experience God? Sirius Publishing Partners, softbound, 180 pages, http://miraclesandmasters.com/ or www.Amazon.com

Here I AM
by Dorothy Lee Fulton, Messenger of Music
A memoir which includes her interactions with Mark and Elizabeth Prophet. Hardbound, 132 pages, $25.00, Cosmic Portals, P.O. Box 525, Emigrant, MT 59027

What God Really Wants You to Know
by C. David Lundberg
The life-changing principles in this book can empower readers to be fully tuned into God, find true love in life, enhance experiences of peace and joy, achieve success, improve relationships, and rediscover a zest for life. Includes the meaning and purpose of life, who we really are, who and what God is, principles for loving living, what are the truths held in all of the world religions? Heavenlight Press, Softbound, 448 pages, www.Amazon.com

RELATED WEBSITES

www.MarkandElizabethProphet.com
(more information on Mark L. and Elizabeth Clare Prophet)
www.MarkandMother.com
(inspiring stories about Mark L. and Elizabeth Clare Prophet)
www.tsl.org
(information on additional publications and free videos)
www.mysticalpaths.org
(free videos and audios of Elizabeth Clare Prophet's teaching on the mystical paths of the world's religions)

The Empyrean (Highest Heaven) by Gustave Doré

We, the seraphim who serve Justinius, Captain of Seraphic Bands, come forth in formation, ring upon ring from out the Great Central Sun . . . to transmit to you portions of our light. . . . Thereby you shall no longer walk in blindness. but you shall walk in the reality of the noonday sun. And you shall pronounce to all people of light that the seraphim have come to rescue the children of the sun.

–Legions of Justinius and Seraphic Bands
Pearls of Wisdom, March 28, 1997

Mother passes the torch of Freedom for the Earth to lightbearers of the world

At the annual July Conference Parade of Flags Mother blesses every nation. The Heart of the Inner Retreat

Beloved! Love his children free! Fulfill your vow! Ascend! I AM with you!
Mother

Mother sends love to the Youth of the World as she holds a devotee's baby

Note to the Reader

If you were moved by this book and would like to share your experience, please contact us at:

Excelsior Publications
Box 64625
Virginia Beach, VA 23467-4625
U.S.A.

Or email: info@ExcelsiorPublications.com

www.MarkandElizabethProphet.com

Check out our book on the unforgettable, life transcending experiences with Mark Prophet:

All for the Love of God:
Life with Mark Prophet, A Modern-Day Mystic

For more inspiring stories about Mark Prophet and Elizabeth Prophet, go to:

www.MarkandElizabethProphet.com

LaVergne, TN USA
09 February 2010
172575LV00003B/40/P

9 781605 309552